To Antoinette
with best wishes

25.06.10

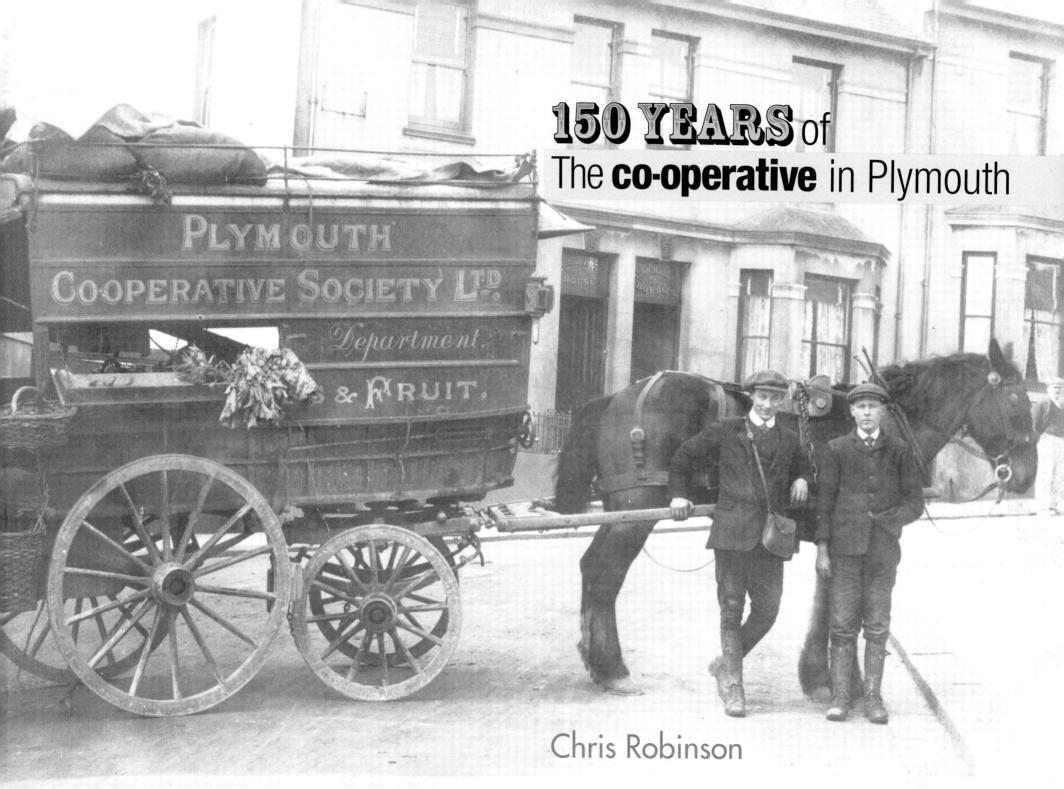

150 YEARS of
The co-operative in Plymouth

PLYMOUTH
COOPERATIVE SOCIETY LTD.

Department.

& FRUIT.

Chris Robinson

British Library Cataloguing in Publication Data

Chris Robinson
150 Years of the Co-operative in Plymouth

A catalogue record for this book is available from the British Library

ISBN 978-0-9543480-8-3

Written and illustrated by Chris Robinson
Design Pen & Ink
© Chris Robinson 2009

First published 2009

Published by
Pen & Ink Publishing
34 New Street, Barbican
Plymouth PL1 2NA
Tel: 01752 705337/228120
Fax: 01752 770001
www.chrisrobinson.co.uk

Printed and bound in Great Britain by
Latimer Trend & Company Ltd
Estover Close
Plymouth PL6 7PL
Devon

CONTENTS

INTRODUCTION

It is a great pleasure and honour to be able to write the foreword to this book representing as it does a key milestone in the history of consumer Co-operation in Plymouth and its surrounding area.

The history of the Co-operative operating in Plymouth interestingly enough follows the economic fortunes of the City itself. Having a strong relationship with the military brought with it economic benefits to those retailers who could service the additional population who came to Plymouth to support the nation in conflict, and, in peacetime the City grew from three separate towns to become the largest city on the South West peninsula.

Co-operation in the middle of the nineteenth-century was for many an ideal and a subject for academic debate. However a small group of men (for they were all men) brought the ideal into being. In Plymouth's case an informal meeting held on Christmas Day 1859 (Christmas Day was one of the few days off for workers at that time) led to the birth of consumer Co-operation in Plymouth on 2 January 1860.

Plymouth grew in tandem with the world economic powerhouse of late-Victorian Britain. The Plymouth Co-operative Society was an organisation prepared to take risks by expanding to provide customers with what they wanted; ensuring that the food purchased was of good quality and free from contamination. Moreover they listened to members' concerns and requests and above all gave something back to those members who spent money with them, in proportion to their purchases – the dividend.

Co-operation became established not just in Plymouth, but throughout the nation in the nineteenth and early twentieth centuries. The Co-operative Movement became a large, diverse organisation, and a bank; an insurance society and a wholesale society, all established to make sure members' needs were met in many different ways.

It was a national organisation with local roots and those roots were very firmly established in Plymouth with a membership base which at that time met monthly to hear what their General Committee (the equivalent of the Boards of Directors) had to say about trading performance, expansion and the all-important dividend levels.

Plymouth became one City in 1914, which gave a further boost to the Society's fortunes. It expanded into Devonport, then westward into Cornwall and eastwards towards Totnes, Dartmouth and Kingsbridge.

However during its early history there was discussion about consolidation; economies of scale were important, as dividend levels could hardly be maintained without those all-important profits. Hence the Plymouth Society took in other smaller Societies around Devon where those economies of scale became difficult to achieve, and where members would be better served by the larger and more profitable Plymouth Society.

In 1910 the Society celebrated its 50th Anniversary, the Co-operative Congress visited Plymouth and many different co-operators experienced the delights of Devon and Cornwall. A history of the first 50 years was written by EC Burton, it was updated in 1960 for the centenary by Bob Briscoe (but Congress did not visit) and here we have this historical account of 150 years written by Plymouth historian Chris Robinson with Congress again visiting Plymouth in June 2010.

Economic recession in the 1920's, just as in the 1990's, created challenging times for the Society, but the continued labours of the Board of Directors, and the Management team, assured progress and expansion. The Blitz of Plymouth in 1941 did not stop its progress although it required the rebuilding of not just the Co-operative Society in Plymouth, but of Plymouth itself.

The 1950's were an exciting time for the Society, creating new buildings from the rubble. Co-operative House Department Store was one of the largest retail units built in Plymouth City Centre but the Society also ensured that it established itself in the new housing estates being built by the City Council at Ernesettle, Efford and Whitleigh. The growth of the Society was paralleling the growth of the City once again.

In the 1960's there was further consolidation with other Co-ops in Devon, leading to the creation of the Plymouth and South Devon Co-operative Society Limited, with Torquay, Newton Abbot, Paignton, and soon after, Buckfastleigh, all joining to create a vibrant consumer retail Society, one that Charles Goodanew and his fellow Plymouth pioneers would have been undoubtedly proud of. However, around that time dark retail clouds were on the horizon; national names like Marks and Spencer, Sainsbury, Tesco, Debenhams and House of Fraser, all with a growing presence in many towns and cities around the country, soon realised that the Co-operative Movement was vulnerable to the changes in retailing that were starting to sweep the liberated, swinging sixties. A growing network of multiple stores backed up by shareholders' capital made it difficult for the Co-operative Societies to retain their market share. The Co-operative Movement had been all things to all men and women and now it was being challenged by other organisations that could do the same as people benefitted from the new-found affluence.

The Movement began to lose touch with its members; dividend levels were lowered or ceased altogether and whilst investment in new stores and new opportunities continued for the most part - particularly in Plymouth and South Devon Society - some of the investment was extravagant and poorly directed.

Just as the Independent, Gaitskill-led Co-operative Commission of 1958 questioned the Movement's ability to retail in non-food and some food areas, so did the Co-operative Commission Report sponsored by Prime Minister, Tony Blair, and published in 2001. This report questioned the overall direction of the Co-operative Movement and urged it to engage more with its Members; to consolidate, re-brand and refocus on things that it was good at.

And so it took two independent reports, written some 40 years apart, to make the sleeping giant of the consumer Co-operative Movement wake up and put in place a coordinated approach that would enable it to compete effectively - otherwise the alternative was to become an incidental retailer and with no sustainable future.

The Plymouth and South West Society took heed of those messages and, in the lead up to its 150th Anniversary, recorded excellent results on a strategy based around co-operating with co-operatives, and divesting itself of retailing activities in areas that offered no sustainable future, while, at the same time, seeking to improve its member proposition and engagement.

The catalyst of consolidation between the Co-operative Wholesale Society, the Co-operative Retail Services and United Co-ops over the period from 2000 to 2007 to form The Co-operative Group; the purchase of the Somerfield food stores chain and the amalgamation with Britannia Building Society, established economies of scale that the Movement had not seen for a hundred years.

The sleeping giant had woken up, its market share was now growing. It was a business model with an ethical base that is as relevant in the twenty-first century as it was in the nineteenth and it had taken consolidation to achieve it.

The question exercising all boards of independent Societies in the twenty-first century, just like those in Devon in the late nineteenth century is, 'when should consolidation with a larger Co-op occur?'

The Board of Directors of Plymouth & South West Co-operative Society made a brave decision to recommend to its Members to consolidate with the Co-operative Group during the spring of 2009. It is undoubtedly the right decision to beat the plc retail monoliths. We had a phrase within our management team – "when the elephants start fighting the ants die first" – by 2009 the Plymouth and South West Society was an ant.

Consolidation creates economies of scale that can be invested to enable members to receive higher dividends; it ensures stores remain open, refurbished regularly and widely located, whilst at the same time providing employees with career progression and training to deliver good service. It also maintains quality member engagement. It echoes all the ideals that must have been discussed by Charles Goodanew and his colleagues on that Christmas day in 1859. Above all consolidation ensures that the Co-operative consumer trading presence is not diluted or lost altogether.

Members emphatically approved the merger of Plymouth Society with that of The Co-operative Group with a 93% vote in favour, in June 2009. Formally the merger took place on 3 September 2009. Further investment is expected from The Co-operative Group for the benefit of the Plymouth & South West members, employees and the retail store portfolio, in the years to come.

It has been my privilege to be the Chief Executive of Plymouth & South West from December 1996 to September 2009 and one of its employees since October 1973. During that time I was elected (in 1998) to be a Director of the Co-operative Wholesale Society, now The Co-operative Group and its Deputy Chair for two years up to June 2009. It enabled me to see a resurgence of the Co-operative Movement, confirming that the business model is still relevant today as it was 150 years ago.

Therefore, I believe that if those men of the original 1860 Committee, who set out to establish a consumer Co-operative in Plymouth, could be here today they would be well-pleased that, 150 years later, a vibrant, successful consumer Co-operative Society serving Plymouth and surrounding areas, is well set for a flourishing and thriving future.

Douglas Fletcher
The last Chief Executive of the Plymouth and South West Co-operative Society.
November 2009

PREFACE

Researching the history of the Plymouth and South West Co-operative Society has been a fascinating experience. Little was it realised, when we formed the History Club some eight years ago and I took on the job of researcher, that the journey would take us so far and be so involved, seeking out the numerous avenues of activity from 1860 to the present day; both trading and social.

Looking at the Co-operative today, we forget that it once had a large lending library, education centre, shipping department, railroad trucks, dairy, laundry, bakery, preserve works, slaughter house, farming, charabancs, furniture repository, as well as house building - to name but just some of the activities long consigned to its historical past.

On the social side, it sponsored choirs, brass bands, drama groups, nursing, youth groups, women's guild branches, football teams, bowling clubs, employees' sports and social club, children's sports days, cycling and swimming clubs, and so on. The list of charities benefiting from donations and grants is far too numerous to quote.

Its history has been researched in much greater depth than ever before, commencing with the original Pioneers and their social ideals, the early trading struggles, the year by year growth, the war years, the emergence into a regional Co-operative, and lastly, the current merger with the national 'Co-operative Group'.

To the Board of Directors, Chief Officials, History Club Members, the many Co-op Members who have kindly deposited memorabilia and photographs, past employees for their memories, and current staff who have assisted - I express my gratitude.

Victor Barton

Victor Barton Former Chief Executive *November 2009*

ACKNOWLEDGEMENTS

This is at least the fourth history of the Plymouth Co-operative Society: the first was written by one of the Plymouth Pioneers, John Webb, back in 1892. It was written with humour, affection, sadness (he had wanted to be the Society's first Manager but was outvoted), but above all, it was written with an intimate knowledge of the events he was describing. In 1910, on the occasion of the Society's 50th Anniversary, Cyrus Edward 'EC' Burton, who had been the Society's librarian for 30 years, produced an updated 'souvenir' history. Then, ten years later, on the occasion of the 60th Anniversary, William Watkins, a former President of the Society, moved the story on a bit further. Bob Briscoe, the then Secretary of the Education Committee, was the next to publish, producing a book to celebrate the Society's Centenary in 1960.

Each writer had brought his own slant to the story, and I would imagine the volume you now hold in your hands is no different in that respect. However, this time the author, although a member, is not and never has been an official of the Society, so in that respect the slant will be quite different again.

It is about four years since Douglas Fletcher first suggested I might like to produce something to commemorate the 150th Anniversary. Back then 2010 still seemed like a very long time away, but now it is upon us and the Plymouth and South West Co-operative Society is no more. The final chapter has indeed been written. Happily, however, Plymouth is now part of something even bigger and stronger - The Co-operative Group - the product of the merger of the CWS and the CRS ... and the Britannia. This last year has undoubtedly been a watershed year in the history of the Movement - not just the Plymouth Society. And so it has been an honour and a joy to bring the story up to the present day.

In producing this book I have leant heavily on the work of my predecessors and in particular on the work of another former Society official, former Chief Executive, Victor Rowland Barton, who produced exhaustive notes on the history of the Society from the earliest days up until twenty years ago. I doubt whether anyone has ever had a better working knowledge of the stories and the characters that fill this volume. Certainly, even in a book this size, it has been impossible to do justice to wealth of material produced by Victor and I commend his typescripts to any future historian of the Society.

For the last twenty years, I have to thank Douglas Fletcher himself; Douglas has been Chief Executive for most of that time, and in the later stages of the book I steal liberally from his notes, as I do Victor's. I have also had many conversations with Mr Fletcher over the last few years and so one or two of the quotes are quite literally from the horse's mouth.

Gillian Lonergan at the Co-operative College Library in Manchester and the lovely ladies who run the Rochdale Pioneers Museum at Toad Lane, were also extremely obliging. Another invaluable reference point has been Johnston Birchall's excellent book 'Co-op - the people's business', published by the Manchester University Press in 1994.

As for the images, Victor Barton, together with the Society's History Club have been relentless in trying to track down any Co-op related Plymouth image they can find. The Society's photographic archives, the majority of which are now held safely at the South West Image Bank, have been immensely useful, while Barbara Dyer, Nicky Demellweek and Clive Weir at the Society HQ in Plymouth, have been enormously helpful. I am also indebted to readers of the Herald in Plymouth, who, over the last twenty years or so, have brought all manner of material in for me to use in my Looking Back columns. There is also a large amount of material on shelves and in boxes in the Robinson residence and at my shop on the Barbican, all of which have been trawled for Co-op material.

So thank you Doreen Mole and especially Rob Warren, who manages our New Street operation and who has also exquisitely hand-painted dozens of Victorian images and maps for the early part of this history. Thank you too, Stacey Dyer and her volunteers at the South West Image Bank for scanning a lot of the Co-operative's pre-digital archive. I would also like to record my thanks to all the un-named photographers who have worked for the Society over the years and whose material does so much to enliven the pages that follow.

On the proof reading front I am indebted to my wife, Clare (who is also my publisher), my mother-in-law, Patricia, my sister-in-law, Helen (a book editor and author herself), and to Douglas Fletcher, all of whom have read the draft manuscript and made comments and observations.

The History of the Plymouth Society, like that of the Movement as a whole, is one of the greatest stories of the last two hundred years. There are lessons here for every individual, every class and every culture - and with 750 million members worldwide, there is ample proof of the efficacy of that legacy and of the basic principles that yield the Co-operative Advantage.

Chris Robinson *November 2009*

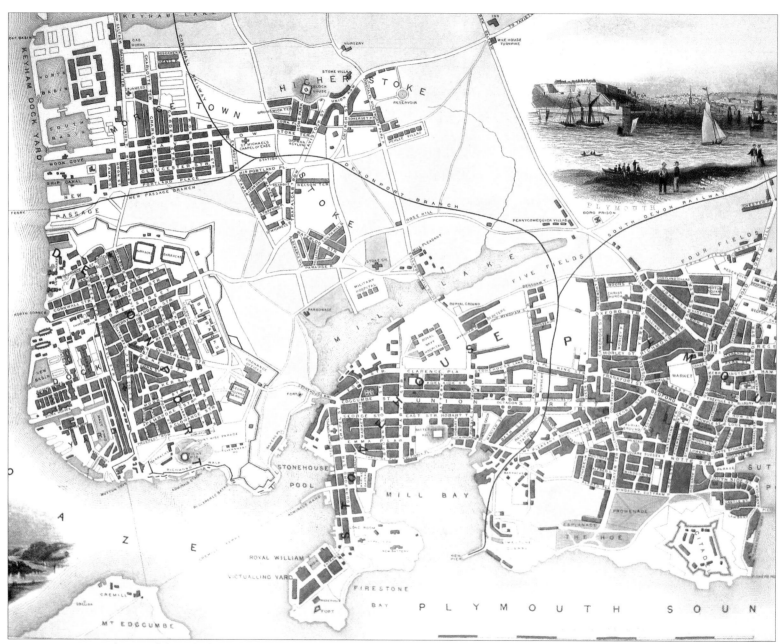

Devonport, Stonehouse and Plymouth - the Three Towns - constitutionally still very separate in 1860, but now linked to the rest of Britain via the railway network.

CHAPTER 1: IN THE BEGINNING

Although there were great celebrations surrounding the passing of the Reform Act in 1832 when thousands gathered in the Bull Ring on Plymouth Hoe, voting rights were still restricted to men who occupied homes with an annual value of £10.0s0d (roughly equivalent to £650 today) which, coupled with certain property qualifications in rural areas, meant that only about one in seven adult males in this country had the vote. Furthermore, while it spelt the end for the so-called rotten borough, there were still some 35 constituencies across the country that had less than 300 electors. It is also worth remembering that voting at Parliamentary elections was not by secret ballot - rather it was open and very public ... at the hustings.

It was Christmas Day 1859, a Sunday, when John Slade and John Shovel, two local craftsmen, called in to visit their good friend and near neighbour, 45-year-old Charles Goodanew, one of Britain's 275,000 shoemakers.

All three working men were unhappy with various aspects of Victorian England and as they sat down over a seasonal drink they started to put the world to rights. Plymouth was overcrowded; the population of around 60,000, was almost four times what it had been when Charles was born. Sanitation was poor, so too were the majority of the population. Food was expensive, and all too often adulterated, and Charles had many mouths to feed, although, tragically, four of his nine children had already died – three of them without reaching their third birthdays. His eldest daughter however had already married and was six months pregnant.

As the three men sat talking Charles pulled out a copy of a book he had recently acquired - George Jacob Holyoake's 'Self-Help by the People' - History of the Rochdale Pioneers' – and he read extracts to his friends.

Charles Goodanew had been an admirer of Holyoake's for many years, the two men were of similar age and, as a 25-year-old Charles had attended a lecture given by Holyoake and had become convinced of the need to change the conditions of the working class. There was no unemployment benefit and many families faced starvation if there were no wage earners in the house or if the wage earners were made redundant. Devonport particularly went through a torrid time after the conclusion of the Napoleonic Wars. The ending of hostilities after more than twenty years of on-off fighting with the French led to great hardships in an area dominated by the armed services. Wages for many in work were very low – it didn't matter how hard some men worked they still couldn't earn enough to fully feed and clothe their families. Literacy levels too were low, many children didn't go to school at all - parents couldn't afford the few pence (a pound

Charles Goodanew

John Leech's opening illustration for Charles Dickens' 'A Christmas Carol' published in 1843. If you want a flavour of the world that the Plymouth Co-operative was born into try any of his major novels, most of which were published between 1837 and 1860.

Charles Dickens: 1812-1870

or two today) that it cost each week to provide their children with any sort of education – and of those children who did go, most left by the time they were eleven and old enough to earn even a small amount of money.

Despite his determination to improve the lot of his fellow man – Goodanew, somewhat unusually, sold 'newspapers, pens, periodicals, ink and paper, and all other gear devoted to the spread of knowledge and information for the people' in his Tin Street shoemaker's shop – he had yet to make a major mark.

A Chartist (the first genuine working class political movement and one dedicated to widening the voting entitlement for men) he had long been inspired by Holyoake's lecturing and his writings, and it may well have been the thought of trying to create a better world for his imminent first grandchild, coupled with conversations with his 29-year-old son-in-law, Thomas Reynolds – another Chartist and shoemaker – that re-ignited Goodanew's youthful ambitions and made him more determined to do something locally.

Certainly he was not alone in his quest to turn intentions into actions. In the six years following the publication of Holyoake's 'History of the Rochdale Pioneers' in 1857, 251 Co-operative Societies were established across the country, a huge increase on the 81 that were set up in the 13 years prior to publication.

It had been just a few days before Christmas 1844, that a group of largely socialist and chartist workers had gathered together in Rochdale, to trade 'co-operatively' on terms advantageous to themselves.

Conditions in the Lancashire textile town were particularly tough; as the Industrial Revolution increasingly saw the introduction of machinery at the expense of man-power, so the displaced workforce struggled. Speaking in a House of Commons debate in September 1841, Rochdale MP Sharman Crawford declared that 136 of his constituents were living on 6d a week (around £1.80 today), 200 on 10d (£2.70) per week, 855 on 1/6d (£5.24) and 1,500 on 1/10d (£6.30). The vast majority of them had scarcely any blankets, 85 families had no blankets, 46 families had only chaff (straw) beds, with no covering at all. Stories abounded of weavers wearing rags, who, having sold all their furniture, worked sixteen hours a

day and survived on a diet of oats, onion porridge, potatoes and treacle. Small wonder that the mean life expectancy for the town of 25,000 was just 21 – a good six years less than it was for the rest of England at the time.

Dreadful as these conditions were, they were by no means new, just as the idea of co-operation itself was not entirely new in 1844. Thirteen years earlier, and less than eleven miles away, in neighbouring Manchester, William Shelmerdine, a local storekeeper, had reported that after one year's co-operation they had increased their membership from eight to thirty-six and had made over £20 profit (£1,200) in their first year's trading. A Co-operative had been established in Rochdale too that year but, like so many of those early ventures, after initial successes, it faltered. The reason – in almost every instance – the granting of credit:

'I look upon the strap (credit) book,' said one shrewd analyst, 'as one of the greatest evils that can befall a working man. He gets into debt with the shopkeeper, and is, for ever after, a week behind; and, as we express it here, eats the calf in the cow's belly.
Hence arose that just terror of credit which the Store from the first betrayed,' wrote Holyoake, adding: 'In their first book of laws—the laws of 1844—the grand fine, the lion fine of the list there given, was to be inflicted on any officer, who, on any pretence, should either purchase or sell any article except for ready-money; which prohibition, as usual when they are emphatic, is given twice over.'

It was a key lesson … indeed it proved to be the vital piece of knowledge in giving strength to the maxim:
'Numbers without Union are powerless—
And Union without Knowledge is useless.'

So many earlier societies had learnt the hard way, but now, in Rochdale in 1844, there arose a wiser group of men (some of them veterans of the earlier organization): the Rochdale Society of Equitable Pioneers.

'Human nature must be different in Rochdale from what it is elsewhere,' wrote Holyoake, at the beginning of his first chapter. 'There must have been a special creation of mechanics in this inexplicable district of Lancashire— in no other way can you account for the fact that they have mastered the art of acting together, and holding together, as no other set of workmen in Great Britain have done. They have acted upon Sir Robert Peel's memorable advice; they have "taken their own affairs into their own hands;" and what is more to the purpose, they have kept them in their own hands.'

'The working class are not considered to be very rich in the quality of self-trust, or mutual trust. The business habit is not thought to be their forte. The art of creating a large concern, and governing all its complications, is not usually supposed to belong to them. The problem of association has many times been tried among the people, and as many times it has virtually failed. Mr. Robert Owen has not accomplished half he intended.'

Notwithstanding the excellent example of the Rochdale Pioneers, not all Co-operatives that followed in their wake were destined to succeed. Perhaps subsequent societies were not as strict in their adherence to the 'Laws' or perhaps they simply did not have access to them, or perhaps they were just naïve or the victims of human frailty, although, more often than not it was the issue of credit. Whatever the reason though, there can be no doubt that more were started, and more thrived, after the publication of Holyoake's account of their origins and early years.

One can but wonder what passages from the Rochdale history Charles Goodanew chose to read to his friends that Christmas day in Tin Street, Plymouth; there are so many sensible, well-written and thought provoking passages within it: 'Poverty is a greater impediment to social success than even prejudice. With a small capital you cannot buy good articles nor cheap ones. What is bought at a small Store will probably be worse and dearer than the same articles elsewhere. This discourages the poor. With them every penny must tell, and every penny extra they pay for goods seems to them a tax, and they will not often incur it. It is of no use that you show them that it – and more – will come back again as profit at the end of the quarter. They do not believe in the end of the quarter – they distrust the promise of profits. The loss of the penny to-day is near – the gain of sixpence three months hence is remote. Thus you have to educate the very poor before you can serve them. The humbler your means the greater your difficulties – you have to teach as well as to save the very poor.

Fourteen of the original Rochdale Pioneers

Top: the first shop in Toad Lane; bottom: the Laws and Objects of the Rochdale Pioneers.

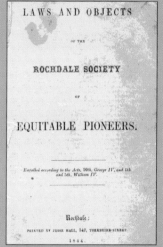

'One would think that a customer ought to be content when he is his own shopkeeper; on the contrary, he is not satisfied with the price he charges himself. Intelligent contentment is the slowest plant that grows upon the soil of ignorance.'

By talking of ignorance in this way Holyoake, far from being condescending, was merely recognising the state of affairs that prevailed in mid-nineteenth century Britain and clearly, by making his shoe-shop double as a newsagents, Goodanew was already doing his bit to spread the word.

It was, as it happened, a job that was becoming easier all the time. The abolition of tax on newspapers four years earlier and on advertisements two years before that, had seen the price of newspapers drop dramatically; the Daily Telegraph, first published just two weeks after the abolition of the tax and named after the invention of telegraphy, which was key to its speedy news gathering, was now available for just a penny (65p) and was rather more affordable than it had been. The move also saw provincial periodicals like the Manchester Guardian, the Liverpool Post and The Scotsman (in Edinburgh) change from being ailing weeklies to healthy daily papers. It also raised the possibility of someone producing a national daily paper for as little as a ha'penny (32p).

Exterior of the room in Tin Street.

Samuel Smiles

It is also likely that Goodanew stocked, sold, and read one of 1859's best selling publications – Samuel Smiles' *'Self Help'*. Largely structured around biographical stories of famous men (there is little or no female content) most of whom had concentrated, like one featured artist – Plympton's Sir Joshua Reynolds – on 'work, work, work', the book was full of inspirational sayings and phrases:

'The spirit of self-help is the root of all genuine growth in the individual.'
'Heaven helps those who help themselves.'

'Help from without is often enfeebling in its effects. Whatever is done for men takes away the stimulus of doing for themselves.'

For men like Goodanew these ideas were by no means new, however the timing of Smiles' publication and its popularity – it sold 20,000 copies that first year and was translated into seventeen languages – meant that the world at large was more receptive to the idea of Co-operation than ever before. Clearly the social climate had moved on a little since that 'longest evening of the year', 21 December 1844, when the Rochdale Pioneers somewhat hesitantly opened their modest little shop in Toad Lane. As Holyoake himself described it:

'A few of the co-operators had clandestinely assembled to witness their denouement: and there they stood, in that dismal lower room of the warehouse, like the conspirators under Guy Fawkes in the Parliamentary cellars, debating on whom should devolve the temerity of taking down the shutters, and displaying their humble preparations. One did not like to do it, and another did not like to be seen in the shop when it was done: however, having gone so far there was no choice but to go farther, and at length one bold fellow, utterly reckless of consequences, rushed at the shutters, and in a few minutes Toad Lane was in a titter.'

It's hard to imagine the sort of worries that the Pioneers shared that solstice day in 1844, but clearly their determination and their solidarity were inspirational and by the time Charles Goodanew came to read excerpts from the Pioneers' early history, fifteen years later, the world had moved on sufficiently for one of Goodanew's two visitors that Christmas day to exclaim: *'I think there is a need for such a Society in Plymouth, and I'll be the one to try and do something like the Owd Pioneers.'*

The man who spoke those words was John Slade, a carpenter who lived around the corner from his host and who, at 52, was a few years older than Goodanew, and of a similar age to his fellow guest, the mason John Shovel. Suitably fired up, it was agreed that a letter should be sent to William Cooper, the Secretary of the Rochdale Co-operative, and one of the founding Pioneers. In the meantime they decided to call a meeting of like-minded souls with a view to progressing the matter immediately.

The First Meeting

The meeting, held two days later, was in a tiny room at the back of Goodanew's shoe-shop-cum-newsagent. Measuring just ten feet by seven feet, the room was by no means ideal and John Slade chaired the meeting from a chair mounted on a table with nine others crowded around as best they could. As well as Slade, Shovel and Goodanew himself, there were: Goodanew's son-in-law, Thomas Reynolds, and his brother, William Goodanew, another shoemaker; Charles John Shovel (possibly a nephew of John and another carpenter); John Webb, Thomas Abrahams, and Thomas Hellyer (who were also all involved in the boot and shoemaking industry); and finally the painter Henry Dryden.

After a long discussion it was unanimously agreed that they should establish a Society along the lines of the Rochdale model and each of those present agreed to go forth and recruit other Co-operators. Thus it was that a week later, on Tuesday 3 January 1860, the same ten men, plus eight new recruits – among them Samuel Lockwood, William Morshead and William Adamson – met in Adamson's workshop in Ebrington Street. Each of the eighteen subscribed a shilling (just over £3) to the enterprise as a joining fee, thereby conferring a sense of commitment to the fledgling organisation.

A week later they all met up at 14 Ebrington Street, again. This time the group decided to appoint a President, Treasurer and a Secretary: Charles Shovel, William Adamson and John Webb, respectively.

A board of six directors were also appointed and a number of other bureaucratic matters were dealt with. As Webb later noted: *'in some measure we rivalled the celebrated Irish Regiment, who mustered a full staff of officers to command one private soldier'.*

Tuesday 3 January 1860 was to be an auspicious day in the history of the West Country, for, not only was it the day that the local Co-operators first made a financial commitment to their new enterprise, it was also the day that William Hunt, Alfred Rooker, William Saunders and Edward Spender launched their new enterprise - The Western Morning News. The background of the four founders stood in marked contrast to that of the pioneering Plymouth Co-operators.

Forty-four year-old, Honiton-born Hunt came from a distinguished Devon family and received a sound education, indeed he was sending material into newspapers in Exeter and Sherborne while still a boy. After gaining further experience in London he came to the Three Towns and worked on the short-lived Plymouth Times, before moving on to edit the West of England Conservative, which later became the Western Courier. It too failed however and Hunt lost a lot of his own money, nevertheless he kept his journalistic hand in, as the Plymouth correspondent for the London Daily News (a post he had been appointed to by Charles Dickens when Dickens was briefly ensconced as editor of that paper). It was not a full-time post though, and Hunt also took over from Llewellyn Jewitt as librarian of the Plymouth Public Library in Cornwall Street.

Alfred Rooker was just a year older than Hunt. The son of Tavistock cleric, he was educated privately by his father, and another reverend gentleman. The much-travelled Rooker came to Plymouth after completing his legal studies in London in 1836. A charismatic and capable figure, he was made a member of the local Corporation without either having been elected or having a ward to represent. No sooner had he been appointed than he was made an Alderman and leader of the Liberals. Three years later he served the town as Mayor (1851-52).

Rooker lived above Mannamead, in Mount View, off Hartley Road, and it was at the end of the 1850s that the 35-five year-old William Saunders moved in to Rooker's neighbourhood. Saunders, an entrepreneur from Bath, had moved to Plymouth with his wife, and his wife's brother, Edward Spender, who in turn had married the daughter of a local surgeon – Dr CE Russel Rendle of The Crescent. It would appear that Saunders and Spender were on the lookout for business opportunities. It was Rooker who first made the introduction when he took Saunders to meet Hunt in the Public Library. Writing later in his memoirs Hunt described the latter as being 'a young gentleman of literary taste and aspirations' who soon 'became a regular gossip of mine'.

Along with Rooker they discussed the local need for a decent daily paper for Plymouth. In the four years since the taxes had been lifted on newspapers, and advertising, not only had Manchester (the first outside London - in 1855) and Liverpool seen weeklies change into dailies, but Sheffield, Birmingham, Edinburgh and Glasgow had also spawned daily papers – so too, in 1858 had Bristol, – something Saunders and Spender had been very aware of when they were in Bath.

Thus it was, that by the time Rooker, Hunt and Saunders started floating such an idea for Plymouth, five of the six largest provincial areas in England had already got their own daily paper; the only exception being Leeds, where the Yorkshire Post would not hit the presses until 1866. And what of the seventh largest conurbation in the country? That was Plymouth, or more properly at the time, the Three Towns (Plymouth, Stonehouse and Devonport).

It is easy to imagine, therefore, the feeling that this was the right idea at the right time and when Hunt was invited to Saunders' Mannamead home to dine with his host and his wife, he met the man who would become the paper's first editor, Saunders' brother-in-law, Edward Spender.

Far left: Brunel's Bridge under construction. Middle: 2 May 1859 opening. Above: the old market.

Hunt, Rooker, Saunders and Spender would have been well aware of the risks they were taking. Despite the fact that these men were, financially, considerably more comfortable than the Plymouth Co-operators, the stakes were much higher and the chances of losing great sums were very real, as Hunt knew only too well. The Western Courier was by no means the only paper to have failed, indeed Crispin Gill in his History of the Western Morning News notes that 'there had been thirty papers that started and died in the four years 1832-6' alone.'

However circumstances had changed enormously since then, not only had the population grown substantially but, more significantly, the ability of the population to move around had increased dramatically - thanks to the arrival of the railway. Plymouth's rail link with the rest of the country had come a decade earlier in 1849 (following Plympton in 1848), however, almost as important for an enterprise looking to break into Cornwall, was the completion of Brunel's masterwork - the Royal Albert Bridge - on 2 May 1859 which opened up exciting possibilities.

Truro and Penzance were now both accessible by train, Tavistock and South Devon were also opened up:

'Every town of any size in the West of England had its weekly paper, but with new ideas, new means of communication, new methods of transport, people wanted their news daily, and did not even want to wait for The Times to arrive from London - at that time it was reaching Plymouth at 6pm. The Western Morning News however could be put onto trains leaving Plymouth at 6.05am (on the up train) and 6.10am (on the down train). The world was moving at a quicker pace and the news from Plymouth was, from a Westcountry perspective, twelve hours more up to date. (Gill)'

Incidentally, as a quite literal sign of the times, one of the stories in The Western Morning News that Tuesday, 3 January was about the alteration of the clocks. This was nothing to do with British Springtime or Summertime, rather it noted that 1 January 1860 was the day that Plymouth adopted Greenwich Mean Time. Previously, like most other provincial areas, it had been using true solar time, which, this far west, meant that Plymouth time was more than quarter of an hour different from London time. In the days of horse-drawn travel and sailing ships, with no radio or telephonic communication, that was fine, but now, in the modern, mid-Victorian, industrial world it was becoming an inconvenience, especially for those compiling train time tables!

Other stories covered in that first ever Western Morning News are equally delightful in the way they unwittingly highlight a very different world. The inmates of Stonehouse Workhouse had had a Christmas treat; so too had Tavistock Workhouse inmates - roast beef and plum pudding. Meanwhile ten-year-old John Ridden was charged with stealing four penny-puddings from a market stall - he was with other boys who snatched the puddings from him - but he was caught. His father said he was always a good boy but he was still sentenced to seven days and a whipping. A drunken man in Looe Street who had beaten his wife and attacked the policeman who tried to stop him was fined £5 or two months jail. At Exeter a clerk received four months for stealing £1.4s.9d from his employer; a soup kitchen had been opened in Tavistock; a report delivered at a meeting 'to aid the working classes' revealed that there were 12,000 people in Plymouth living in single rooms and a proposal was put forward to build 60 cottages for them, with investors receiving no more than 5% interest - quite a good return at the time. Alderman Rooker himself proposed the formation of an association to oversee the work and by the end of the meeting £5,000 of the £8,000 needed, had been subscribed. A far cry indeed from the few shillings that the co-operators were looking for from members.

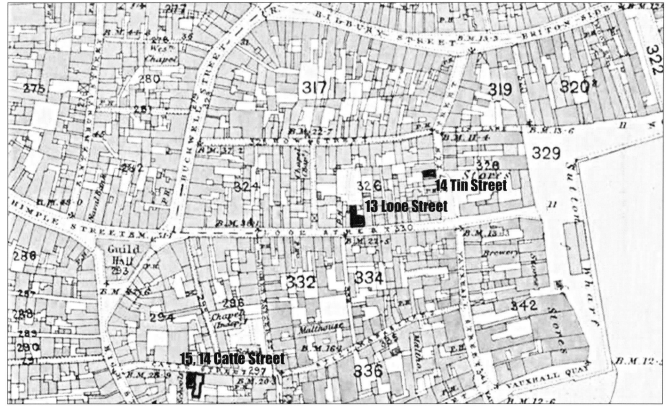

14 Tin Street

13 Looe Street

15, 14 Catte Street

14 Tin Street: the home and workshop of Charles Goodanew where he met with John Shovel and John Slade on Christmas Day 1859.
15, 14 Catte Street: properties of John Slade. 13 Looe Street: John Webb, the Society's first Secretary.

Left: George Holyoake
Above: Robert Owen.

George Jacob Holyoake was born in Birmingham in 1817. His father, George, was a printer, his mother, Catherine, a button maker. After enjoying a basic education he was apprenticed to a foundry and became a whitesmith. While still in his teens he became socially and politically active and joined the Birmingham Reform League.

He attended lectures by the Welsh socialist and social reformer Robert Owen, the man widely regarded as the father of the Co-operative Movement.

Owen (1771-1858) was to be a major influence on Holyoake's own thinking on socialism and co-operation. Replying to a 'loaded' question posed by a clergyman in Cheltenham when lecturing on Owenite socialism, Holyoake achieved the unusual distinction of being the last person in Britain to be arrested for atheism. Upon his release from prison six months later, Holyoake coined the term 'secularism' to express his views on the subject – views which he subsequently expounded in 'The Movement' (which later became The Reasoner). Critical of Christianity, he proposed instead a belief system based on reason and science. By the mid-1850s The Reasoner was selling around 5,000 copies a week and more than 40 secular societies had been established around Britain.

Over the next couple of weeks further meetings were held, each time members paying their entrance fee and weekly subs towards their eventual goal of each member contributing a pound (£65) towards a share capital with which they could begin to start purchasing.

In the meantime meetings were held at John Webb's house to lay down a set of rules for the constitution of what they agreed would henceforth be called the Plymouth Mutual Co-operative Society.

By the beginning of February, treasurer Adamson announced that they had almost three pounds (nearly £200) in hand and the directors decided that it was dangerous to have such a large amount of money lying idle and duly resolved that *'the sum of two pounds and ten shillings be invested in purchasing groceries which could be sold at a profit'*.

That decided, the next question was – from where they should run the business?

Thomas Reynolds

Looe Street, with Webb's house half-way up on the right.

The First Shop

As it happened a room in one of the three properties that John Slade had in Catte Street had just become vacant. Although it was an upstairs room it was a reasonable size and the Committee agreed to rent it from their fellow founder for one shilling and ten pence a week, starting on Wednesday, 2 February 1860.

Wasting little time, they set about furnishing the premises. With a few chairs and tables they created a shop area with a counter, an office, a reading/meeting area and a committee table. Stock was stored in a three-cornered cupboard, and with borrowed scales, a measuring jug, some weights and a set of tea caddies (bought for ten shillings), the Plymouth Mutual Co-operative Society was ready to do business.

Goodanew's son-in-law, Thomas Reynolds, was charged with acquiring the stock and he went off to the market with William Adamson, the Society's Treasurer, who carried the money in a bag and kept a meticulous account of all the purchases. Just as the Society intended only to sell items for cash, so they also determined only to purchase items for ready money.

'The starting stock possibly consisted of flour, oatmeal, lard, dried fruits, tea and sugar; the main ingredients from which a meal could be made at the time' (Webb).

It is hard now to appreciate the plight of the poorer customer in mid-nineteenth century Britain; subsistence levels were very low and yet there were many unscrupulous merchants who lost little sleep in selling corrupted goods to the general public.

The Food and Drugs Act, designed to stamp out many of the more evil practices, was still a decade away and among the more commonplace misdemeanours were the addition of: alum (aluminium sulphate) to bread, white lead to flour, copper sulphate to bottled fruit and jam, iron sulphate to tea and beer, lead to wine and cider, red lead to coffee, ground glass to sugar and lead sulphate and bisulphate of mercury to sugared confectionery and chocolate.

Over time such wicked tampering and adulteration brought on chronic

gastritis and often fatal food poisoning. A lesser side effect, notably prompted by the addition of alum, was the inhibition of digestion and thus the lowering of nutritional value from other foods.

Most basic commodities were potential targets and as late as 1877 the Local Government Board found that almost a quarter of all the milk they inspected had either been watered down or bulked out with chalk or both. Animal and human waste were other unwelcome ingredients that often found their way into foodstuffs, along with fleas, lice and bed bugs.

"Little girl: If you please, Sir, Mother says, will you let her have a quarter of a pound of your best tea to kill the rats with, and an ounce of chocolate as would get rid of the black beadles."
Punch 4 August 1855

And it wasn't just adulteration that the buyer had to be wary of, in 1862 the Privy Council estimated that a fifth of all butcher's meat in England and Wales came from animals that were 'considerably diseased' or had died of pleuropneumonia, and antacid or anthracoid diseases.

Thus it was that in addition to the more distant Co-operative promise of a share of profits based on amount spent, members had the more immediate potential benefit of buying better quality produce with their money. Small wonder that the Committee were keen to spread the word – and play their part in the enterprise.

Saturday, 11 February 1860, was the red-letter day in the fledgling society's diary, for it was on that evening that the first customers were welcomed into the upstairs room in Catte Street. In those first few weeks, Wednesday and Saturday evenings were the only times the shop was open for business, but such was the enthusiasm of the 'salesmen' and the demand from the customers that it wasn't long before other evenings came into play. A healthy competition arose among the members, as John Webb was later to recall: 'how we vied with each other in those days as to who should be allowed to do the work for nothing, and how petty jealousies grew if any one undertook a duty another thought belonged of right to him.'

Meanwhile, the proprietor of the small shop immediately below the new grocery-store-cum-office and education centre soon tired of all the activity around him and moved out. Straight away the Society seized the opportunity, and having agreed to pay John Slade a further one shilling and sixpence a week, added the ground floor premises to their operations. The new room, albeit a small one, was at least on street level and it was illuminated by gas light.

However thereby hung a tale. The gas lighting hadn't been installed by the landlord, but rather at the personal cost of the vacating tenant, who was understandably keen to get some return on his investment. Certainly the Society were glad to have the use of these fittings. Catte Street was a narrow, ill-lit thoroughfare (it is wider and lighter today – and it's now known as the eastern end of Palace Street) and on a gloomy winter's evening such premises could be particularly dark. Doubtless the outgoing tenant hoped that once they got used to the gas light they would not want to do without it and would meet what he considered to a reasonable agreement.

Unfortunately, the Committee did not feel that the price was right for those 'bits of brass' and refused to pay - although they continued to use the lighting ... until, that was, one busy Saturday evening when, having reached the end of his patience, the erstwhile tenant returned and on being refused again, produced a set of tools and proceeded to dismantle his fittings, leaving the shop in a state of darkness: 'very dull and woeful did the stuffy little place look by candlelight, after such brilliancy as we had hitherto enjoyed.'

It was not long however before the Committee had secured the services of a gas fitter who was employed to do the work - costed at 18 shillings – 'on the understanding that the payment be placed on his account as part payment of his share capital.'

Gas was still a relative novelty in 1860. Introduced into the Three Towns in the 1820s, it wasn't until 1845 that the Plymouth and Stonehouse Gas-light and Coke Company was established at Coxside, thereby improving the provision to those two towns. Writing in 1870, RN Worth reported that Plymouth 'enjoys the advantage of having the cheapest gas in the kingdom, 2s 9d per thousand feet. Gas street lighting, incidentally, was first seen in Plymouth in 1832 and by no means were all streets lit in those early days. Prior to that Plymouth's first proper street lighting dates back to 1770 when the town procured and mounted 200 oil lamps around the town – before that, once the sun had set, the town was very dark indeed.

From little acorns – Plymouth's first Co-operative shop in Catte Street

From 1732 to 1757 Benjamin Franklin, the American statesman, publisher and inventor, writing as 'Poor Richard' or 'Richard Saunders', produced a hugely successful almanac containing a calendar, poems, astrological and astronomical information and a good many of his own aphorisms and proverbs. These included such familiar gems as;

A penny saved is two pence clear.
There are three faithful friends—an old wife, an old dog, and ready money.
Lost time is never found again.
A rotten apple spoils its companions.
and
God helps them that help themselves.

Accountancy periods followed the calendar year and although that meant that by the end of the first quarter of 1860 the Society had only been trading for some seven weeks, it was with a certain degree of pride that the Directors announced their first Quarterly Report to the membership:

'Gentlemen - in presenting this the first Quarterly Report for your approval, your Directors are pleased to congratulate you on the result of the trade carried on by them during the last seven weeks - a result they believe which has rarely been attained, and never surpassed by any similar Society during the first quarter of their existence.

'Success which may be considered due to two causes: first, the small expense of management, and, second, the large trade done in proportion to the number of members: but they confidently hope the dividend will be still more satisfactory in the ensuing quarter, a hope founded that, while expenses will not be greater in proportion, the trade will go on steadily increasing. But we cannot disguise the fact that the result would have been still more gratifying had a larger number of the members availed themselves of the opportunity to become purchasers, a result which they hope to secure by impressing on the mind of every member the fact that the more they spend at their own shop, the more they save, and following the maxim of poor Richard, that a penny saved is a penny earned, earnestly desire to impress on all the advantages of laying out every halfpenny they can in Catte Street, and further, with a view to foster that habit, the Directors hope they shall soon be able to make arrangements to afford the members the opportunity of supplying themselves every evening (Sundays excepted). They also hope that, having appropriated a small sum for educational purposes, this room will be made available for that purpose, and would suggest the propriety of electing a committee for that object (according to the rule) as soon as practicable, and conclude with the hope that you will stamp with unqualified approval the following accounts ...

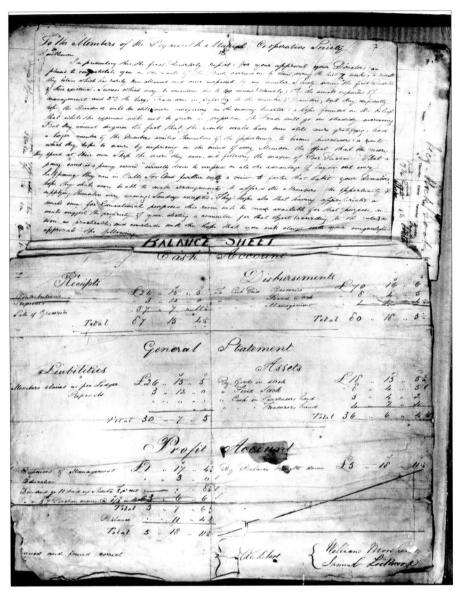

The first account and balance sheets for the Plymouth Mutual Co-operative Society. March 1860

The accounts were audited by William Morshead and Samuel Lockwood, both of whom were almost certainly at that first major meeting in Ebrington Street at the very beginning of the year. Remarkably, in those short few weeks and months the membership had increased from the 18 that met then, to 72 as of 27 March, each of whom had contributed a minimum of a shilling and each of whom had earned a significant dividend of one shilling and two pence in the pound spent. To date those 72 members had, between them, invested almost £27 (around £1750) and spent, in the shop, £57 (£3700) – that's over £8 (£520 a week), not bad for a business that started out only being open two evenings a week.

As Secretary John Webb was later to note in his history of the Society (1892): 'No subsequent quarterly return gave so much satisfaction as that humble record of our early efforts; it came to us a mother's firstborn, a perfect promise of the issue that was to be, proving to us by the grand dividend of one shilling and two pence in the pound that we were on the high road to success, and solved the question of our ability to make Co-operation in the West of England a living factor in our daily lives.'

Within that quest to make co-operation *a living factor in our daily lives* was the earnest desire to help educate and improve the lot of the members and to that end three shillings were allocated from that first seven weeks trading surplus for 'educational purposes'.

Education: An Important Key

Educational provision within the town, indeed within England, was a little like the lighting in the Catte Street store without gas – woefully inadequate. Secretary Webb was one of the privileged few who had had a reasonable schooling. He had been a pupil at Jago's school in Cobourg Street and doubtless he, more than most, appreciated that having some form of education is like living with the light on: it is easier to find your way around, you can see things for what they are and, having identified a distant goal there is a better chance of attaining it.

Webb also knew the value of doing things by the book, and of learning from past experience. From the very outset he had been in touch with the Co-operative Pioneers at Rochdale about their rules and how they might be adapted for the Plymouth Society. Such correspondence and subsequent

deliberation with his Directors took up many hours of the shoemaker's valuable time. Duplicate copies were laboriously produced in longhand, before the working day began and after it had ended, only to find that the drafting had been done in line with legislation that was in place in 1844 when the Rochdale Society had started, but changes to the law in the meantime meant that they would have to be re-drafted.

Meanwhile, trading in Catte Street continued to prosper. More stock lines were added, and more stock generally was bought, the increased cash purchase power of the Society enabling more advantageous buying and a greater profit margin – and/or cheaper prices. Notwithstanding that, it soon became apparent that an even more substantial capital fund would allow even greater stock holdings and greater bargaining capabilities thereby making the Society's shop even more attractive. A special meeting was held to discuss the matter and a subsequent appeal to increase the Society's capital was well met with increased subscriptions – one man, John Rogers, agreeing to invest a pound on the spot … a huge amount of money for the working man at that time.

Clearly, confidence in the infant organisation was growing, however as the levels of success went up and up, so too did the degree of paranoia on the part of some investors. Remember this was a time when there were a lot of worthy, Chartist, socialist, co-operative ventures started, aiming to improve the plight of the poor and many failed – a worrying prospect for those for whom every penny was important.

'It will be recalled that the little shop at 15 Catte Street was owned by John Slade, one of the pioneers, and he held the door key during the hours of day and night, when the shop was closed. It was not long before some 'demon among the pack' whispered or made the suggestion that it would be easy for Mr Slade to enter the shop at any time during the closure hours and help himself to stock – not that there was any basis for this slur – but the Committee thought it wise to affix a second lock to the shop door; the key of which to be held by the person whose turn of duty it was to open the shop for trading. A notable plan in theory but not in practice; for if the duty person failed to turn up through illness or work, or forgot to bring the key or left it in the pocket of his other clothing, then the shop could not be opened until the key was located. So it was not long before Mr Slade had custody of both keys, living as he did in the next door property.'

'Publick School … for the Education and Improvement of the Morals of Poor Children' was constructed in Cobourg Street in 1812. Free at first, thanks largely to various philanthropic subscribers, the school was obliged to implement fees after the terrible cholera epidemic of 1832. Initially a penny per week, this was later raised to tuppence and then around 1860 it was increased to sixpence for pupils in the upper school.

The 16-year-old Catherine of Aragon arrived in Plymouth in 1501 en-route to London and marriage with Henry VII's eldest son, Arthur. The marriage had been set up to secure an alliance with Spain and foil the link between France and Scotland. In the event the fifteen year-old Arthur died within six months of the marriage and so as not to lose the 200,000 crown dowry, Henry made plans for Catherine to marry his second son, Henry.

John Slade must have smiled wryly to himself at this, but you can't help feeling that the man must have been a little upset that it was deemed necessary in the first place.

Happily, none of this nonsense thwarted the progress of the enterprise and when the accounts were drawn up at the end of the second quarter, at the end of June, it was revealed that weekly turnover had improved by around 30% despite the fact that membership had only increased by 10%. In other words, members were spending more in their shop. Thanks also to a new initiative, members were also able to benefit from buying meat as well as groceries, bread and flour, as an arrangement was reached with a local butcher who undertook to pay the Society a commission of 5% on all the meat he sold to members and in strict turnover terms, that market was equal to just over a third of the Catte Street sales.

However the profit margin was down slighty, reducing the value of the dividend from 5.8% to 5.4% – nothing too worrying it would seem but sufficiently concerning to one or two agitated members who called for - and got – a new set of Committee members.

Notwithstanding the level of dividend, business was clearly picking up on a week-by-week basis – over the next thirteen weeks, thirteen new members were recruited – and turnover again edged upwards. More significantly though it was during this summer quarter that the decision was taken to move out of John Slade's Catte Street property. Lack of space was apparently the driving factor, but doubtless there were other issues, not least of which was the location itself.

Time was when Catte Street housed some of the most desirable residences in Plymouth. Indeed, directly opposite the shop that the Co-operative was operating from was Palace Court: *'which yet stands, and may long stand, so substantial are its massive limestone walls, so sound still its oaken timbers,'* wrote 33-year-old Richard Nicholls Worth, a former feature writer for the *Western Morning News*. Worth was writing in the first edition of his first, and indeed the town's first formal history, published in 1870. Worth had started out as an apprentice journalist on the *Devonport and Plymouth Telegraph*, in 1858, so would have been well aware of the progress of the Plymouth Mutual Co-operative Society. He was also well aware of the history of the buildings in Catte Street, notably Palace Court, which

was *'reared by the rich merchant, Painter, towards the end of the fifteenth century. The evidence is not quite clear,'* he continued, *'but there seems little reason to doubt that this is the "goodly house towards the haven" which, according to Leland, Painter erected: and wherein he entertained the Princess Catherine of Aragon on her arrival in England; and the nobility and gentry of the neighbourhood who flocked to Plymouth to do honour to their future Queen.'*

'Palace Court, entered by an arched doorway, is situated in Catte-street, not far from the Old Guildhall, and is, at the present time, so far removed from anything palatial in appearance, or, in fact, that it has simply become the residence - being let off in separate floors or rooms - of people of the very lowest ranks of society. It is, indeed a place to be but once visited, and that, a visit of but short duration. Still, putting aside all feelings of disgust at the modes of living of its denizens, or of the filth and squalor of the place, it is worth a visit, and some few interesting features will repay examination - especially a carved corbel on the landing of one of the principal staircases. Of this "Palace Court" denuded of an excrescence, which has been built up in the quadrangle, and so cuts off some portion even of the little amount of free air the inhabitants formerly had to breathe, we give an engraving' **Llewellynn Jewitt's History of Plymouth, 1873.**

Social Conditions

By the time the Co-operative members opened their little shop here, however, the character of this old Plymouth street had changed, along with many of the other erstwhile up-market parts of the old town. As Worth himself noted, these changes were described in a *'very faithful but by no means flattering picture of the town as it appeared in 1852 drawn by Mr Rawlinson. He describes nearly every house and shop as having an independent style of its own; the macadamised streets as very dirty in wet weather and very dusty in dry; the old back streets as narrow, crooked, and steep, with narrow passages leading into dirtier and still more crowded courts.'*

'One privy serves the whole court, and this is usually filthy; the cess pool full, overflowing and the foetid refuse stagnant over the surface. An external standpipe, the water on only for one hour in twenty-four, supplies water to an entire court with many tenants; tubs, mugs, pots, pans, and troughs being placed in the yard, on the stairs, landings, or in the filthy rooms, to absorb all the deleterious gases of the place. Within, the furniture accords with the premises; it is old, rotten, broken, and ruinous. One room serves for a family of father, mother, and children - not unfrequently grown up sons and daughters. Dogs and fowl inhabit the same apartment, and, in some instances, ten human beings.

'Originally many of the houses now in ruins were erected as residences for the nobility and gentry of the town; but from being the abodes of those possessing wealth they now give partial shelter to the improvident, the vagrant, the vicious and the unfortunate. The quaint carving on the stonework looks out of place; the walls are half in ruins; the gables are shattered, and foul weather stains of damp blotch the surface. Within, matters are even worse; the rooms are now divided and subdivided on every floor; the staircase is darkened; its massive handrail and carved balusters are croppled and broken; the once firm stairs are now rickety and dangerous; the stucco-finished plastering is blackened and in holes.'

Many of the issues touched upon by Robert Rawlinson were common to many towns in Victorian England and in his capacity as an Inspector from the General Board of Health, he went around the country assessing the state of sanitation provision and/or the lack of it. Great changes followed in the wake of such reports as Worth noted: *'To the Commissioners the town is indebted for the improvement of Treville Street, and the widening of Whimple Street, in its narrowest part only fifteen feet across, to thirty-five feet. Since the Local Board superseded that body £50,000 has been expended in street improvements. Union Street, George Street, Bedford Street, and Old Town Street on the main line of thoroughfare, have all been cared for. To the commercial district of Plymouth, where the streets, old and narrow, proved utterly inadequate for the reception of the traffic to and from the quays, very great attention has wisely been paid. Notte and Woolster Streets have been widened almost throughout their whole length. Southside and Vauxhall Streets have received very little less care. At the same time, Plymouth has been transformed by the construction of a complete system of sewerage, at a cost of upwards of £35,000, from one of the unhealthiest towns in England into one of the healthiest.'*

However, while the principal arteries of the town were being widened, cleared and cleaned, in the back streets it was a slightly different story. Here the so-called slum clearance schemes were still decades away and doubtless provided the Members with further incentive to move their Co-operative base away from Catte Street to a location *'only separated from the main thoroughfare of Treville Street by that ancient hostelry known as the Spread Eagle public house.'*

A Better Location

The new premises were a complete property – a house with a shop frontage – 17 Kinterbury Street. On 19 September 1860, Catte Street was vacated and the following day, a Thursday, the Kinterbury Street store was ready for business. Among the many advantages offered by the new location were a store-room behind the ground floor shop and a dedicated room above the shop which could be used as an office, a committee/meeting room and a reading room/library. The spare upper and rear rooms were all let, the April 1861 census revealing that four couples, with twelve children between them, shared this accommodation with a couple of in-laws and lodgers. All in all the 25 tenants yielded a quarterly income of £4.10s0d, which, provided that it all came in, went a considerable way towards paying the £6.0s0d rental that was due for the whole building. In other words they now only needed to find 2/3d per week rent, instead of the 3/4d they were paying to use the rooms in John Slade's Catte Street property.

Robert Rawlinson was a successful engineer and sanitation expert and was one of the first inspectors appointed in the wake of the 1848 Public Health Act. His findings did not always endear him to Local Authorities, however his expertise in sanitation would have made him a very popular figure in a service area like the Three Towns. Sent out to the Crimea in 1855 where many men were losing their lives to disease rather than to the enemy, Rawlinson and his team were responsible for measures which, by the end of the year, meant that the health and hygiene of the British Army out there was in a better state than it was back home.

William Gibbons - Chemist and Druggist - 15 Kinterbury Street, the building to the right is probably No.16 making the taller building, next right, No17. With more floors and space at the back this, then, would appear to be the Plymouth Co-operative's second base.

Perhaps the principal advantage of the move however was the location itself – Kinterbury Street – running eastwards of and parallel to Old Town Street, this was a proper place of commerce. In addition to the Spread Eagle there was also The Lamb and the Treville Street Vaults, there were a handful of drapers, including J&S Stidston's, a handful of boot and shoemakers, a couple of cabinet makers, several warehouses, including that of Moon & Sons, the piano and sheet music specialists, there were printers, stationers, book sellers, ironmongers, wholesale fruiterers and grocerers, toy sellers, a watchmaker and jewellers, a baby linen warehouse, a paper-hanging warehouse and a painter and decorator. To put it simply there wasn't much you couldn't find for every one of life's requirements in the short stretch between Treville Street and Whimple Street and, by a strange quirk of fate, right next door to the enterprise's latest home - at 15 Kinterbury Street - was William Gibbons' pharmacy.

In the late summer of 1860 this was still pretty much an ordinary 'chemist and druggist', however, within the shop there was a small counter given over to the overriding passion of Gibbons' son, Edward Stanley - and that passion was the relatively new phenomenon of postage stamp dealing.

At first Gibbons was reluctant to indulge his son's whim, however, by 1862, that is within eighteen months or so of the Co-operative concern moving into Kinterbury Street, the young Gibbons was achieving a higher turnover with his stamps than his father was with the core pharmacy business.

Turnover, meanwhile, was increasing for the Co-operators too, although the dividend was down – a consequence, it was suggested by the Committee, of the cost of moving premises. This time the drop in dividend didn't prompt a change of committee, as confidence was clearly growing in the venture all the time. Another thirteen members had joined in the thirteen weeks up to the end of September and, having moved to a more commercially viable part of town, the decision was taken to open the shop during the daytime as well as in the evenings. As this would have placed unreasonable demands on the time of a volunteer workforce, the decision was further taken to employ a full-time sales person – Mrs Esther Carter.

The appointment, however, was not without its problems. Firstly, Mrs Carter, was, obviously, married and, at that time, there was widespread prejudice against the employment of married women; and secondly Mrs Carter's husband was a member of the Committee and during very busy periods Mr Carter would help his wife – the problem here being that rules forebade any committee member holding office if they had a pecuniary connection with an employee. However, as Mrs Carter was paid seven shillings a week and her husband was paid nothing, the view was sensibly taken that the Society was getting two workers for the price of one.

However, during that first autumn period of trading, an unpleasant, but minor, disagreement arose over the presentation of the accounts. John Slade, the Treasurer, and the man from whom the society had leased their first premises, was unhappy with the auditors marking the value of fixtures and fittings at their purchase price – he wanted to see them written down for a little less, allowing for depreciation. Making his views clear at a crowded meeting, he managed to upset most present by his dismissive responses and a motion was passed to expel him. Having not been properly conducted, the motion was judged invalid, however Slade saved any further embarassment by resigning his post. This unfortunate turn of events was compounded at the end of the next quarter when the value of the fixed assets were depreciated by 2.5%, vindicating Mr Slade, but he'd already left the Committee. Remarkably though, Slade's membership number, 4, was the only one of the original numbers to survive - although following the 2009 merger with Co-operative Group, it has now gone.

Taking Stock

Wednesday, 26 December 1860, saw the end of the Co-operators' first year of trading. They had come a long way since that previous Christmas Day when John Slade and John Shovel had called in to visit their friend Charles Goodanew for a bit of seasonal cheer. To date they had enlisted over 100 members (although eleven had come and gone already) and their modest enterprise had turned over almost £700 (£45,000); small wonder that they decided to hold a celebratory, Boxing Day, tea party at Buckland Hall, in Station Road off Union Street.

A severe frost made conditions difficult for the ladies ferrying the china and supplying the tea to the venue – on foot of course – but the event was a great success and made a handsome profit. And, to further round off what had undeniably been a good first year, a decision was taken to invest that profit in the purchase of a number of second-hand books; which together with donations and loans from members, was to form the basis of the Plymouth Co-operative Society's first library.

Above: mid-nineteenth century Union Street - Station Road was just this side of the railway bridge on the left. Right: the shop in Kinterbury Street.

The move to set up a library had been a neat solution to the problem encountered by the refusal of the Registrar of Friendly Societies, sixty-three year-old civil servant, John Tidd Pratt, to allow the co-operaters to siphon a small percentage of their profits off for the purposes of educating their membership. Three members – Thomas Reynolds, Joshua Gliddon and Edward Travers – were detailed to visit Mary Forward's second-hand bookshop in neighbouring Ebrington Place and buy books that they *'considered suitable for the reading and general enlightenment of the general membership'*. Forms (long benches) and a table were also purchased for *'the comfort of the members'* and Joshua Gliddon was appointed the Society's Librarian.

The Government Official in charge of registering and ratifying Friendly Societies - John Tidd Pratt (1797-1870).

And so ended the first year. The Plymouth Mutual Co-operative Society members had every reason to be pleased with themselves. As they set forth on their second year of trading their new hours of opening were testament to the fact that this was now a proper business and no longer one that operated on a part-time, entirely voluntary basis.

The shutters were off by seven o'clock every morning, until 8.30 every evening – Monday to Friday – with an extension soon introduced on Saturdays to 11pm! Not surprisingly the turnover showed a consistent increase and while the membership in 1861 only increased by around 50% the turnover was almost double that of the first year. The range of stock, too, was greatly increased.

The facts spoke for themselves – the Society was consolidating its already impressive status and well the members might exhort their Plymouth peers to jump on the bandwagon:

'Join us, Working Men, for we assure you, when you examine the groundwork of this Society you will find it holds all the seeds which, properly matured, shall grow and prosper for the working man's benefit, socially and morally, and will prove, when thoroughly developed, the charter by which our class shall be emancipated from the majority of the evils which afflict us - social or political. Above all, remember the poorer you are the more immediate and valuable to you will be the benefit.'

The purpose of the message was twofold: partly it was to persuade more people that it was in their interests to join the organisation, and thereby making it bigger, making it stronger too; and partly because there had been one or two conspicuous failures in the area of other co-operative ventures.

There was an average dividend of 1/6d for every pound spent and when the average annual spend per member was between eight and nine pounds this represented about twelve shillings (almost £40) of payback and was a very attractive incentive indeed, especially when members were already being rewarded by buying what was generally a much better quality product in the first place. Indeed by the end of that second year a significant amount of produce was being sold to non-members. In other words people who, even though they may not have been benefitting from

Plymouth Mutual Co-operative & Industrial Society's first secretary and historian - John Webb.

'the divi', were happy enough just to be buying more reliable groceries, bread, meat and other product lines as they became available.

However, against the rosy picture painted by the flowering Plymouth Society there were other, less encouraging stories to be told.

Part way through the year a local Bread and Flour Co-operative venture failed partly thanks to the mismanagement of the *'directors of the rotten concern'* (as Webb called them). *'The affair went to the Court of Chancery, and, there being no limited liability, the unfortunate shareholders had to pay several pounds per £ share to cover the losses and law costs associated with the bankrupt business.'* A change to the law (following the passing of the Companies Act in 1862) would stop shareholders being responsible for the debts of a company they invested in, but that change came too late for this society and given that some of the members of this concern were also members of the Plymouth Society, Webb says: *'We had to wax eloquent ere we could persuade people that ours was not a second edition of the swindle, and our system was based on a different practice.'*

The unsuccessful saga of the Bread and Flour Co-operative failure was by no means the only local failure of its kind and Webb's early history contains several references to other societies in the Plymouth area which failed. *'There is for example, talk of a society, "a sickly little concern, which had small capital, less credit and no energy". For a time in response to an appeal for help, Plymouth Society supplied it with goods at the cheaper rate, made possible by better buying. This only delayed "the inevitable crash that will always attend a co-operative society which trades on insufficient capital and gives credit to their members on such security".'*

The Plymouth Committee suggested members increase their stake in the share capital to breathe new life into their concern, but it was too late - instead *'members withdrew what money they could, and when the society's credit was stopped its existence soon ceased. Some of the members joined the Plymouth Society - sadder, but wiser.'*

At around the same time a couple of societies at Keyham, then very much a new town built up around the Keyham Steamyard (the new Dockyard development, which had opened nine years earlier), also failed. So too did a society in Exeter, in 1863. Anxious to find out why, and with a view to making sure it didn't happen here, the Committee sent secretary Webb to investigate.

'Downright dishonesty' on the part of some of the principal players in that organisation, was Webb's finding. Clearly, according to his later account, the simple nature of Webb's verdict prompted one or two members of the Plymouth committee to think that his fact finding journey had been a waste of their time – and money – despite the valuable information and advice that had been gleaned.

Not that the Plymouth society was itself immune to 'downright dishonesty' although fortunately the scale of their internal problems, while big enough to rock the boat were never big enough to capsize it.

The first culprit was a certain Mr Stribling, who was appointed purchaser for the society early in the summer of 1861. It would appear that previously much of the purchasing had been overseen by Webb's brother, Thomas, who had many years experience of the grocery trade. The purchaser's job was to attend every committee meeting and keep it informed of the vagaries of the market.

Having provided a Bond of £5 as security, Stribling was allowed a weekly cash float of two pounds (£130) to cover the cost of small purchases. However before the year was out 'Stribling went away to parts unknown', taking £1.12s5d with him which would appear to have been 2/5d more than his quarterly wage. 'This caused some friction between members of the Committee, particularly when Stribling's Bond proved to be worthless.'

Even from our perspective, 150 years on, we can probably imagine the atmosphere of those committee meetings and reading between the lines of Secretary Webb's early history it is very obvious, and by no means surprising, that the bigger the whole enterprise became the more serious the meetings became.

The opening of Keyham Steam Yard in 1853 was swiftly followed by the development of new estates at Keyham and Ford and was a great boost to the population of Devonport, Stoke and Morice Town.

'The Committee, as privileged individuals at their meetings in those primitive days, were of a very free and jovial disposition; pipes were lighted, jokes indulged in, all spoke at once when they were so minded, and the lord of misrule reigned merrily indeed. This state of affairs became intolerable from a business point of view, so in July 1862 the Committee resolved that 'all irregularities during business hours should be visited on the head of each offender by a fine of one penny: smoking and failing to keep order when requested by the chairman so to do, or not rising in his place when speaking, being specially named for which a fine shall be imposed.'

This resulted in more orderly conduct at Committee Meetings except for one objecting member who resigned his office in disgust, but as Webb recorded, 'we managed to do without him and elected a better and more reasonable man.'

A Serious Business

The increasing seriousness of the business quite simply reflected the increasing onerousness of the business. The more produce that was sold the more work that had to be done ordering, recording and administering that activity and, not surprisingly, the hardworking Committee began to feel that perhaps they should have a modest slice of the action to reflect the fact that they were putting in more hours and more effort than the average member.

So it was that in March 1862, just two years after Committee men had jealously guarded their rights to take their turn to do voluntary shifts in that first Co-op shop, the Committee now commenced the payment of the rota sub-committee, responsible for the supervision of the store.

'Two Committee members had to take charge of the goods each week, see them weighed and equal to sample, enter them in the invoice book, and bring up at the next meeting a list of articles required. For this they were to receive two shillings per week. At the same time it was decided to pay the Treasurer five shillings per quarter, though, later in the year this was increased to ten shillings.'

This decision was doubtless partly prompted by the huge amount of work involved simply in recording in massive ledgers every member's purchases. It was tedious and terribly time-consuming work and so the Committee decided to enter the world of metal checks and tokens. From a die-maker in Birmingham, a Mr Smith, they ordered ten different value dies, presumably; a farthing, ha'penny, penny, threepence, sixpence, shilling, florin, half-crown, crown and a pound.

The checks were impressed with the name of the Society and the value represented, and the Society ordered 14,000 of them and straight away had the job of counting them to make sure they had exactly the right number. That was just the beginning of what would prove to be an ongoing headache, for the next task was to commission a carpenter to make a box with ten separate compartments to take the tokens.

At first problems with an ill-fitting lid meant that checks kept slipping into the wrong compartment, much to the irritation of all concerned and the carpenter wasn't paid until he'd sorted the problem.

The system was set up in such a way that whatever cash the customers spent they would be issued with checks to that value – their dividend being calculated on the value of the check holding at the end of each quarter. Clearly this meant that the amount of checks issued should be exactly equal to the amount of takings across the counter, and that meant from non members, as well as members and so a special drawer was also fitted into the shop to take all the checks generated by sales to non members.

No sooner had the new system been put in place, than the Committee resolved to pay Bartholomew Fox, a general labourer and one of the Society's first three trustees (appointed in the summer of 1860), sixpence a week *'for his trouble in keeping the checks and supplying the saleswoman (Mrs Carter), and keeping and balancing the accounts of all those handed to and received from her.'*

Of course the new system presupposed that every member was organised enough to store and cash their checks at the end of each quarter and practice soon showed that this wasn't always the case. Thus it was decided that henceforth the dividend should be calculated on the basis of the checks returned rather than those issued, a decision that resulted in a 3% - 4% rise in the dividend.

As the implications of the system made themselves more and more obvious a twin-locked box was made to store the checks and two Committee members were detailed to jointly issue the checks to Mrs Carter. However while the Committee could take various measures to make sure everything was as watertight as possible at their end, there was no guarantee that members would be entirely straight in their check dealings. As Robert Briscoe noted in his centenary history:

'The Committee was never very pleased with the metal check system. It permitted trading in checks, since there was no means of identifying the member with his purchases. The counterfeiting of checks, particularly the brass ones of £1 denomination was another problem. Rumour had it that an unofficial quota of checks was added to the official store.'

Victorian coinage ranged in value from a farthing (a quarter of a penny) through to penny and a guinea (a gold coin worth £1.1.0d.). Above a crown (5/-) and a penny.

'Finally, in 1886, five members of the Society, including a committee member, were expelled on suspicion of having stolen a quantity of them. The Society reverted to the old practice of booking in duplicate members' purchases.'

It should be remembered that these could be, and often were, very hard times for the working man and for those living in cramped and crowded conditions, where every penny was precious, trust was a very valuable commodity. It wasn't easy to find a safe place to keep what little money one might amass, a bank account was beyond most people, as were savings accounts.

Nationally there were only 600 savings banks, many of which were owned and operated by local employers, and workers were often reluctant to make deposits, however modest, as they were worried that their employers might cut their wages if they – the employers – thought that their employees could afford to save anything from their wages.

Happily however, as the Plymouth Society entered its second year, the Chancellor of the Exchequer, William Gladstone, announced, in the House of Commons, that new savings banks for low-paid men were to be established in every Post Office in the land. For Plymouth, that meant the new facility would be in Whimple Street, where, as it happened, the Plymouth and South Devon Savings Bank had just moved and where Plymouth's second oldest bank, the Naval Bank (established in 1773) had moved a decade earlier.

Gladstone's news was roundly welcomed, one MP observing that, *'the state provides beer shops for working men to spend their money, but has not been forward in giving them facilities for saving.'*

To put that in some sort of context, the 600 savings banks nationally in 1861 could be contrasted with in excess of 300 pubs and beerhouses operating at the same time in Plymouth alone (that is not counting Devonport and Stonehouse). Drunkenness was a great problem. The Government's attempt in 1863 via the Revenue Act to steer drinkers away from spirits, and towards beer, was a step to try and reduce the problem as was the closure, the following year, of all London pubs between the hours of one o'clock and four o'clock in the afternoon.

The problem of where to keep cash wasn't just a problem for the individual however: as the Society's turnover continued to rise the question of storing surplus funds became a growing responsibility. As they entered their third summer the Society's average weekly take was well over £30 (£2,000) and it was decided that every penny in excess of £10 (*'to meet petty expenses and bills due'*) should be taken fifty yards or so down the road and deposited in the Naval Bank – on the corner of Kinterbury Street and Whimple Street – every Monday morning.

Kinterbury Street, looking towards Whimple Street

The Society, after little more than two years, was now on a fairly solid footing and over and above their annual fire insurance premiums they were also now looking to protect themselves against altogether unknown hazzards.

On 1 April 1862 the decision was taken to commence a guarantee (reserve) fund, initially this was on a sliding scale depending on the level of dividend, but later it was commuted to a simple 2.5% of the trading surplus.

All these measures placed an increasing burden on the Society's principal administrator, John Webb, and in order to save him going back to the committee, *'like Oliver Twist, quarter after quarter asking for more'*, each time that increase became demonstrable *'a most interesting method was evolved for paying the secretary. Educationists will be interested to note that this is the first recorded instance of the "per capita" basis being used for anything. The first payment the secretary received was in the third quarter when he was paid 10s.; at the end of two and a half years, the remuneration had risen by leaps and bounds to 30s. for the quarter's work, at which figure some members considered him too well paid for the amount of work involved and, in any case, the Secretary was placed in the invidious position of having to ask continually for more. This caused members to introduce the piecework principle into co-operative practice. The Secretary was to be paid 3d. per quarter for each bona-fide member on the books, and this was to be checked by the auditors.'*

The simple logic of these and other payments, including some remuneration for the auditors, seem to have raised few eyebrows among the membership, however the decision to hire crockery and meet certain other expenses at the Society's second Christmas party, caused *'much argument'* when an overall, and reasonably substantial, loss was reported on the event. It was a different story the following year however, and the third festive celebration raised over eight pounds (£500) and it was decided to donate the whole lot to the Lancashire Famine Relief Fund.

On the one hand this acknowledged the Plymouth Society's debt to the inspiration and ideals of the Rochdale Pioneers and on the other it was a call for help that had been circulated around all the Co-operative Societies on behalf of the Lancashire MIll Workers. With no unemployment benefit to be had, the cessation of the supply of cotton, a consequence of the ongoing American Civil War, had brought even greater hardship to that part of the Midlands.

Nor was it just individuals who were struggling. In April 1864 it emerged that *The Co-operator* – the organ of the Co-operative Movement – was in financial difficulty.

Predecessor of the *Co-operative News* and logical successor to the monthly periodical that William King had produced, between 1828-1830, the then current incarnation of *The Co-operator* was a fortnightly publication that had been started by the Manchester Equitable Society in 1860, rapidly enlisting the services of local journalist Henry Pitman.

Pitman soon found himself editing *The Co-operator* – he even suggested the name – and after just nine months was forced either to take full control, and be responsible for all charges and liabilities, or see it fold.

Happily it managed to survive and for their part, in 1864, the Plymouth Co-operators sent a grant of one guinea (around £70) from the Reserve Fund, plus an undertaking to buy as many copies as there were purchasing members in Plymouth (around 250), a third of the cost of this being borne by the education fund.

The second youngest of eleven children, one of Pitman's elder brothers was Isaac (the phonography man) and the young Henry was one of the first to learn his brother's system of shorthand. Undoubtedly it gave his reporting a more accurate touch and as the 1860s unfolded *The Co-operator* covered one of the most exciting decades in the development of the Co-operative Movement. Certainly through it's printing chapters of Holyoake's History of the Rochdale Pioneers, it did much to spread the success of co-operation.

The Plymouth operation was clearly one of those success stories. Getting ever stronger and more financially stable they were not only in a position to help other organisations, but also, themselves. Under new rules they decided, in May of 1864, to elect Samuel Lockwood as their first President (he had been the Society's original auditor) and moreover to pay him sixpence a week, a level of remuneration that Secretary Webb estimated as working out at a penny an hour (less than a pound!), which suggests

Brighton physician, and philanthropist, Dr William King, had started the Co-operator back in May 1828. A monthly periodical, it promoted the principals of co-operation and even gave practical advice about running a shop along co-operative lines.

King, who had thought about the church as a career, was very well-educated (Ipswich Grammar/Cambridge University/Paris) and settled in Brighton soon after his marriage in 1821. Quick to become involved with charitable work and the welfare of the working classes, he advocated that people should not cut themselves adrift from society but rather should create a society within a society and whereas Robert Owen had written of the way forward being through a utopian vision of 'villages of co-operation', King's way forward was for a more step by step pragmatic approach - to start with a shop.

'We must go to a shop every day to buy food and necessaries - why then should we not go to our own shop?' To that end he proposed a regime of rules, audits, trustees ... and the avoidance of pubs for meetings (lest the profits should get drunk). If the working man would only fund his own shops, contributing small regular sums, then such shops could sell a basic range of goods (mainly food - as a medical man he was well-aware of the adulteration that went on) and then the profits on these commodities could be used to pay the unemployed to make other products to sell.

For just over two years King used The Co-operator to expound views that justifiably place him in the eyes of many as the true father of Co-operation – at least in terms of the ultimate practical success of the movement. However, while never forsaking his beliefs and principals and while maintaining a relationship – as a friend and advisor - with Lady Noel Byron, King concentrated on his medical career after 1830 and The Co-operator ceased publication.

Dr William King - 'father of the modern Cooperative Movement'. Right: First edition of The Co-operator, the monthly magazine King produced in Brighton.

THE CO-OPERATOR.

KNOWLEDGE AND UNION ARE POWER:
POWER, DIRECTED BY KNOWLEDGE, IS HAPPINESS:
HAPPINESS IS THE END OF CREATION.

No. 1.   MAY 1, 1828.   1d.

A Co-operative Society, like all other Societies, such as benefit Clubs, Trade Societies, Savings' Banks, is for the purpose of avoiding some evils, which men are exposed to when they act singly, and of obtaining some advantages which they must otherwise be deprived of.

The evils which CO-OPERATION is intended to combat, are some of the greatest to which men are liable, viz. the great and increasing difficulties of providing for our families, and the proportionate danger of our falling into PAUPERISM and CRIME.

Let us consider these more at length.

The rate of wages has been gradually diminishing for some hundred years, and now it is not above one-third of what it used to be—but this is not all, for the same causes continuing to act, the wages must go on diminishing till a workman will not be able to maintain a family; and by the same rule, he will at last not be able to maintain himself. This conclusion it is frightful to think of, but whether we think of it or not, it will march on in its own silent way, till it unexpectedly overwhelms us like a flood.

But are we certain that this is true?—are we really approaching any thing like starvation, in spite of any labor and industry we may exert? I am afraid that this is certainly true; and I will give you other reasons for thinking so.

PAUPERISM.

Why do people become paupers?—because they must either go to the parish, or starve. And this necessity has operated so widely, that the independent day laborer has almost ceased to exist. The country laborer who can, in many respects, live cheaper than we can in a town; who can have his garden, and raise his own potatoes, &c. can now very seldom live without the parish aid: and it is a common rule to make an allowance for each child, above a certain number. The same situation has begun to beset the mechanic. He is frequently obliged to go without work a day or two in the week, or to have his wages lowered. If this goes on, he must also come to the parish.

1

that the President was involved in around six hours work a week on the part of the Society. The Committee had, incidentally, already voted themselves expenses of 6d a week the previous year when they had upped Mrs Carter's wages to 11/- (just under £40) a week.

Furthermore it was also agreed that should any member be in severe financial difficulties - 'extreme distress' - then they could receive a grant of up to a pound, provided that 'the unfortunate applicant' had at least two and a half times that amount to their credit in the account of the Society. Such was the Plymouth Society's confidence in their enterprise that they now felt that they were in a position to offer an albeit limited form of credit.

Business was good and about to get a whole lot better.

Derry's Clock - erected to commemorate the wedding, on 10 March 1863, of the 21-year-old Prince of Wales, Albert Edward (the future Edward VII) to 18-year-old Princess Alexandra, daughter of Christian IX of Denmark. Plymouth's Mayor, William Derry, paid for the clock and the Corporation, through Derry's efforts, financed the drinking fountain which supported it. Many people treated the day as a holiday, including the Co-operators: 'Although we are essentially a democratic movement, yet we were so loyal to the Throne, and those connected therewith, that we determined, on the occasion of the marriage of the Prince of Wales, to forego our convenience, and close the shop on that day, the objectors thereto being in a hopeless minority.'

CHAPTER 2: EXPANSION & EMPLOYMENT

The Freemason's Hall, Cornwall Street, 1832 - this neighbourhood was a far cry from the back street premises in Catte Street.

As the Plymouth Mutual Co-operative Society approached the end of its fifth year of trading it was felt by the members that the time had come to move again. *'Since we were getting so great and the little shop in Kinterbury Street becoming inadequate to our wants, a sub-committee was appointed to look out for a shop that would be more suited to our purpose and many houses named by them were overhauled and rejected; meanwhile we jogged on, doing our best in our restricted premises, where, in a quarterly meeting of 5th January 1864, we decided to remain.'*

'By August 2nd we had become savage at being cooped up in Kinterbury Street, and panted for more room and we resolved "that the Committee be empowered to take more commodious premises at once".'

Thus it was that just six days later, on 8 August 1864, after almost four years, the Society moved on again – this time to 3 Cornwall Street, just along from the impressive Freemason's Hall and not far from the Public Library.

Mrs Carter took the opportunity to retire and was presented with an illuminated testimonial in recognition of her exemplary service, meanwhile a new shopman, Mr Oliver, a man with some experience of the furniture business, was appointed.

The new building allowed a degree of expansion. In addition to the ground floor shop there were eight other rooms which meant that the Education Department could have separate rooms for the library and the reading room. The shop opened every morning as before at 7.30am and closed Monday-Friday at 8.30pm (11pm on Saturdays).

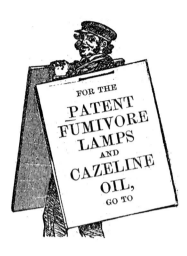

FOR THE
PATENT
FUMIVORE
LAMPS
AND
CAZELINE
OIL,
GO TO

The Reading Room itself, however kept the building open 8-10pm each evening and was stocked with *'books, papers, chess and draughts, for the information or amusement of members and friends.'*

To promote the change of address some 10,000 handbills were printed and distributed and such was the impact of the increased confidence of, and in, the Society, that turnover in the three months of the year was almost as much as that of the first six months. Membership too rose spectacularly with the biggest number of new recruits joining up since the first year.

Small wonder, therefore, that when, in November, members were asked to increase their investment in the Society so that a larger and more varied stock could be held and sold, the response was more than equal to it.

The new shopkeeper, Mr Oliver, however, was apparently not equal to the task of running the shop in quite the way the members hoped – or expected; *'A poor venture'* who *'caused us much loss and trouble through his careless habits and dishonesty. Though not clearly proven, we were morally satisfied that such was the fact and so we parted with him, to our great relief, before he had served twelve months behind the counter.'*

As the Society paved the way for Mr Oliver's departure so they turned their attention to his replacement; *'members clamoured for a professional to conduct their business, thinking it undignified in their greatly growing position that a man not born in or brought up to the trade should stand behind our counter and do our business.'*

What they wanted was a grocer, not a former furniture salesman and so another sub-committee was constituted to *'enquire into the character and skill of the many applicants'* that came forward for the post. However as the secretary himself was later to note; *'I fear we chose the worst - at least, we chose one bad enough.'*

After four years of steady growth and prosperity under Mrs Carter in Kinterbury Street, the Society clearly had great hopes of their move to Cornwall Street, and certainly, sales in the last quarter of 1864 were close to double what they had been in the last full quarter in the old place, but the dividend was the same as it had been for that quarter and already questions were being asked of Mr Oliver. With that unfortunate gentleman

out of the way, however, it was anticipated that the true rewards of the move would at last be reaped.

However such was the scale of the problems generated by his successor, Robert Kennard, that Secretary Webb devoted a whole chapter of his history to the saga and titled it *'Peril'*.

Peril: The Kennard Saga

The episode is undoubtedly significant as at its lowest point it threatened the very survival of the Plymouth Society, however it is also fascinating for the details of the whole sorry affair reveals a great deal about the wider world in which it happened:

'Robert Kennard, on whom the choice of the Committee fell as the professional grocer to undertake the management of our shop, was a nice-looking, well-spoken, good-tempered little man some 25 or 26 years old (the son of a minister of the gospel of Christianity, and who stood as bondsman for him), entered our service at the end of July, 1865, a guard of two Committeemen being set on the premises during the time that Mr Oliver was clearing out and Mr Kennard taking possession.'

Clearly the Society had come a long way in five or six years; turnover was almost four times what it had been in that first year and the stock could no longer be stored in a corner cupboard, however it is interesting to note that for the benefit of the incoming – and the outgoing – shopkeeper a full and thorough stock-take was carried out by two committee members in the presence of both men.

It is also worth recalling that Mr Oliver was not the first employee to cause the Society headaches, there had already been the saga of Mr Stribling, the purchaser, who not only absconded with ready cash but whose £5 bond had proved worthless. Consequently, and in due consideration of an altogether more responsible post, the Committee decided to levy a £40 bond on their new man. However the Reverend Kennard objected to this, being only prepared to make himself responsible for £20 and, notes Webb, *'the Committee tamely made the alteration in accordance with his wish'*. *'It was,'* adds Webb with the benefit of hindsight, *'the first foreshadowing of our coming trouble.'*

The second cause for concern came just two days after the quarterly meeting that had ratified young Kennard's contract. There was general unease within the Committee that not only did the figures for the Society's last quarter's trading (and the first under Kennard) not show a profit, they appeared to reveal a loss, and, therefore, no dividend.

Anxious not to face the members without being able to explain the situation they gave orders for another stock check, but by the time of the adjourned quarterly meeting no further light had been shed on the matter and so they appointed two of their members to check again, *'entrusting to this task a mason, who was on his own showing an undoubted authority in all matters connected with figures, and another, who, without vaunting, really did know something of accounts'*.

Of itself this serves to highlight the degree of amateurishness that still pervaded the whole endeavour, a situation compounded when these new efforts failed to throw any insight into the affair and a resolution was passed suggesting that the mason should have the sovereign paid to him for his troubles withdrawn. They did however relent, but clearly that still didn't solve the problem and rather than face *'scornful tongues and fingers'* the Committee resolved not to issue a balance sheet for that quarter.

Night after night they met to try and get to the bottom of the matter. In the meantime the weak-kneed and greedy, in the absence of a dividend payment, demanded repayment of their share capital, prompting a resolution from the Committee that *'all applications for withdrawals from the Society not be entertained until the loss incurred by us during the twenty-third quarter be satisfactorily settled by the meeting of to-morrow.'*

However the meeting the next day, Thursday, 23 November 1865, revealed little other than that the stock auditor's account was *'generally correct'*.

By now the frustration of the members was almost at boiling point and it wasn't helped by the fact that the prime object of their anxiety - their new storeman - was at the meeting: *'Feeling against Mr Kennard ran high, and the place became as excitable as a political meeting, with this exception, that all the irritation set one way, and that was 'Kennardwards'. Threats of all sorts, stopping short of putting them into execution, were hurled at the young man by the majority of members.*

'Fearing an outbreak of lynch law and moreover feeling they ought no longer to trust him with their cash now their confidence was gone' the meeting was adjourned, but the Committee met the following day and *'boldly stepping outside the strict interpretation of the law'* resolved that *'Mr Carter should take the place of Mr Kennard on Saturday'* and that the Committee would hold themselves responsible for him (presumably this was the very same Mr Carter whose wife had retired when the Society moved from Kinterbury Street and who was experienced himself in the running of the business).

Of course it hadn't helped in relation to the above that the Society's cash box had *'in some mysterious way escaped from the custody of Mr Robert (Kennard), and by some equally mysterious manner turned up at Stoke, somewhere in the neighbourhood of Penlee, dreadfully mutilated and minus the coin.*

'We fancied we saw the rogue stealing at dead of night, with the battered box hidden from public view, seeking a place wherein to deposit the mute witness of his crime.'

Thus it was that Mr Carter, the Secretary, John Webb, and *'as many of the Committee as we could manage to assemble at that unusual hour'* - that is before breakfast - met outside the shop in Cornwall Street. One can imagine that the street was quite quiet, on that last Saturday morning in November and certainly that the Committee men themselves would have been hushed as they waited for Robert Kennard to *'throw open the doors at the regular time for business'*.

By Webb's account we learn that Kennard was *'rendered for a moment speechless ... I suppose he saw the game was played out, and he, the loser, checkmated in a way he had not looked for.*

'Politely they all bade him a "Good Morning" ... 'though I believe there was not a man among them who would not have preferred taking him by the ear and thrusting him into the street; but as that would have been contrary to the Act made and provided for the public peace, we acted the hypocrite with honied words that found no echo in our hearts.'

Once inside the shop they read Kennard their resolution and Mr Carter took over from the young man who protested throughout at the high-handed manner with which the proceedings were being conducted. This, however was just the beginning of what would become a very protracted affair.

The adjourned quarterly meeting was held on the Tuesday, the day that Mr Carter's temporary employment was due to end, according to the previous week's resolution, but a decision was taken to suspend Mr Kennard for a further week and in the meantime John Webb was charged with the task of looking into 'the whole account of the Society's trade from the date of Mr Kennard's employment'.

Webb picks up the story: 'Now that matters had reached this critical state, and our faith in the man having been so rudely destroyed that we could only think evil of him, and having arrived at that morbid state that fears a highwayman in every bush, we were frightened lest he, during the silent watches of the night, might so far seek revenge for our summary treatment of him as to roam the premises unchecked and remove so many of our goods as may have suited his requirements.'

The author then goes on to defend the Committee's paranoia by stating that rumour was rife concerning a previous shopman, who worked at the premises, and 'baskets belonging to nobody knew who, filled with nobody knew what, had been seen to leave No.3 at very unholy hours, and betake them to another house in the neighbourhood'.

Clearly this wasn't entirely relevant as the Co-operative were not in occupation then, however, Webb continues: 'Therefore to prevent any suspicion of loss in a similar manner, it was deemed necessary that some other person should be engaged to sleep somewhere on the premises, and keep watch between the shuttering of the shop in the evening and the advent of the temporary salesman in the morning.'

However nobody wanted to accept the challenge: 'one after the other declined the thankless and uncomfortable duty, until the Secretary, in despair, agreed to be the victim.'

Thus it was that Webb himself ended up sleeping on a mattress on the floor of the room used by the Committee. For three weeks he maintained this

vigil, 'thereby preventing any wrong doing on the part of the enemy if such had been his intention - the only loss, as far as he was aware, being one sheet, which disappeared on the very last night.'

Somewhat dryly Webb notes that while he wasn't reimbursed for the loss of the sheet at least the Committee 'generously declined to charge him for his lodging, which I presume they considered a fair equivalent for the lost linen'.

A week later, on 5 December 1865, Kennard was dismissed by a resolution of the Quarterly Meeting … 'but seeing that it would be rather sharp practice to turn him into the street without some little preparation, they kindly allowed him to remain one week longer in the apartments allotted to him.'

Quaint as all this maybe appears from the present age of product tagging, electronic cash transactions and CCTV, it was a major problem for our early Co-operators. Although, on the face of it, life went on in the new Cornwall Street premises, and trade continued to grow - behind the scenes there was great consternation, especially as more and more of the more timid members wanted to withdraw funds 'as each fresh act of turpitude came to light, and losses small in themselves became, through the uncertainty, magnified immensely'.

What's more, simply relieving themselves of their second consecutive corrupt storeman was not the end of the matter. Having terminated Kennard's employment the Society demanded the £20 bond that had been grudgingly agreed. Kennard, however, was not happy with the suggestion, nor, more importantly was his reverend father, and a counter claim was made for a month's wages and the return of the £20 that young Kennard had invested as his security … 'which £20 we shrewdly suspected was paid out of the money taken on our account, as it was not paid for some short time after he took charge of our business'.

In other words it rather looked as though Kennard had appropriated the funds from the Co-op's daily takings to pay his deposit to his Co-operative employers. 'Consequently a minute was made to the effect that no person should in future take charge of our business until the whole of the money agreed on as security was safely deposited in the Treasurer's hands.'

Remember, while not exactly amateurs, none of these men had ever run anything bigger than their own business, and already, after just a few years, their Co-operative endeavour was much bigger than anything they had achieved individually, and there were still areas of operation in which they were very much novices. Arbitration was one of them.

In accordance with the Act under which the Society was registered, *'If any dispute arose between members of the Society and the Committee, the affair should (all other means failing) be settled by arbitration.'*

As an internal matter, the police not having been involved, this was regarded, by law, as a private quarrel, and the Society's constitution decreed that as long as the person making an appeal was prepared to deposit the sum of ten shillings - *'as proof of his being earnest in his demand for justice'* - then he was entitled to that arbitration. Kennard paid his ten shillings.

In accordance with the Act that legitimised their activities the Society had named five arbitrators and three of them now had to be chosen, by lot, to consider this issue. *'The three allotted, being informed thereof, duly met, and their first act in the drama was to look out for number one; that is, to know who were going to pay them for their trouble.'*

Another lesson for the Society.

But who was to pay? *'After some demur on the part of the Committee, and positive refusal on the part of the Kennards, we at last, after much negotiation and discussion, agreed, by February 26th, that 'we would guarantee the arbitrator's full payment for the service rendered by them'.'*

Taking Webb's stock account as their starting point they set to work. The arbitrators, being working men, could only meet outside working hours and consequently the meetings, in the Cornwall Street committee room, were at irregular and often very late hours - *'several times well into the next day'. Each meeting had to have all three judges, plus Kennard and Webb:*

'Mr Kennard, whose reputation and cash were at stake, fought bravely at every point where he could hope to gain a penny in his favour ... while the Secretary, stoutly opposed his claim to any unfair leaning in his favour; and the arbitrators, not being pressed for time, and knowing the remuneration would depend on the hours spent in the investigation, listened with exemplary patience to the oft-recurring wrangle ... finishing their nightly labours with a reasonable amount of good refreshment kindly provided for them in the form of high teas.'

And so it dragged on, until, in the middle of April, the arbitrators found, in the Society's favour, that Kennard was deficient in his cash account by nearly eight pounds (approx. £500), but they were only prepared to release their verdict after they had been paid (6 May) and their bill was nearer £30 (£2,000).

Throughout all these proceedings Kennard had not only been, quite rightly, attending the arbitration proceedings, but had also, through *'bad manners and mistaken notion of his due'* (Webb's words), been attending Committee meetings, as a member of the Society. Thus it was that two days after the arbitrators released their verdict the Committee expelled Kennard from the Society ... and *'so we got rid of him, as we thought'.*

However the Society's angst was far from over. The Reverend Kennard, having been made aware of the situation, *'naturally refused to believe in his son's ill conduct, threatened and blustered about what he would do if this, that, and the other thing were not done according to his direction, or at least to his satisfaction and proved to be a harder nut than his son.'* And so, *'being doubtful of our skill in legal matters, we hired a lawyer.'*

John Beer, who lived at 2 Albermarle Villas, was engaged to fight the Co-operator's corner; *'but the old gentleman had no experience of Co-operative law or Co-operative Societies, and was not a success in the opinion of the members'.*

Solicitor number two was no better *'but was honest enough to confess his ignorance of our requirements'*, and yet notwithstanding that he still had to be paid, just like the first gentleman they'd hired.

Every step of the proceedings had been a learning curve, and an expensive one at that. Happily however it was a case of third time lucky, and lawyer number three concluded the Kennard affair; apparently with a minimum of fuss and a bill of £3.18s.6d.

Albermarle Villas, Stoke

For all correspondence: selection of contemporary postage stamps, each one slightly enlarged

At last the whole nightmare was at an end, or so it seemed, there was, however, to be yet one more twist in the tale: *'We had one burly gentleman, a great friend of the Kennards, who often sat in the Presidential chair. Being elected thereto in July 1865, he not only refused to believe the facts as verified by the arbitrators, but he also presented for dividend a large number of checks that were said to represent the purchases of one Mr Bright. The Committee, doubting his word, seized the checks, and consulted the lawyer on the advisability of prosecuting him for fraud in attempting to obtain money under false pretences - we presumed the checks to have been purloined by Kennard and handed to him.'*

'This we did at the Plymouth Police Court, but were unable to show a sufficiently clear case of roguery to induce the magistrates to convict him; but he left us, and I have not heard that anybody regretted his departure.'

The upshot of the whole Kennard saga was that for the first time the balance sheet at the end of the quarter (it was a double period on account of the earlier adjournment) showed a deficit of £25.11s.3d. which included the uncertain asset of the £20 bond due on Kennard's account.

After two unsuccessful appointments and the protracted proceedings that followed in their wake, the Committee were wiser, but poorer - quite literally, for on 28 May the decision was taken to write off 5/- from the accounts of each of the 200 *'whose hearts had never failed them, or whose faith in our ultimate success had never been shaken'.*

Implicit in those words is just how fragile the enterprise still was and clearly some members had abandoned ship soon after those troublesome waters had been encountered. The failure of the Devonport and Keyham and Exeter enterprises were still fresh in local minds, while nationally, news of the horror story from Scotland where the large Glasgow society, having expanded too rapidly, failed in 1864, would have no doubt spread like wildfire.

Moving On

These were testing times and although it was now twenty years since the Rochdale movement had established itself, and inspired a hundred or so similar experiments across the country, there were still many areas yet to jump on to the Co-operative bandwagon. London itself came quite late to the movement; indeed nothing much happened there until 1860 when a group of railway workers started to get together.

Co-operation was still a very novel phenomenon and one that not only had its doubting Thomases within the movement, but many jealous detractors outside it. It was fully two years since the Plymouth members *'to counteract the prying tendency of our enemies to spy out our nakedness (now we had gained some notoriety), and curious folk who were desirous to know the secret of our success, resolved that no person should tread our holy ground unless under the supervision and guidance of one of the Committee'.*

At the same time, within the movement our local Co-operators recognised the value of learning from the experience of others and decided to buy in ten shillings worth of *The Co-operator* each week and make them available to members at half-price. To that same end the Committee *'ventured to spend fourpence a week in the purchase of The Grocer, a paper published in the interest of the retail traders, the knowledge derived from which was well worth the money, although we often had the mortification to read some bitter words directed against our movement; but we could afford to laugh at their interested babble, seeing their unkind words broke no bones or frightened a single member so as to cause him to desert our ranks'.*

Not everyone saw the value in this however and a vote was necessary to endorse the decision; indeed not everybody appeared to see the value in the Secretary. In the summer of 1865 Webb's right to open all the mail addressed to the Society was challenged and eighteen months later, thinking him to be overpaid, they advertised his job at £3 per quarter instead of the £4 it had grown to. There were just two candidates for the post – a Mr R Woods and Webb himself:

'At the election the members thought the old one was good enough, now that the payment was reduced twenty-five per cent, and continued him in the place he had filled from the foundation.'

Webb was clearly an important figure in the early success of the Plymouth Society and, as Secretary and probably the best-educated, and most articulate, of the members, doubtless dealt with all the paperwork and administration in those early years. Clearly such a degree of power would have made some envious, others resentful, but most almost certainly appreciated the advantage of having such a strong, supportive, and capable character in their midst.

It's interesting to note that in his early history of the Plymouth Society, first published in 1892, and written two years earlier, we read that Webb *'has been connected with the* Western Daily Mercury *for some considerable time, and a regular contributor to* Doidge's Annual *for several years past.'*

The *Western Daily Mercury* was started by Isaac Latimer just six months after the *Western Morning News* - and the Plymouth Co-operative Society - had been born into the world, and was originally situated almost directly opposite the Morning News office in Bedford Street; while *Doidges Annual* started life in 1869, in Whimple Street, right next to the Society's first bank.

One wonders when Thomas Doidge first met Webb; they were both of a similar age, Webb was five years older, and, doubtless thanks to Webb, the Plymouth Co-operative Society had produced its first almanac – *'following the fashion of the day that was fast becoming universal,'* – in 1862, not long after the move to Kinterbury Street. *'Containing such special information as might be useful and interesting to all concerned'*, the almanacs partly served to advertise the Co-operative Society locally.

Webb, short of saying when they stopped producing them, merely states that it was a *'custom continued for some years, but now (1890) and for many years past discontinued'*. Perhaps it was the appearance of Doidge's Annual that brought about the change.

But to return to 1865; having dismissed Kennard, after some several months with presumably the restored and temporary Mr Carter in charge, the Society made a new appointment, and little could they have known it then, but their new man - Mr Crews - would turn out to be a much more reliable figure.

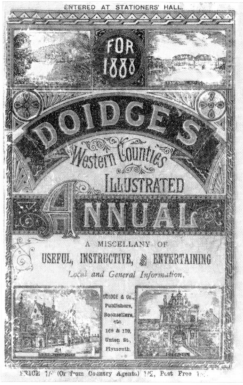

THE HISTORY
OF THE
PLYMOUTH MUTUAL
Co-operative & Industrial Society, Limited.
BY JOHN WEBB.

Plymouth Hoe in the 1860s, the Trinity obelisk occupying the site later to be taken by Smeaton's Tower

CHAPTER 3: DIVERSIFICATION

Despite all the headaches occasioned by troublesome employees, and the problems generated by the cash withdrawals made by the more fainthearted members, the Society managed to hold its own.

In February 1865 an arrangement was entered into with a local coal merchant, Richard Pilditch, of 95 Union Street, whose depot was in Newport Street, off Stonehouse Creek. It was a similar deal to that which the Society had previously entered into with bread and meat suppliers, and Pilditch agreed *'to allow us one penny per cwt. off the market price'*. Within three weeks three other coal dealers were offering the same deal.

Later in the year the Plymouth Society *'agreed to open communication with the Wholesale Society.'*

The Co-operative Wholesale Society (CWS) had started life just two years earlier and was to become one of the greatest features of the Co-operative Movement. Twenty years after the initial success of the Rochdale store in Toad Lane, some 100,000 working men and women had become members of one or other Co-operative Society.

There were still some parts of the country yet to be touched by the Movement - as already mentioned, London was slow to take up the challenge, while other areas, particularly in and around Rochdale and most notably in Manchester, were rich in co-operators.

Although it was by no means obvious at first, one thing about having dozens of shops set up by working people with the express aim of selling quality produce at reasonable prices, with all profits either going back into the business, or the pockets of those people who joined in with the Movement, meant that you had, for the first time ever, anywhere in the world, a network of shops. It wasn't exactly a chain of stores, but they were linked by a common purpose and for the most part by the Rochdale Principles.

As the number of these independent co-operative operations spread across the country, and as improvements in distribution and communication continued apace, so the exciting possibility of a co-operative central agency buying in even greater quantities from manufacturers and therefore being able to supply co-operative stores with produce at more greatly reduced prices, began to present itself.

The seeds for such an idea had already been sown back in 1850 when an independent group of the Rochdale committee members set up the Rochdale Co-operative Corn Mill. At first it almost collapsed through the employment of a dishonest miller, who had a fondness for drinking, and volunteer book-keepers who, it was claimed, bungled the books for nothing.

Happily, however, it was turned around by drafting Abraham Greenwood in as manager. Greenwood had joined the Society a few years earlier and very quickly managed to make a loss-making concern into one that, by the end of 1852, was supplying 22 separate societies, with each one receiving a dividend in relation to their spending, in the same way that individual Co-operative customers did.

Amusingly the Rochdale Co-operative Corn Mill had to overcome one minor problem with respect to many of those customers, and that was that the flour was too pure - people had become accustomed to the taste of adulterated bread!
'Eventually,' wrote Holyoake, years later, 'members learned the nature of good flour when they had it; their tastes were better educated than that of many gentlemen of the middle class, and the Directors were able to tell the purchasers, in a reckless manner, "if they wanted to adulterate the flour they could do it themselves".'
It helped that the Society agreed not to sell anyone else's flour, and consequently they were, in 1856, able to leave their rented accommodation and move into a purpose-built mill of their own. By the time the Plymouth Co-operators were establishing their Society, in 1860, the Rochdale Mill was turning over more than £100,000 a year (roughly £8 million in today's terms).

By this stage, the twenty-eight year-old, well-read, Greenwood could already see the potential in the wider co-operative network and the following summer the idea of wholesaling first appears in the co-operative records, with James Smithies, the Rochdale store secretary, minuting the appointment of Joseph Clegg to look after the wholesale department.

Later in the year following a co-operative conference at which it was agreed that Rochdale should become the Central Depot, the *'first laws of wholesale were adopted'* (Holyoake). The first two were:
1 The business of the Society shall be divided into two departments, the wholesale and the retail.
2 The wholesale department shall be for the purpose of supplying those members who desire to have their goods in large quantity.

The third concerned the constitution of the committee appointed to oversee the operation, and the frequency of meetings, while the fourth 'law' was about the level of interest that would be charged on the capital loaned to the wholesale department by the Board of Directors, and fifth and final 'law' described the process by which profits would be divided. Among the four signatories to the document were Smithies and Greenwood.

The idea was not only that goods could be supplied in large quantities, but also that nearby co-operative stores in Lancashire and Yorkshire, whose capital was too small to allow them to buy in the best markets or to afford them the services of a skilled buyer, could take advantage of a bigger, centralised organisation.

As Holyoake notes; *'A few stores did join in, but they never gave that hearty support necessary to make the scheme thoroughly successful.'*

Furthermore, *'after a time the demon of all working-class movements hitherto - jealousy - crept in.'* Certainly that distinctly unattractive trait was to beset the Plymouth co-operators on more than one occasion and in various different contexts, in this instance though it emerged that *'the stores dealing with the wholesale department of the Pioneer's Society thought it had some advantage over them; while on the other side, a large number of the members of the Pioneer's Society imagined they were giving privileges to other stores which a due regard to their immediate interests did not warrant them in bestowing'.*

Charles Kingsley, E Vansittart Neale, Thomas Hughes, John Ludlow and Professor Maurice

A philosophical Greenwood would later look back on this early attempt to start a Wholesaling operation and conclude that the Equitable Pioneer's Wholesale Department had failed because it was *'too early in the field'* - it was an idea ahead of its time. Just like the slightly earlier (1850) attempt by a group of Christian Socialists - among them Edward Vansittart Neale, Professor Frederick Maurice, Reverend Charles Kingsley, John Townsend Ludlow and Thomas Hughes - to institute the Central Co-operative Agency to *'counteract the system of adulteration and fraud prevailing in trade, and for supplying to co-operative stores a quality of goods that could be relied upon, and in the highest state of purity'.*

Like other 'failed' co-operative initiatives in other areas, this was a scheme that the world was not quite ready for, but its lack of success was not without its positive side and the lessons learnt along the way were to be of help a decade or so later when, having twice been put up, the wholesale house, at last, had *'sufficient solid ground to stand upon.'*

In the meantime, however, there was another initiative from the Pioneers - the Rochdale Manufacturing Society.

Established in 1854 this was another mill-based enterprise, this time focused around cotton and wool ... and like the flour operation, this too was a success. Again those responsible started by renting premises and again it wasn't long (1859) before they were able to build their own mill. Small wonder that the Rochdale example was inspiring others far and wide.

But it wasn't just the possibility of manufacturing co-operative produce for co-operative stores that was exciting, it was also the possibility of importing cheaper foreign produce through improved channels of communication that offered up new market opportunities.

The introduction of steam trains had made it much easier to move goods across the country, but the introduction of steam ships made it easier to move goods around the world. And just as Britain was at the forefront of the Industrial Revolution that was driving all these advances, so the Co-operative Movement, being in the right place at the right time, was able to pioneer changes in the Retailing Revolution.

Distribution was undoubtedly the key and with hundreds of affiliated outlets the Co-operative Wholesale Society had a head start on the rest of the field.

Remember, prior to the middle of the nineteenth century there were no department stores, in fact most shops were modest affairs, very few people owned more than one and the likelihood was that if they did it would be run by another member of the same family. Essentially the type of shop available and the pattern of shopping had been the same for generations:

There were 'proper shops' - grocers, mercers, milliners, hosiers, hatters, and haberdashers; there were 'general shops' which sold all sorts of everything, but not in designated departments; there were travelling salesmen - hawkers, peddlers or packmen - who would come with the fair or the market; and lastly there were 'workshops' - these were the domain of the producer-retailers - the bootmakers and blacksmiths, the butchers and bakers, the tanners and tailors, the upholsterers and undertakers, and the carpenters and cabinet makers - these were the very core of the Co-operative Movement. Whatever the worst excesses and the fall out of the Industrial Revolution, these men still had a degree of control over their output and their destiny. Aware that nothing came from nothing and that all their produce came from their own time and labour, their attitudes were informed with a degree of honesty and gritty realism not always present in other quarters. They were quick to appreciate the benefit of co-operation amongst themselves and between like-minded organisations elsewhere.

Whether you're looking at the Rochdale Pioneers or the founders of the Plymouth Society it is these producer-retailers who dominate.

Of course, not everyone bought the idea. Some factory owners, some shopkeepers and other retailers were suspicious and hostile to the new

Bon Marche, literally the bargain store, is often recognised as the world's first true department store. It was set up in Paris in 1838 by Aristide Boucicaut and by 1852 had recognised 'departments'. Jenner's in Princes Street, Edinburgh was established in the same year, but perhaps the honour should go to The Bazaar in Manchester.

It started trading in 1831 and unusually for the time had a rule that: 'prices shall be marked on all the goods, from which no abatement shall be made' - we take this for granted now in shops but then bargaining was very much the order of the day.

Also The Bazaar, unlike so many other shops at the time, was prepared to allow people to walk around and see what was on the counters, without any undue obligation to make a purchase. In 1836 Kendal, Milne and Faulkner acquired The Bazaar and the following year they announced 'a sale of silk mercery, linens, shawls, Tuscan and straw bonnets and other items essential to the lady of fashion' - this, it would appear, was the world's first shop sale.

Kendal, Milne and Faulkner, soon afterwards added other lines to their stock and moved into the next door property when it became available.

The first true department store, according to more current conventions, though, was probably William Whiteley's London shop opened in 1863. Inspired by the vast array of merchandise under one roof at the Great Exhibition of 1851, Whiteley's 'Universal Provider' became famous for selling 'Anything from a Pin to an Elephant'.

movement. Some societies failed, usually as we have seen either through extending credit to their members or by the poor choice of employees, however, as the number of societies grew inexorably there was also the ridiculous situation where two or more societies could be vying with each other in the market-place thereby driving prices up.

By the time Greenwood advanced a new plan for what would become the North of England Co-operative Wholesale Industrial and Provident Society Limited, in 1863, there were several hundred Co-operative stores in the country, and the Rochdale Pioneers themselves were operating nine grocery stores, all supplied and managed from the Central Store in Toad Lane.

'The transactions between the branches and the Central Store are very simply managed. The head shopman at each branch makes out a list of all the things wanted on a form provided for the purpose, and forwards it to the Central Store. The manager upon receiving it gives directions to the railway or canal company, where the Store goods are lying, to send the parcels of articles required to each branch named on the delivery order. The Central Store in Rochdale,' adds Holyoake, 'stood in precisely the same relation to its branches as the proposed agency would to the federated states.'

And that is precisely the reason that the Rochdale Pioneers, having so successfully launched a working model of co-operation - one that was now being emulated in all parts of the country - were so well-placed to get a working model of wholesaling under way. Even so after two false starts no one could have *'foreseen the great ascendancy which one day would be attained by this Society. It is very seldom that anyone does see the ascendancy of anything while it is upon the ground. When it is roaring over the mountain tops, the prophets of its failures declare that they predicted its rise, and now believe they made it float'.*

Addressing his remarks to some 200 Co-operative delegates (some from as far as Dublin and London) who had assembled in Manchester on Good Friday, 1863, Abraham Greenwood spoke of how there were now over 120 Co-operative stores just in the three neighbouring counties, Lancashire, Yorkshire and Cheshire - that is around the heartland of co-operation centred on Rochdale. Of these, the top 26 stores alone were now turning

The hall, off Kirby Street, Ancoats, where the Good Friday Meeting was held in Manchester on 3 April 1863.

over between them more than £800,000 a year (over £50 million now). Add in the other stores and assume that the average spend per individual member was around ten shillings a week (and it was known to be more than that) then 40,000 members would generate over £20,000 a week, that is over a million pounds a year - *'an ample field for a wholesale agency to work in'.*

The maths seem simple enough now, with the benefit of hindsight, but remember nothing like this had succeeded before - the previous two attempts having both withered on the vine. For Britain and indeed for the world, this was another first.

What is truly fascinating however, from our twenty-first century perspective, is not so much the bottom line accounting behind the wholesale scheme, but the grocery list of consumables that Greenwood based his sums on - these were the main product lines of the northern co-operatives in 1863.

Taking a million pounds as the approximate annual turnover, then it appears that just over half of the members spending went on:

Sugar	18.2%
Butter	17.8%
Tea	5.2%
Coffee	1.4%
Tobacco	4.3%
Soap	2.7%
Syrup	1.8%
Total	51.4%

Remarkably therefore it would appear that a third of the northern Co-operatives' annual turnover was on sugar and butter, with tea and tobacco accounting for another ten per cent.

It didn't, of course, matter what the members were buying, what mattered were the quantities they were buying things in, for this was the key to the launching of the third attempt at wholesaling. Having demonstrated the existing working model of the Central Store at Toad Lane and run through a basic, but persuasive, business plan, Greenwood secured the backing for the new endeavour, which was to be based in Manchester.

Forty-three Societies signed up for the new venture, representing an investment of £1,400 (calculated on the basis of five shillings per member). Rooms were rented in Manchester and two men and a boy were employed to run the operation. In no time at all they had moved into a warehouse and they began to hold stocks.

Not everyone was behind the plan however; there were many who had been steadfastly opposed to the idea, mainly newer members, not wholly committed to co-operation in the first place, and although outnumbered when it came to making the decision for the Rochdale Society to invest in the scheme, they were sufficiently strong to hinder a business connection with the new organisation. Notwithstanding that, it was to the manager of the Rochdale Store – Samuel Ashworth – that Greenwood looked for someone to head up the new enterprise. However, even Ashworth wasn't entirely convinced and although he eventually accepted the post, he was anxious that his position at the Central Store would still be there if this experiment should also fail.

It can't have been easy for Greenwood. As he, himself, was to note, he had 'to stand the fire of the criticism, doubt, and distrust of the plan, of which no one else was willing to undertake the responsibility or defence of.'

But succeed it did, and spectacularly so. Unlike the Scottish version, which, launched that same year in Edinburgh, was tainted by the earlier failure of the Glasgow Co-operative Society, and struggled to make headway. It folded after four years, although in 1868 another north-of-the-border wholesale scheme proved to be altogether more successful.

'Men must be taught as though you taught them not,
And things proposed as new as things forgot.' (Alexander Pope)

Building A New Future

Wholesaling wasn't the only unconquered territory the Rochdale Pioneers were looking to move into as the 1860s dawned however; it had been paramount among their early aims to provide accommodation as well as provisions for their members. Spurred into action, at last, apparently through the decision of a local shopkeeper-and-landlord to increase the rents of some of his tenants simply because they were Co-op members, and therefore not his customers --'they should not have all the dividends to themselves' – the Rochdale Pioneer Land and Building Company was formed. Their aspiration: 'to build a superior class of dwelling for the working man'.

Twenty-five extremely modest-sized houses were built in equally modest terraces and yet even these were beyond the pocket of most members. Nevertheless the company kept going for a number of years, before being taken over by the main Society, the Pioneers themselves having gone into the construction industry.

Pioneer Street and Equitable Street were two of their early achievements in 1867, part of a forty-eight house Co-operative estate still standing in Rochdale today. At the time, such success was intoxicating and in Plymouth 'several enthusiastic members of our Society' determined to attempt something similar. The Plymouth Co-operative and Industrial Building Society was formed.

'Pygmies in practice, but giants in theory', was how Secretary Webb was later to describe this earnest offshoot.

'As journeymen masons, carpenters, &c. they, of course, had no insight into the employers' side of conducting building operations, but were satisfied that, as the said employers were all making a fortune by employing them, this coveted fortune they fondly hoped to divert into what they considered its legitimate channel; namely, the pockets of the men whose active labour made the capital of value, without which it would certainly be altogether unproductive.

'Probably their failure arose partly from attempting too much, partly from working on borrowed money, partly from the unwise selfishness of the men employed, who demanded and received the best wages, whether the work done was equivalent to the pay, which in many instances it certainly was not; but in short days and frosty ones they expected to be paid their full wages, as though the summer was always with them.'

Webb's cynical tone here would doubtless raise an eyebrow or two among the building fraternity today, but we must remember he was, in his own time,

*Abraham Greenwood 1824-1911
Trained as a woolsorter, Abraham was born in Rochdale and educated at his uncle's school near Leeds. Secretary of the Rochdale Chartist Association in 1842, when just 18, he was an originator of the Pioneer's Education Department. In 1877 his paper on the Department was printed by the Co-operative Union and was to have a major influence on other societies.
Principal promoter of the Co-operative Wholesale Society, he was its first President. He was also founder and a director of the Co-operative Insurance Company (CIS as it became) while his daughter was to become one of the founders of the Women's Co-operative Guild.*

a free-thinking socialist and certainly one who very clearly understood the difficulties that could blight ill-founded attempts at co-operative endeavour.

With *'many pounds borrowed from the Naval Bank, together with certain quantities of wood and stone on credit'* this was not, from the very outset, being run on a cash-only basis. *'They took two pieces of ground in a field at Lipson Hill, the part now known as Sea View Terrace, where they set to work in good earnest, and were fortunate in finding a purchaser for the first house finished, one Mr Gullet (a miller), at the price of £490. Emboldened by this they at once took up another and a larger plot adjoining the second house; and ere the second house was in any way near completed began the third, neither of which did they exist long enough to finish.'*

Unfortunately, although they sold their house at a good price *'£50 more than those of a similar appearance'*, they *'discovered that the profit on the transaction was a very meagre one; so they were compelled to fall back on the practice so hurtful to their feelings, and so opposed by their utopian dreams, and so ruthlessly condemned by them when resorted to by employers'* - they had to subcontract some of the work.

But it didn't end there; during the course of the work on the second house they also entered into a contract with the authorities in Devonport to build a sewer at the bottom of Stoke Hill, close by the wall of the Military Hospital. *'But the contract price proved all too small for the work. Unexpected difficulties turned up that had never occurred to the framers of the estimate. The water would come down when least wanted and stop the work; and the ground that they believed to be nothing harder than mud and shillet, or loose slate, turned out in places so dense as to oblige a resort to gunpowder to remove it. Yet they struggled on bravely, and finished, at a loss of over £50, the job, which remains to this day, and is likely, being thoroughly well-made, to last for many generations, a lasting monument to their skill as builders, and a warning to others not to venture on an undertaking without the necessary skill or reasonable data on which to count the cost.'*

It was a shame, for as Webb rightly observed, the failure of the venture *'retarded movement in that direction for some time ...'*

The Flour That Blooms

Happily though, it didn't stop movement in other directions, and among the various initiatives proposed for that new year of 1867, came one from that class of member who disliked the drudgery of *'carrying heavy parcels from the stores to their homes'*.

Remember the motor car was still the stuff of science fiction, the horse-tram was still five years away - for Plymouth - and most working men would not have been able to afford a hackney carriage or even a hansom cab. One of the great achievements of the Co-operative Movement generally was that at last parents could contemplate sending their children to the shop to buy things in the relatively safe knowledge that the children wouldn't be palmed off with inferior or poor value produce. However, not everyone had children on hand to fetch and carry, hence members of the Society *'considered it was time we did as other shopkeepers did, and keep an errand boy'*.

However, concerned that one boy might not be enough and that were more than one to be employed, the expense of it all might start eating into the amount of cash available as dividends, others ensured that the *'project was strangled as soon as it was born'*.

There was less opposition, though, early the following year, to the idea of the Society taking on an apprentice. *'Unfortunately,'* as Webb was to note, the young man appointed *'did not turn out so well as we had fondly hoped, and we were, in a few months, glad to sever the connection.'*

Another new undertaking that the Society embarked upon in 1867 was *'the selling of meat'*. Having previously entered arrangements with local butchers to operate on a commission basis, the Society now determined to enter the meat market on a formal basis. Starting in November from a counter in the *'furthest corner'* in the Cornwall Street store, they were, within five months, prompted to extract that element of trade and set it up separately on a stall in the market. It would seem that members preferred their shopping to be done in the one place, however, and as the meat sales diminished in the market place, they decided, after just three months, to move back into Cornwall Street.

As all this was happening another Society's sub-committee was constituted to look into the viability of establishing a bakery.

A sense of urgency soon overtook the project and the Committee were instructed to find suitable premises. A couple of weeks later, 14 April 1868, an offer was made on a house in Clifton Street, but the landlord wasn't prepared to install an oven, and so attention shifted to a property in what was then a very new part of town, up near the Cathedral - Neswick Street. No.30 was already fitted out as a shop and bakehouse and the Society appointed John Moyse as their first baker and his wife as the shopkeeper there.

Having already had their fingers burnt with their first storeman at Cornwall Street the Society extracted £20 in shares from the couple with a guarantee of the same amount from the baker's brother who agreed to act as bondsman. The couple were allowed two rooms at the top of the house to live in, for which they were charged £8 a year, however within a few months the Society *gave them the rooms rent free, instructing the man to make first, second, and third class bread to suit the tastes or pockets of the members, promising him also if he baked any number of sacks of flour in excess of ten, he should be paid one shilling extra for every sack so baked*. But, relays Webb in his history, *'our first baker, like our first professional shopman, was not the right man'*.

Following complaints about loaves being under weight, inferior flour being used and *'unpleasant chidings respecting the management of the shop'* the couple were found to be *'much further behind in their returns than our first defaulter'*. Close examination of the accounts confirmed the Society's suspicions, prompting the baker's brother, Robert Moyse, to try and extricate himself from the bond.

John Moyse and his wife were suspended and one of the original Plymouth members, Thomas Reynolds, who had been looking after the meat sales, was put in temporary charge at Neswick Street. Moyse's arrears were found to be almost £40, half of which was sort of covered by his share holding, prompting an attempt to claim the other half from his unhappy bondsman and brother, Robert.

In the event it was to be another expensive lesson for the Society. As Webb was to record; *'between ordering a thing to be done and getting that order obeyed there is at times a slight difficulty, especially when the party ordered objects to obey, and the person ordering is unable to enforce the command'*.

'Claiming and getting were two different things,' added Webb, *'as our lawyer found it very easy to ask Mr Robert Moyse for the money; but as he found, that individual, if* proceeded against and ordered to pay as promised, would be utterly unable to do so, the prosecution was abandoned, we considering it unwise to invest good money in trying to get a shirt from a naked man, although the shirt, if it existed, belonged of right, to us.'

Having suspended Moyse there appeared to be no shortage of applicants to take his place, unfortunately, however, the Society's second choice, Thomas Richards, was little better than the first: *'the bread that under John Moyse was certainly not the good thing we wanted, was no better under his successor, so that in about a month we had to threaten him with dismissal if he did not or could not produce a better article, a threat which a few days after we put in practice'*.

A third baker was taken on but found *'a fortnight of our work not suited to his constitution'*. By this stage the Society had already taken on a baker's assistant and after this third disappointment the decision was taken to up the wages for the fourth appointee and to increase those of the assistant.

Notwithstanding the problem of finding the right personnel for the posts, there appeared to be little doubt about the viability of the move into the bakery business and by January 1870 the Committee *'grew anxious to get a bakehouse in the eastern end of town'*.

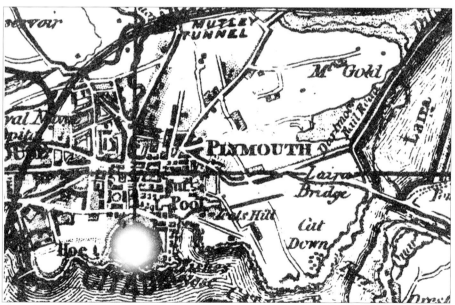

Plymouth in 1868 - the eastern end still didn't really extend much beyond the old heart of the town

Above: Bedford Street in the 1860s. Right: 1868 35th Quarterly Report and Balance Sheet.

By 10 February 1870 they had settled on *'a house in Britonside, next door to that ancient coaching-house, ere the railway reached Plymouth, known then and now as the "King's Arms".'* Not to be confused with the neighbouring King's Head, which stood (and still stands) but a few yards to the west of it - the King's Arms was at the bottom of Whitecross Street (Moon Street today).

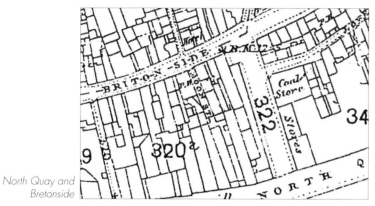

North Quay and Bretonside

No sooner had this addition to the Plymouth Mutual Co-operative & Industrial Society's portfolio been made than *'we began to hanker after the opportunity of selling drapery.'*

Cutting Their Cloth

Those members assembled at the quarterly meeting of July 1870 *'gave their gracious sanction to the Committee's desire, and in one month from that time we had fitted up a room at the top of the house in Cornwall Street, and there our lady saleswoman, the wife of one of our members, took charge on Tuesday, Friday and Saturday in each week.'*

Within two months, however, the said lady, who also had a family to care for, found the duties too much and her place was given to a widow, who must have been quite a young widow as she was to stay in the department for nearly twenty years, before emigrating to join her only son in America.

Clearly with all these new ventures achieving a degree of success there was a high degree of optimism around the Committee table, so much so

that at a special general meeting convened at the end of February 1871 it was agreed that *'in view of the increasing trade and prosperity of the Society, and the very inadequate accommodation for the transaction of business, this meeting is of the opinion that it is desirable to purchase or build more extensive premises for its further development'.*

Another sub-committee was appointed to progress the scheme, its composition was typical of the core membership - they were all skilled craftsmen; two carpenters, a shipwright, a painter and a tailor. Agreeing to meet every Monday until their mission had been accomplished, they decided to advertise in the local daily papers. Replies were soon forthcoming and at the next Quarterly Meeting they were happy to recommend a house should be purchased in Charles Street for £1,450 (almost £100,000). The meeting, however, deemed the price to be too high and would only agree to offer £1,300.

As it happened the building was held in trust by a man who headed up a firm of wholesale grocers and although, as Webb noted, *'we did a great deal of our trade with him'* … he was *'decidedly opposed to all things Co-operative, although in all other respects a liberal-minded man, he became rigidly unbending in the matter of price.*

'His curt treatment setting up our backs, we would not stoop to offer a penny more than the £1,300 and set about seeing Nos. 12 and 12.5 Bilbury Street – now 42 Treville Street' (as it was at the time Webb was writing - it is now long gone – its site just to the west of the aforementioned King's Head). The Committee this time instructed that no more than £700 was to be paid and in the event Messrs Bray and Webb managed to effect the purchase for just £675.

Webb again picks up the story: *'we set to work with our usual energy'* and had the property conveyed *'as quickly as the lawyers felt inclined to work'*. There was a slight issue over a party wall, and one of the Society's wealthier members withdrew his money to *'to put it in, as he expressed it, a safe place'*. The scheme went ahead nonetheless and the said member, despite repeatedly re-applying for membership, was, each time, denied. A tea party was held for the Society's lady members and wives and a new shopman was appointed (this too caused a minor furore as the man was not a member of the Society).

The 1874 Factory Act at last brought in the ten-hour working day. Henceforth it was illegal for women and adolescent boys and girls to be employed for more than ten hours a day between 6am and 6pm. Furthermore, no child under the age of ten could now be employed at all. For men, ten and a half hours was the new limit, but in practice they were not expected to work longer than ten hours.

By the end of that year, 1871, membership and turnover had increased by around 50% while the annual profit had doubled - from £657 to £1,314. Small wonder therefore, after a brief period of consolidation, that the Committee again looked to expand their operations; *'On October 14th, 1872, we fancied it would be wise to provide against the cold season rapidly approaching, and resolved to engage in the selling of coal, and placed notices in the shops asking the members to increase their shares for that puprose; so the money came in, and in fourteen days after, we had secured a coal store in Vauxhall Street.'*

A week later they had hired one man to sell the coal and two others to deliver it. Such was the potential in this area that the following spring the Committee were authorised to take up shares in a Co-operative colliery, however no further action was taken. This was quite possibly due more to the failure of the colliery in question rather than reluctance on the part of the Committee. The Derby Co-operative Society lost £500 in an abortive attempt to set up a colliery in Ripley, lack of capital being the main problem. There was another Co-operative colliery established at Halmer End by the West Yorkshire and North Staffordshire Co-operative Coal Mining & Building Society, but it too struggled and was bought by the Yorkshire Miners' Federation in 1880, before failing altogether.

High Days and Holidays

Notwithstanding some of the problems being experienced in other quarters however, these were heady times for the Co-operative Society in Plymouth and, in generous mood, and almost in anticipation of the Disraeli Government's Factory Act of August 1874, the Committee graciously decided they would *'close our shops on Wednesday evenings at five'* ... *'our first movement towards the weekly half-holiday'*.

From our current perspective the idea of closing at five instead of ten o'clock at night doesn't seem like a very big deal at all, however, working conditions were a little different then and there were very few opportunities for leisure time during the prime hours of daylight.

The situation was improving, though, which largely accounts for the increasing amount of sporting activity around this time, with many cricket, football and rugby clubs tracing their origins back to the 1860s and 1870s.

The Football Association came into being in 1862, drawing up universally accepted rules for the game for the first time; the Rugby Football Union was born in 1871. Plymouth Cricket Club records go back to 1862, the Albion Club was active as a rugby outfit from 1876 and the Argyle Athletic Club played their first football match in October 1886. Interestingly enough, reflecting the half day holiday that was in place in many parts of the country the Wednesday Cricket Club in Sheffield, in 1883, gave birth to the Wednesday Football Club, by which name it was known until 1929 when it officially would become known as Sheffield Wednesday Football Club.

Prior to 1871, Sundays were for Christian worship and for rest and not for sport or entertainment and, prior to 1871, that left just Good Friday and Christmas Day as the only guaranteed holidays - literally holy days - work-free days, that most working men and women enjoyed. Hence the informal meeting on Christmas Day 1859 that had sewn that first true seed of the Plymouth Co-operative Movement.

One or two enlightened employers did however grant their workforce other days off, like Easter Monday, but no matter how many employers observed such days, the banks were still obliged to stay open for at least part of the day to meet their commitments to pay Bills of Exchange that were legally due on that day.

In 1871, however, Sir John Lubbock, a wealthy banker and MP for Maidstone, introduced a bill which led to four extra days a year - Easter Monday, Whit Monday, the first Monday in August and Boxing Day - being days on which banks would close and bank staff, together with other workers in England, Wales and Ireland would have a day off work.

Anticipating problems from those who would not appreciate having to have their Bills of Exchange early, however, as they already had to with bills due on Christmas Day or Good Friday, he proposed that such bills should be settled on the business day after the new holiday. Clearly the extra day's grace appealed to most and the bill sailed through, however there needed to be some way of differentiating the two types of holiday and so Sir John proposed that these new work-free days be designated 'bank' holidays.

John Lubbock 1834-1913
The son of Sir John William Lubbock, John Lubbock was educated at Eton and afterwards taken into his father's bank. He was 22 when he became a partner in the bank, and 31 when he inherited his father's baronetcy. Five years later he was elected MP for Maidstone and in his long political career he was responsible, not only for the Bank Holiday Act, but also the Ancient Monuments Act of 1882. A naturalist and archaeologist, he published the influential text-book; 'Pre-historic Times as Illustrated by Ancient Remains, and the Manners and Customs of Modern Savages'.
An acquaintance and neighbour of Darwin, Lubbock was responsible for inventing the names Palaeolithic and Neolithic to describe the Old and New Stone Ages.
In 1884 he founded the Proportional Representation Society, which later became the Electoral Reform Society.

Not surprisingly the Bank Holiday Act was well received by the working population and the August Holiday was popularly dubbed St Lubbock's Day, in Sir John's honour. Notwithstanding that however, not all employers were ready to simply fall in line, much to the annoyance of those affected:

'To some minds little things as well as great ones prove a grievance, and the closing of our shops on bank holidays as a matter of course, was elevated into the first place, which induced the Committee to compromise the trouble by determining to deal with the question of closing the stores on these occasions separately as each such holiday came round, and that the next ensuring August 7th (1876) they would make a beginning in this direction by ordering all the stores to be closed on that day.'

Writing his account many years after this, Webb was pleased to record that the question of whether or not to honour bank holidays was no longer an issue 'as for years we have observed the day as religiously and as much a matter of course as the most devout believer of St Lubbock in Plymouth.'

Certainly the Committee, generally, did not seem averse to allowing their employees an opportunity to celebrate and on Thursday, 13 August 1874, all the Plymouth Co-operative stores were closed at 10am to allow everyone to enjoy the spectacle surrounding the visit of the Prince of Wales and the opening of Plymouth's new Guildhall and Municipal Buildings. A red letter day in the history of the rapidly expanding town.

49

Four years after the laying of the foundation stone, Plymouth's new Guildhall was opened by Queen Victoria's eldest son, 33-year-old Albert Edward, Prince of Wales and Lord High Steward of the Borough of Plymouth (and the future Edward VII).

As the assembled crowds waited for the Prince to be handed the silver key, trumpeters played a Grand Festival March, specially written for the occasion by the 30-year-old organist of Sherwell Church, Frederick Lohr. After the formal opening there was a 'Dejeuner in the Great Hall' of the new building.

The opening of the Guildhall was later to be the subject of one of the fourteen great stained-glass windows that ran down the sides of the Great Hall, while another depicted the reception held here the following day when the Freemasons of Devon and Cornwall met and welcomed the Prince of Wales as their Grand Master.

Above: The Dejeuner on the opening day. Right: The grand opening of Plymouth Guildhall, 13 August 1874.

Curiously enough Banking was another area that the Plymouth Committee considered branching into in 1873, thanks largely to the efforts of another wealthy banker and Member of Parliament, Walter Morrison. Morrison, an *'active person in matters Co-operative'* was one of Plymouth's two MPs at that time and was responsible for introducing into the House of Commons a bill for the amendment of the Industrial Societies Act, which would enable organisations like the Plymouth Mutual Co-operative & Industrial Society to set up their own banking organisation.

'The Secretary was instructed to engage a person to take around a petition in its favour, and get members to sign in its support - which he did,' wrote Webb, who was, of course, referring to himself as Secretary, adding that *'a large number of signatures in support thereof were obtained; but up to the present day we have not availed ourselves of the privilege, as some kindred societies have with fair success and profitable results'.*

Branching Out

The Co-operative Wholesale Society (CWS) began operating *'a loan and deposit business'* - the forerunner of The Co-operative Bank, as early as 1872, although until the law was actually changed, in 1876, it was of *'doubtful legality'.*

The Committee's reluctance to enter the banking world was not a sign that they were not open to new ideas, however, and around this time they even went to the trouble of providing suggestion boxes: *'neat little boxes, with nice gilded letters on them - 'For The Committee' - hoping thereby that the unruly and dissatisfied, seeing in every shop an invitation to disburden their minds without taking the trouble of travelling to Treville Street on nights when the Committee met, would deposit their grievances or friendly counsels therein'.*

However few took advantage of this new avenue of communication and when one or two of the female members of the Society *'set to wondering why the Committee could want begging boxes for their private benefit, the climax came, and 'For The Committee' slunk out of sight, no one thinking it worth his while to enquire after their whereabouts.'*

Meanwhile another Committee minute referring to yet another mode of

correspondence determined that *'no communications of our Society should on any account be made on Post Cards'.*

One wonders if some specific missive, able to be read by all the postal employees who handled the card, triggered such a resolution, or whether the Committee were just sharing the general feeling among the better educated that to expose one's business to the gaze of the postman was neither seemly nor discreet. Certainly the new postcard phenomenon was a popular one - a million cards were sent out in the first week (from 1 October 1870) of their being issued in this country. Each one sold for the cost of the stamp, which in this case was the tiny new ha'penny lilac.

 The new halfpenny lilac issued on 1 October 1870 to coincide with the introduction of the new Post Office postcard. Picture postcards were not circulated or allowed until September 1894 (nb actual size of stamp).

Interestingly enough, Webb's comment on the Committee's minute on Post Cards appears straight after his reference to the Plymouth Society sending their first ever delegate to the Conference of Co-operative Societies meeting at Gloucester - perhaps he sent a post-card from Gloucester with some sensitive information on it!

Letters were coming in from all quarters at this time, reflecting well on the success and status of the Plymouth Committee: *'We had a request from our Devonport members to send bread to that town, but declined to entertain it just then, believing the quantity ordered not sufficient to pay the cost of carriage, yet promising to do so as soon as we could without loss in the transaction.'*

And then there was an application from the *'inhabitants of Brixham, for information touching the founding of a Co-operative Society in that town, and we directed the Secretary to do his best in assisting them in their endeavour'.* Here then was the now well-established Plymouth Society, playing the role of the Rochdale Pioneers to their Devon neighbours. They had successfully negotiated a number of potential problems in their first few years and could now hold their heads high in the county.

The Plymouth Co-operators were no longer a small back-street enterprise, rather they were a force to be reckoned with and when, in December

Walter Morrison: MP for Plymouth from 1861-74. Born in 1836, he was the son of James Morrison who had made his fortune, first in haberdashery, then in banking. Walter was a keen supporter of the Co-operative Movement while in office; he also did his best to further Women's Suffrage. In 1872 he introduced the first Proportional Representation Bill, which, of course, was successfully opposed and defeated.
A keen educationalist and churchman, he was later a Liberal MP for Skipton (1886-92 and 1895-1900). John Stuart Mill, Charles Darwin and Charles Kingsley were among his guests, the latter casting him as John Hartover in his book 'The Water Babies'.

Stonehouse was in a strange position three-quarters of the way through the nineteenth century. Like Plymouth and Devonport, it had grown spectacularly in recent years, notably in the wake of the construction of the Naval Hospital (1760s), the Royal Marine Barracks (1780s), the Military Hospital (1790s), and then the Royal William Victualling Yard (1820s and 30s). In 1850 they built their own Town Hall 'with accommodations for the County Court, police station ... and apartments for the Stonehouse Library and Scientific Institution, and a handsome Ball Room, 85 feet by 45 feet. With Devonport having already built a new Town Hall a generation earlier, this was doubtless part of the stimulus that provoked Plymouth into building its even more impressive Guildhall and Municipal Buildings. However Stonehouse, the peninsula town, could grow no more, development having expanded right up to its boundaries with Plymouth and Devonport. In terms of an independent township, it had peaked, consequently it is no great surprise that there appears to have been insufficient appetite for its natives to start their own Co-operative venture.

1874 they received in the post 'an outstanding request from the master bakers of the town to raise the price of bread in common with them ... they were told very politely that we should do nothing of the sort, that when we wanted to raise or lower the price of bread, we should do so irrespective of the master bakers or any other persons, whoever they might be.'

'Goodness knows,' reflected Webb, 'what induced them to look on us as fools ready to fall into the hands of the enemy, but they held us in dread, no doubt, now we had become a powerful corporation, and were desirous to engage us in their conspiracy.

'We have had no application of that kind since,' he added, 'presumably because of the rudeness of our reply.'

One group that the Committee were responsive to, however, were 'the Stonehouse men'. It's interesting to note that while there were men attempting to set up an effective Co-operative in Devonport, the third of the Three Towns – Stonehouse – was still without either an organisation of its own, or a store. Thus it was that in April 1875, the Plymouth Committee determined to open a branch store in Stonehouse.

A deputation of three committee men was charged with 'house-hunting' and by the end of August they had not only found premises - in Adelaide Street - but appointed a shopman 'to minister to the wants of the people of Stonehouse'.

With a significant revenue stream now being generated, the idea of establishing further branch stores suddenly seemed seductive and before the doors of the Stonehouse store had even opened, a special meeting was convened to consider even 'greater progress'.

On Thursday 15 July 1875, the membership 'desired the Committee to take Stores in the best neighbourhoods'. They also voted to remove the Drapery 'to a more central position and to add the tailoring thereto ... and to consider the advisability of grinding our own corn'.

Of course one consequence of having ever more stores to service and supply was the need to develop an effective means of getting goods from A to B. More than a question of having a delivery boy for their customers, this was an altogether more practical concern about moving increasingly greater quantities of goods around the Three Towns. Remember one of the reasons for deciding not to service Devonport with Co-operative bread was the cost of carriage, hence the Committee minute from that year, 1875: 'to supplement our strength, we resolved to buy a horse'.

True to almost every other resolution adopted by the Plymouth Society a three-man sub-committee was appointed. These three men were, according to Webb, who tells the tale with obvious relish, 'supposed to be learned in horse-flesh, and capable of counteracting the wiles of rogues who deal in that species of quadruped'.

Adelaide Street

'Presumably,' he writes, 'we selected the best three individuals for the purpose - a tailor, a clerk, and a Jack-of-all-trades - who did the work so well, that the beast (a beauty to look at) went on very well for some few months, and then from some unknown, or at least unexplained, cause, although there were no end of theories propounded on the matter, turned out to be a pronounced kicker, and put the lives of sundry persons connected with her ladyship in imminent danger; indeed, the animal's conduct became so outrageous that, in despair of curing her vicious propensity, although we had any amount of gratuitous advice on the matter, and had fitted her with a kicking-strap, we were eventually forced to part with her; but as her scandalous conduct had become public property, one of the committee rode her to Tavistock fair, and sold her unconditionally and without warranty for £20.'

Doubtless the said committee man got the train back into Plymouth, though Webb doesn't tell us. He does, however, add by way of a postscript to the story, that the horse 'became a famous hunter, and ended her career in that calling by nearly killing her rider and breaking her own neck'.

Clearly, however the episode left the Plymouth Society without their own transport once more. We must assume that they hired in hauliers or men with handcarts when they needed to move more than a man could carry on his own.

Public transport around the streets of Plymouth was, by this time at a more advanced stage than almost any other city in the country. Following the passing of the Parliamentary Tramway Act of 1870, the Plymouth, Stonehouse & Devonport Tramways Co. became the first such company in Britain and their tramline – which ran from Derry's Clock to Cumberland Gardens (Devonport), via Union Street, has been described as the 'grandfather of all legitimate tramway companies'.

The route opened on Monday, 18 March 1872, and was a single track with eight passing places along its 1.9 mile length (it was officially one mile and seventy-four chains, there being eighty chains to a mile). Two years later the route was extended deeper into Devonport, taking in Fore Street and Marlborough Street, adding just over half a mile to the length of the route; a route that was serviced by eight tram cars and some seventy-eight horses.

Known locally as 'green trams' on account of their pale green livery - which had a white lining - the trams were pulled by two horses each of which were required to do around 10-12 miles a day (about two complete circuits). Negotiating the 1-in-11 incline of Devonport Hill would require two extra horses and no-one on board was allowed to stand as the trams went up or down the hill.

The depot for all the horses and trams was, interestingly enough, off Manor Street, just yards from the Stonehouse shop that the Committee took possession of in August 1875 - a shrewd move on their part.

Transport, generally, was a far cry from what we are used to today and Webb's account of the early history of the Society references another interesting incident that took place in 1875: 'A good looking ship, bearing the encouraging name of Sunbeam, put into Plymouth Sound with her crew in a high state of mutiny; and being hauled before the magistrates for their rebellious conduct, they averred that the ship was utterly rotten, and that they preferred a prison to an untimely death. The truth of which assertion being fully proved, they were dismissed of the charge of mutinous conduct' and here's the reason for Webb recounting the story: 'and to show our practical sympathy with them, and to assist them in their loss and distress, we voted them £5.'

Going up Devonport Hill. Stonehouse, and the bridge form the backdrop.

This was a time when the Co-operation across the country was progressing by leaps and bounds and suddenly men who previously only had experience of their own small businesses found themselves at the helm of a huge, cash-rich enterprise. Happily common sense directed most of the decision making:

'In July, we resolved, in consequence of our having a mass of money earning nothing, that a sum of £1,000 should be invested in the funds of the Wholesale Society, at the same time proposing to become members of the said Society.'

The Wholesale Society wasn't the only central initiative that the Plymouth Society bought into that month as they *'determined to remove our policy of insurance with the County Fire Office, so far as the Grocery and Bakery in Treville Street were concerned, and transfer our favours to the Co-operative Insurance Society'* - the CIS, another of the Rochdale Pioneers early offshoots.

In the South West though, it was Plymouth who were the Pioneers, and some members clearly found the burden greater than others. Secretary Webb was just about to discover that his relative satisfaction with the status quo was not shared by all. Indeed the signs had been there since 1873, when after dropping the idea of appointing an accountant, *'a new idea dawned on the restless minds of some, that a head should be fixed on our body, believing that although we had done uncommonly well considering the many toils and troubles incident to such an innovation as ours, without one, yet as we were now steadily growing it was no longer advisable to go staggering on without a crown.'*

That he was not one of those restless minds himself becomes quite obvious in the way he carries on the narrative: *'This notion went on developing in the minds of its adherents as rapidly as did the fervour of the ancient Hebrews who, dissatisfied with their republican form of government, and envying the neighbouring nations who were in the proud possession of kings to rule them, abandoned their simple form of government to chose a king with all its attendant consequences; so tired of unpretending practice, they would do as other firms did - have a head more or less capable and responsible for conducting the Society's business.'*

Leading Issues

It was in November 1873 that the process began, when a meeting was called *'to consider the advisability of electing a Manager for the Society.'*

One wonders if Webb would have been quite so caustic in his comments had he been elected himself, for in the event, after popping in and out of view, without any action being taken for a year or two, the matter eventually came to a head and an election was held.

By this stage the affair had become a very tense one: *'meeting after meeting, discussion followed discussion, formal and informal, at all times and places were held, until the tempers of the opposing forces were at fever heat, nor did it cool a bit even after the election of a person to fill the office had taken place, which was not until another six months had elapsed. The middle of 1876 saw the matter settled, the choice being narrowed between the two candidates, namely, the Chairman of the Society, and the man who had held the position of Secretary from the foundation in 1860, sixteen and a half years service, when to serve in that capacity was not a sinecure, and brought much more honour than compensation - both working men whose sole knowledge of the Society's requirements had been gained by experience of the constant growing and ever-changing conditions inherent in such a social life as ours. The former, a cooper by trade, a cellarman by practice; the Secretary, a humble follower of the useful but despised and unpopular craft of shoemaking. Thus the respective candidates stood at the time of the election, which resulted in the Secretary being passed over, and the Chairman elevated to the coveted position, to the great disgust, anger and annoyance of the vanquished.'*

Secretary Webb, having argued against appointing a manager, having worked tirelessly for the Society for many years and for little reward, and having then stood and been rejected, was a bitter man.

However he was not alone: *'So strongly did the beaten section feel on the subject, a section of all the oldest members, with very few exceptions, men who had weathered the adversities and obloquy of the earlier history ... registered themselves to form a new Society.'*

And, according to Webb's far-from-impartial account, they very nearly succeeded. The problem was they couldn't get their money out quickly enough, and one of the main - and wealthiest - malcontents, pulled out at the last minute, fearing that his actions would be detrimental to his brother who supplied the Society with their butter and eggs.

Writing some fourteen years after the incident, Webb's vitriol was undiminished: *'So passed the storm,'* he wrote, *'but the effects remain; the clash of the tempest is no more heard, but the distant thunder growls from time to time, and at election times the partizan spirit then first engendered and brought into existence, is freely exhibited, and the bond of brotherhood broken past repairing.'*

Not only then did Webb's wound not heal, but he also maintained a rueful wistfulness about what might have been: *'Had the separation taken place, it would have afforded an interesting and instructive chapter in the history of Co-operation to have seen and been able to compare the relative merits of dissimilar modes of procedure running side by side, and have gone far to settle the question that has troubled more than the Plymouth branch of the Co-operative movement.'*

Whatever the whys and wherefores, the deed was done - the Plymouth Society now had a Manager; a Manager who was to have: *'the general supervision of the Society's business in all its branches: 'the power to purchase to the extent of £750 (around £50,000): control of all the Society's servants,'* and his orders, once issued, to have the *'like force or effect as if given by the General Committee.'*

He was also to have a salary of £100 per annum. He also had a name, Joseph Henry Young, but, thanks to Webb's ever festering rage he could not bring himself to identify his adversary in his account of the first thirty years of the Society's history. For him, this was the end of an era, the financial reports that the Committee requested he prepare later that month, would be his last. And as soon as Young took on the role of Manager, William Henry Lethbridge was elected to succeed him as Chairman.

Nor was this the only decision made with regard to the payment of staff that year, for it was further resolved that *'the system of paying employees by commission be abolished'* and that henceforth, *'all the Society's employees be paid a weekly wage and a bonus.'*

The previous practice, was, wrote Webb, *'felt by the majority to savour of sweating, or at least to be getting a profit out of the labour of other persons, and consequently antagonistic to their ideas of what a democratic society like ours should cultivate and enforce'.*

The new wages structure took effect in January 1877. That same month in response to a long-held feeling that *'our markets were too far from a large number of our members'*, No.1 Ross Street, Morice Town was purchased and was *'soon found of so great convenience for members in that neighbourhood as to become the most successful of all our stores for the sale of groceries'.*

Joseph Henry Young the first General Manager of the Plymouth Mutual Co-operative Society, was born in 1838, and was at the time of his election, ten years younger than John Webb, his only rival in that first election.

A Growing Concern

Small wonder that, year on year 1876-1877, membership increased dramatically by almost 1,000 – from 1,750 to 2,695. It was altogether a good year for members and employees alike. For employees a further bonus came that year with the Committee's decision, arrived at after a certain amount of dispute and debate, *'to close our shops on Wednesday afternoons at one o'clock.'*

While for members there was the enticing prospect of yet more outlets to shop in: having decided that it was *'our bounden duty to increase the required accommodation demanded by our Drapery Department'* an existing drapery in Cornwall Street was bought out and the Society moved their own department out of Treville Street and into the new premises.

Less than a week later, 17 May 1877, having just freed up space in the Treville Street stores, the Committee bought a house, tenements and workshop that stood at the back of the stores. The reasoning here was to create space for further bread production as they were struggling to meet demand for *'that necessary, known as the staff of life'*.

Charles Goodanew.

EC Burton

Treville Street premises.

'In a short time we were busy pulling down, altering and building such extensions as seemed to be absolutely necessary,' and yet even then it wasn't enough and 'like the half-starved pauper boy, Oliver Twist, we were asking for more' and just a few months later 'hankered after the adjoining property that bounded our Treville Street premises at the west and northern extremities'.

And so the premises of the Old Lion Brewery or Green Street Brewery, were added to the rapidly growing empire, followed, in September by the purchase of the Barbican Coal Store – close to the western pier – and soon after that, the Phoenix Coal Store.

These were giddy times as September also saw the purchase of the property in Cornwall Street next door to the drapery they had just bought out. This new acquisition became the grocery, allowing that department to vacate its current setting across the road and thereby free up the whole of the ground floor of that building for the Butchery department and providing more room for the library and reading and recreation.

Knowledge was another avenue that the General Committee were anxious not to neglect and the Educational Committee were granted additional accommodation for reading rooms, both in Cornwall Street and in the new Devonport store in Ross Street.

Books and newspapers were beyond the means of most and much use was made of the limited opportunities available. The printed word was the only medium available for the dissemination of information and learning and, initially, the Society spent the vast majority of its education budget on such material. The Co-op librarian was on hand every Thursday and Saturday evening from 8pm-10pm and by 1872 some six hundred volumes were available, as well as copies of the London and local daily papers. An assistant to the librarian was appointed in 1876, with a quarterly salary of ten shillings.

Three years later, to meet the ever-increasing demand for the facilities, it was agreed that the library should be kept open all day. The librarian at this time was one of the Plymouth pioneers, sixty-four year-old Charles Goodanew, and Mr EC Burton was his assistant. The following year Burton succeeded the retiring Goodanew and oversaw the gradual expansion of the library and newsroom service around the Three Towns.

A Woman's Place

From 30 January 1877, the new deal for all salesmen was 22 shillings a week for those who took £50 or less per week, rising to a little over double that, if as much as £500 a week was taken. Note, however, that was for the sales*men*: sales*women* were different: *'the lady who conducted the Drapery department, being a woman, was considered worth no more than three-fourths the above scale for men'.*

The fairer sex they might have been but there was nothing inherently fair about the attitude towards women at this time. It took a ruling, later that year, about the legality of women becoming members of the Society *'without first getting their husband's consent'*, before they could resolve the issue of married women becoming members in their own right and of a woman being entitled to *'her own separate use of all money invested or accumulated profits.'*

The whole issue was wrapped up with the suspected *'fraudulent entry of married ladies [to meetings] by presenting the [membership] cards belonging to their lords'* (note the use of the term *'lord'* not *'husband'*). Henceforth, it was decreed that lady members should in future have white cards and therefore the red were no longer of use as *'passports to any of the Society's meetings for any of the fair sex, married or single'*.

As you might imagine such sexism was by no means confined to Plymouth - it appears that the daughter of one of the Rochdale Pioneers, didn't find it particularly easy gaining access to the Rochdale reading room. However, before long, the Movement would start to play a major part in ushering in change.

It all began innocuously enough. In 1883, Alice Acland, whose husband was a pioneer of adult education, started a column – Women's News - in the *Co-operative News*. Setting out her stall, she suggested the column could help bring co-operative women together through talking about cookery, childcare and needlework. But there was a sting in the tail; *'why are we held in such little esteem among men?'* she asked, adding, *'why is the feeblest type of man called an old "woman"'*.

Mary Lawrenson, whose father was a printer and active in the Society,

was first to take the bait. She wrote in suggesting that perhaps they could set up *'an independent body to promote instructional and recreational classes for mothers and single girls'*. Alice Acland thought this was a fine idea and proposed a *'guild of women'* working to promote Co-operation and, furthermore, thereby create a support group for women so that they no longer felt their *'efforts were isolated and of little value'*.

By the end of that year, 1883, three branches of Women's Co-operative Guild had been formed and three years later, when Co-operative Congress was held in Plymouth, Mrs B Jones, supported by a number of well-known lady co-operators, presided over a meeting of some 300 women, as a consequence of which twenty-four names were submitted and a Plymouth branch was soon formed.

The Women's Co-operative Guild *'was the first working women's organisation in the world and marked a completely new departure for, at that time, the wife of the wage-earning workman had no recognised rights of her own, no independence, and no cultural leisure; and even in the Co-operative Movement she was not expected to hold an official position, although nominally the Movement stood for the equality of men and women. The indebtedness of women's organisations of all kinds to the Guild can hardly be overstated; the subsequent indebtedness of the Co-operative Movement, not only in Plymouth, but all over Britain, is clear'* (quoted in Briscoe).'

Other Advances

The ladies' first Guild meeting locally was held in 42 Treville Street in 1886, but we've wound the clock on a little, and back in the late-1870s there were yet other significant steps being taken:
'Having up to this time – June 1879 – catered for the wants of our brethren while in health, we now turned our attention to their necessities in case they fell sick, and to that end, disregarding the doctors, we took out a licence for the sale of patent medicines, not out of any tender regard for the health of the community, but because some desired to be supplied with the special nostrum they fancied and patent medicines carry a good profit in their selling.'

'There are not any statistics of the number of persons we have cured or killed,' added Webb, *'but as the sale goes merrily on, it is only fair to presume that the cured are in excess of those who are done to death by the fourteen secret mixtures that were ordered to be brought into our stock, as a first instalment of what many consider a risky proceeding.'*

Plymouth already had a number of chemists and druggists in town - among them Balkwill, White and Loye - the latter being in Treville Street, where Stanley Gibbons' father had also been based, but such were the advances being made in medicine that more and more people were turning to pharmacists. Jesse Boot (founder of Boots the Chemist) had opened his first outlet in Nottingham two years earlier, so the Plymouth Co-operative venture was timely.

One move, the success of which seemed less certain to start with, was the decision to open a second store in Devonport in the summer of 1879. The location - 69 Duke Street - was right in the heart of old Devonport, as

69 Duke Street (from The Monthly Record August 1900)

opposed to the Ross Street venture which was part of the more modern Morice Town. For the first four years of its existence its turnover was virtually stagnant, however, thereafter it enjoyed some six years of improvement only for trade to then start to fall away. Added to this was a distinctly lukewarm response to the establishment of a reading room above the shop.

However, while Devonport, which, after all, was no stranger to failed Co-operative ventures, spluttered, the main Plymouth operation continued to go from strength to strength.

The development of the Old Lion Brewery site adjacent to the Treville Street premises in Green Street, was completed and the new stores opened there on Wednesday 12 November 1879. HJ Snell, who would go on to do a great deal more work for the Society, was the architect, and was doubtless among the party of employees and officers of the Society, as well as all the workmen 'who have been employed continuously on the erection of the buildings,' who were 'invited to be entertained at a high tea at the Society's expense'.

Falling just two weeks short of the twentieth anniversary of that first ever meeting in Charles Goodanew's house in Tin Street - barely a hundred yards from the impressive new Treville Street complex - it must have been a very happy occasion. It seemed like no time at all since eighteen men had subscribed a shilling each to launch the new venture in the first week of 1860 and now, here in 1880 the membership owned and were running seven grocery stores (in Neswick Street, Treville Street, Adelaide Street, Ross Street, Cornwall Street, and Duke Street), one butcher's shop (Cornwall Street), a drapery/tailoring shop (also in Cornwall Street), a footwear shop (Treville Street), as well as two coal stores, a boot and shoe making factory, a bakery and a grocery warehouse. All of it financed from the Society's own resources - there were no bank loans or mortgages.

By the end of 1880 the annual turnover would be nudging £100,000 of which almost £13,000 was surplus, yielding a handsome - two shilling and fourpence - dividend for the membership, which, incidentally, now stood at over 5,000. Impressive figures indeed. The Plymouth Co-operative was now one of the major traders in the area and one of the most successful Co-operatives in the country.

An early view of Plymouth Hoe before Elliot Terrace and the Grand Hotel appeared and the transformation of the 1880s which saw the arrival of the Pier, Smeaton's Tower, Drake's Statue and the Armada Memorial.

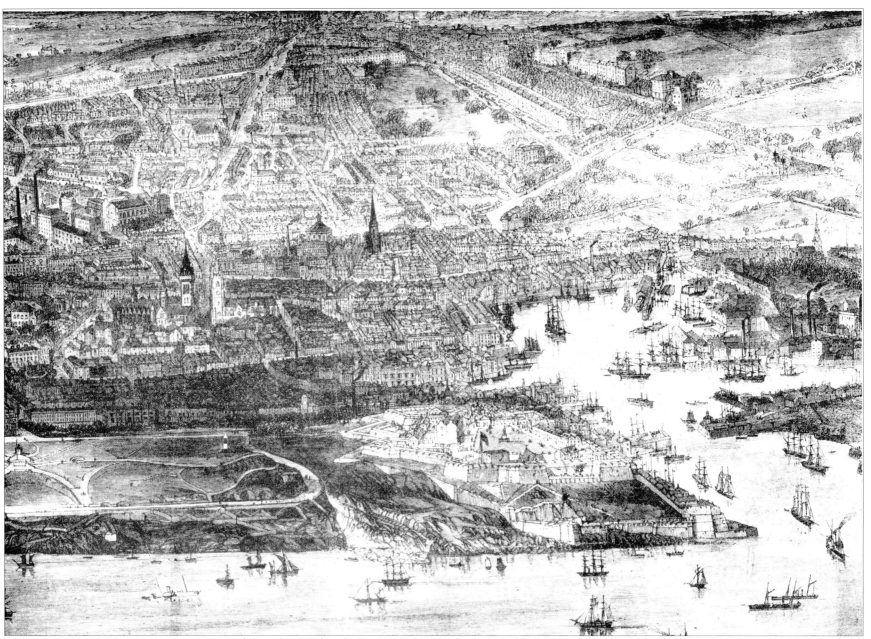

Bird's eye view of Plymouth, 1873 from the Illustrated London News: note the Guildhall, which was completed the following year, is shown the wrong way around.

CHAPTER 4: CONSOLIDATION

Into the Eighties

As the new decade dawned, so the Society continued its programme of expansion; that summer three freehold properties at Ford, in Alexandra Road, were purchased and converted to a grocer's, butcher's and shoe shops respectively. Two months later negotiations began on the purchase of a further premises in Plymouth, in Armada Street, also destined to become a grocery store.

In the meantime, on 27 July 1880 a decision was made *'to appropriate £2,000 to the building department'*: *'the first investment made, I believe,'* wrote Webb, *'for the benefit of members who desired to become the owners of the houses for which they had up to this time been paying a rent.'*

This meant, in effect, that the Plymouth Committee had set up their own building society.

Again the Plymouth Society were astute in following developments in the market place; with the population of the Three Towns (especially Plymouth) expanding as rapidly as any other part of England there was an ever increasing demand for home ownership, particularly among shopkeepers and tradesmen.

Three Towns Population figures.		Plymouth	Devonport	Stonehouse
	1801	16,040	23,747	3,407
	1811	20,803	30,083	5,174
	1821	21,591	33,578	6,043
	1831	31,080	34,883	9,571
	1841	36,527	33,822	9,712
	1851	49,673	37,499	11,971
	1861	62,599	50,440	14,343
	1871	68,758	49,449	14,585
	1881	75,094	48,775	15,125

Devonport, to some extent, had peaked already, although the construction of Keyham Steam Yard in the early 1850s provided a significant boost. Stonehouse, albeit on a much smaller scale, grew more than fourfold between 1801 and 1881, thanks in no small measure to the construction of the Royal William Victualling Yard. Meanwhile Plymouth, commercially, grew like topsy, from just over 16,000 in 1801 – making it smaller than the much younger Devonport at that point in time – to over 75,000 by 1881 making it bigger than the other two combined. What is more, over the next ten years Plymouth's population increased by a further 10,000. Small wonder therefore that over that same ten-year period the Co-op's 'building' investment figure went from £2,000 to £25,363.

It was apparently a win/win situation with Webb adding: *'Doubtless the moneys advanced have proven of great advantage to the borrowers, and a more extended use of our capital (lying idle in the banks) in that direction would be found a benefit to the Society and the individual members who may desire to avail themselves of the advantages held out by this branch of our enterprise.'*

Nor was it long before the Society went even more directly into the housing market: *'finding more ground than we wanted at the premises in Ford, and feeling anxious to make the most of our property, the Committee, entered into a contract with a builder to set up four cottages on the unused space, and appointed a man to keep watch and ward on him during their erection'.*

It was a far cry from previous local Co-operative foray into house building which had seen members doing the building work themselves, paying themselves well but ultimately not turning a profit. Having long-since banished the self-build approach, however, the Society were no longer

The National Building Society was formed in 1849, the Abbey Road Building Society was born in 1874 - the same year that the Building Societies Act was passed in order to regulate the way in which building societies operated. Incidentally one of the other big names in the frame, the Halifax was established as the Halifax Permanent Building and Investment Society in 1853.

Armada Street grocery.

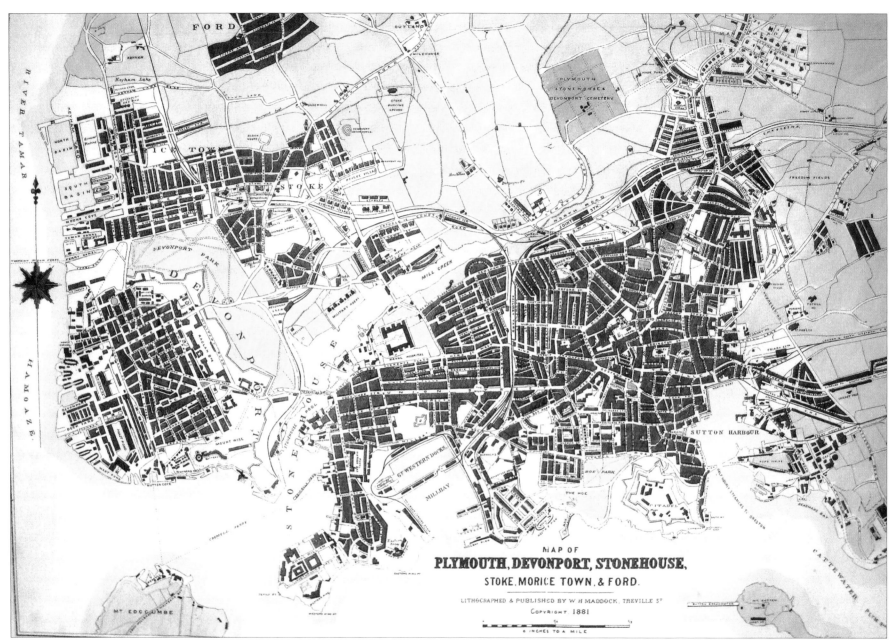

The Three Towns as they appeared in 1881, with Stonehouse almost fully developed up to its border with Plymouth.

simply setting their sights on existing premises, and as Plymouth spread out over its rural hinterland, the Society were keen to establish a presence in all the newly populated parts of town:

'Since our advent in 1860, Plymouth has extended at a very rapid rate,' wrote Webb, 'especially at the north and east ends of the town; and many members having migrated in these directions, it was found necessary to extend our facilities to these neighbourhoods. Accordingly, in May, 1883, we bought a house in Holborn Street, which, like all the property we buy, we still retain. Business was commenced there by us in the last week in the following July, and the usual success has attended our efforts.'

The following year, 1885, 'still further afield, and this time to the other side of the Tamar, where stands a little town named Torpoint. With many members residing there, it was thought a good movement to make by setting up a branch store, which we did to their great comfort and joy, departing a little from our usual practice of selling groceries only in grocery shops, by adding the sale of boots and shoes to our miscellaneous stock in this particular case'.

Next on the radar came the emerging estate around Wilton Street, Stoke, and two years later, in the spring of 1887, 'tenders were invited for the erection of buildings according to plans and specifications to be seen at the office, the said tenders to be delivered, sealed and endorsed, not later than March 29th, which was done, and the building erected and occupied by us before the end of 1887' (Webb).

Another development that same year, saw a second property purchased in Armada Street. Demolition followed and the site was refashioned with a butcher's shop, so that now 'the northern part of the town was more efficiently served'.

But that northern boundary was by no means cast in stone. Greenbank Hospital had just been built a little to the east of this neighbourhood and beyond that was the Old Workhouse, destined to become Freedom Fields Hospital. That building had been erected in the 1850s, during one of Alfred Rooker's terms as Mayor of Plymouth, and at a celebratory dinner marking the occasion he had said:

Left: Holborn Street   Below: Wilton Street

'One cannot help looking back to the time when the present workhouse (in Catherine Street), now clearly in the centre of the town, was in the suburbs and, in the present rapidly increasing state of the town I have little doubt that that which we are now building will, in 200 years, be included in its limits.'

As fate would have it, Rooker would be Mayor again when the old workhouse was demolished to make way for the new Guildhall, but little could he have anticipated that the new Workhouse would find itself within the town boundary before the nineteenth century had run its course.

Mutley Plain became the new north in as much as the boundaries were stretched to include the latest developments there in the mid-1890s. Anticipating the inevitable, on the last day of December 1889, the Society bought ground there, 'building thereon two of the best and most handsome and commodious shops to be seen in the neighbourhood, carrying on there a Grocery, Butchery, Dairy and Boot Department: and being thus built by us and for our special use, they are among the most convenient premises we occupy'.

The properties stood obliquely across from Mutley Baptist Church which had been completed twenty years earlier, and just along from the even newer Methodist Church, on the same, eastern, side of the Plain.

Conveniently situated for the railway station that had been created to serve the area at the beginning of the 1870s (just below the Baptist Church), it was not surprising that the Society took full advantage of the opportunity presented to them for this particular new build and had a number of apartments built into the handsome, four-storey development, all of which they rented out.

There could be little doubt now that the idea of using capital in this way to generate future revenue was much better than leaving the money 'lying idle in the banks' and each successful venture to the Committee widened the extent of their ambition.

Not all the ventures were successful however.

Above and left; late-Victorian Mutley looking north - it wasn't long before the Society had exploited the advertising potential of that big blank wall.

Floating: A New Idea

'Having much property on land, we hankered to have some at sea,' said Webb, *'and the South Devon Shipping Company, having advertised to sell their fleet of schooners, our ambition was fired not only to sell coals, but also to import our own, in furtherance of which desire we said we would buy one, and appointed two shipwrights to inspect the vessels, attend the sale, and buy one of the bargains, if they were worth buying - sending them on their way rejoicing with £50 in their pockets, to pay (if they succeeded in their design) such a deposit on the transaction as should convince the auctioneer we were in earnest in the business.'*

That was on 22 August 1881. Four days later a minute was entered in the Committee's record book *'that we approve of the purchase of the schooner Plymouth for £600.'* At the same time, it was resolved to advertise for a master and to purchase a cargo of coal.

'In one week we had engaged a practical seaman to manage the new affair for us,' recorded Webb, adding ruefully, *'but the result of the speculation has not been of that nature which encourages men to continue in any line of trade in which they may embark, and, up to the present time (he was writing ten years on), having taken our warning by the good schooner Plymouth's conduct, we have confined our purchases to terra firma, and sent no more cash adrift upon the uncertain sea.'*

It is difficult, from this distance, to work out exactly why this venture failed. Perhaps they were unlucky with the weather, the choice of captain or some other factor, but undoubtedly for the CWS and for the British population as a whole, the improved trading routes that were opened up via the rather more reliable steam ships resulted in great changes in the marketplace.

The importation of wheat, first from America, then Canada and India, saw that principal dietary staple come in at half the price of British wheat. Add to this a dramatic improvement in the performance of refrigerated holds, enabling ships to bring foreign pork, lamb and beef into the country and it's easy to see why the cost of food dropped so spectacularly during the 1880s.

'In the ten years from 1877-87, the price of food in a typical working class family budget dropped by 30%. In the last quarter of the century the price of wheat, sugar and tea cheapened by more than 50%, while that of butter and bacon fell by 25%' (Birchall).

Good news for those passing on the price cuts, and that meant, in Plymouth particularly, good news for the increasingly well-organised Co-operative Movement. Where local independent stores were well-run it might be difficult to make inroads, but many little local independents were not well run and the idea of chains of stores outside the Co-operative movement was still largely in gestation. And so successful Co-ops cleaned up and the Plymouth Society in particular was forging ahead at a rate unmatched in any way by any other group in Devon and Cornwall.

But as the very essence of Co-operation was co-operation, it was a welcome move, in March 1882, when *'a long-wished-for and much-desired step was taken to form a District Union of the various Co-operative Societies in the West of England'* (Webb).

Co-operation within the Movement

In Devon there were nine Societies: Barnstaple, Bideford, Buckfastleigh, Devonport (Coal Association), Exeter, Newton Abbot, North Tawton, Tiverton and, of course, Plymouth. Of the nine together Plymouth with its 7,769 members accounted for over three-quarters of the county membership and, with a turnover of £122,989, over 85% of the trading done.

Remarkably Exeter had fewer members than all but Bideford, Tiverton and North Tawton, the latter being the only Society to have a smaller turnover. The Exeter Society, in fact, was turning over little more than the Plymouth group had achieved in their very first year.

Meanwhile in Cornwall, where there were ten Societies, the combined membership was less than a fifth of the Plymouth total and their turnover was correspondingly similar.

Small wonder therefore that *'being proud of our position,'* the Plymouth Society *'determined to celebrate the twenty-fifth anniversary with a grand gathering in St George's Hall, Stonehouse, and prominent men connected with the Movement, from near and far, to mount the platform, and give us advice, censure, or encouragement as seemed best to them.'*

Webb's phraseology suggests a degree of smug self-satisfaction as evidenced in his next line: *'That we escaped their censure was to be expected, seeing how successful we had been during the quarter of a century we had been at work ...'*

It was, by all accounts, a glorious gathering and doubtless sewed the seed for the proposal the following spring to *'recommend to the Quarterly Meeting the advisability of inviting the Co-operative Congress to hold their 18th Annual Meeting at Plymouth'*, later that year of 1886.

The invitation was given and accepted, and, *'at the appointed time, the delegates, men and women (hundreds of them), swarmed into the town, and were feted, and held great business meetings touching the many and varied phases of the ever-extending Movement, reading and hearing the papers read, and holding great discussions thereon, winding up the interesting function of the last day of their visit by being grouped early in the morning in front of the Municipal Buildings.'*

'After which they were taken for a day's ride by rail through Cornwall to Penzance, and thence by coaches to the Land's End - a trip that gave great pleasure to the tourists gathered from the length and breadth of the kingdom, most of whom were unaware of the impressive and unique scenery of the sister county.'

Cornwall would certainly have been uncharted territory for most of the 600 or 700 souls who, it was estimated, made the train journey to Penzance. It is not known how many of them then made the further, twelve-mile, horse-drawn journey by wagonette to Land's End, but it would appear that the extra excursion was something of a dusty one on that dry day in the middle of June 1886.

Compared to the heavily industrialised hot-beds of Co-operation around the country, rural Cornwall, where fishing and farming were the main economic drivers, stood in marked contrast to so much of Victorian Britain and doubtless gave the delegates plenty to remember.

Above: Land's End. Top: Sennen, by Land's End . Top left: Guildhall Square - all c 1890.

For the local contingent an undoubted highlight was the presence at the Congress of 69-year-old George Jacob Holyoake, whose *History of the Rochdale Pioneers*, written some 30 years earlier, had been so instrumental in spreading the Co-operative word, particularly in Plymouth.

The Earl of Morley had taken on the role of Congress President, and had given the inaugural speech, lasting about an hour, on the first day of the proceedings, Whit Monday, 14 June. While the General Manager of the Plymouth Society, Joseph Young, chaired events on the third and final day of the official business - Wednesday 16.

It was a great day for the local Co-operators, climaxing with a grand occasion on the Hoe when, *Co-operator No.2*, the second lifeboat to be built with cash donations from Co-operative Societies, was launched at West Hoe Pier.

Tens of thousands of people had gathered on the Hoe to witness the event which had been preceded by a procession through the Three Towns. Starting at Friary Station on what was a gloriously sunny day, the ensemble was led by a volunteer band and carriages containing the leaders of the Co-operative Movement as well, of course, as the lifeboat itself, which was drawn by three pairs of horses, and which was later to be based at Ilfracombe.

As already mentioned, one of the immediate consequences of the Congressional visit to the Three Towns that June was the formation of the local Women's Guild, however, it is also tempting to think that thoughts of mechanisation were spurred on as a result of having so many candidates in town from the bigger centres of industrialisation. Either way, up until that summer Webb records that *'we had made and repaired boots and shoes by the ancient system of hand-sewing'*, but by the autumn *'we considered ourselves capable of producing our own riveted and machine-sewn boots and shoes, thereby reaping the profits that went into strangers' pockets.'*

Machine Driven

Thus it was that the Plymouth Society invested *'many hundreds of pounds in machinery and materials'* and *'hired a man who was said to be an expert in that class of trade'*. Note the hint of sarcasm from Webb when he writes

'said to be an expert', clearly as an old shoemaker himself he was none too convinced.

Nevertheless, within a few years the business was turning over nearly £8,000 a year - respectable enough, but as Webb himself observed, *'the bootmaking business has never ranked among the very profitable sources of income, nor has ours proven an exception to the general rule'*.
It was by no means the first venture into the mechanised world, seven years earlier it had been found necessary to invest in a machine that could tackle the *'laborious business of making dough'*. To that end £60 had been spent on a piece of equipment that could *'do the work more easily and expeditiously'* and *'by which the great amount of manual labour was considerably lessened and the want of the community more readily met.'*

Finding ways of improving service and profitability is always a concern of any successful business and it was the guiding principal behind a variety of decisions taken by the Plymouth Society, some of which were executed more swiftly than others. For example, at the beginning of 1885 the Committee determined to enter the farming business, again with the idea of *'reaping the profits that otherwise went into strangers' pockets'*.

'From that time, down to July 1888, we never lost sight of the matter, until on that date we secured Poole Farm of 104 acres at a rental of £280, and have worked it with varying success or failure from that time, living in hope that the ugly word 'failure' will no more be heard in connection therewith.'

Co-operator No.2 *having been launched in Plymouth in 1886 by MP's wife Mrs Acland, saw service at Ilfracombe from that summer through to 1893. Throughout that time George Williams served as its coxswain.*

'Some of our livestock'.

Top: Duke of Cornwall Hotel opened 1865. Above: General Post Office, Guildhall Square, 1888.

No.1 Neswick Street, bought in January 1889 and opened as a butchery.

The Committee had been looking for something at least twice that size, however the Forder Valley premises was to be by no means their last agricultural venture and there were better times ahead.

Another development that took several years from conception to birth was to be the greatest project undertaken to date - the creation of a purpose-built central premises.

One Giant Step

The first move in this direction had come just a few months after the flirtation with the schooner as, in November 1881, the Committee sanctioned the purchase of No's 17 &18 Frankfort Street - the combined cost, £3,600, being the biggest single investment the Society had made to date.

For once the Society did not rush to occupy the premises themselves, indeed they didn't rush to do anything, rather, six years later *'after much cogitation, we determined on utilising the property by building thereon a mighty erection worthy of our wealth, to which end we directed Mr Snell, the Society's architect, to prepare full plans for the new buildings to be erected. That was on November 1st 1887'.*

Another year passed, and then, in January 1889, the existing tenants were finally given a month's notice and a Mr Shellabear was contracted to demolish the old buildings. After a little gentle prodding from the Committee, Mr Snell eventually produced a set of plans for the site and later that year Alfred Debnam was awarded the contract for the new development. The contract price - £17,617 for the building alone.

This was an enormous commitment and prompted Webb, in his history, to pause *'and consider the mighty power contained in pence properly directed and judiciously applied. Barely thirty years had passed since our first outlay of between £2 and £3, and here we found ourselves contemplating the outlay of at least £30,000 in one great block only ...'*

It was indeed a testament to the extraordinary success of the Co-operative Movement in Plymouth, and, following the purchase of No's 15 & 16 Frankfort Street (in 1890 and 1891 respectively), that the whole scheme grew bigger still.

'That my readers may form a fair notion of this magnificent building let them imagine a house 150 feet long, 70 feet high to the parapet, and 85 feet to the ridge of the roof, with a noble tower rising to 120 feet, the whole designed in the style known as Renaissance, built of red brick, with dressings of Portland stone, and a plinth of polished granite running the whole length and breadth of the massive pile, adorned with suitable carvings wherever the taste of the architect considers it proper, so as to make it not only a useful erection, but a "thing of beauty and a joy forever".'

It is hard now to appreciate the impact this new building would have made: apart from the Guildhall and Municipal Buildings, which were then less than twenty years old, and the odd naval or military building or church, there was little else on anything like this scale in the area. There was the Duke of Cornwall Hotel opposite the principal railway station at Millbay and the new Post Office in Westwell Street, both built in a similar grand Gothic style, but you only have to look at the neighbouring properties here to see just how spectacularly the new Co-op's new Central Premises stood out. Within a few years redevelopments in Old Town Street and Bedford Street would see structures on a similar scale but, as of 24 February 1894, this was something a little special.

The Western Daily Mercury described the building as being superior to any other block of business premises in the Three Towns, while the Western Morning News called the great pile a *'prominent feature'* and *'an enduring monument to the architect'*.

Great were the celebrations surrounding the opening ceremony. All those working for the Co-op in the Three Towns were allowed to attend (all the Society's shops were shut at 11am, and, at 1.30pm, an impressive procession of rolling stock assembled at Friary. In all there were almost fifty wheeled vehicles: eleven horse-drawn bread vans, three milk floats, sixteen hand-pushed milk barrows, three grocery vans, five oil wagons and eight coal wagons.

Headed up by the Plymouth Borough Band, they processed up to Treville Street where they were joined by a 500-strong contingent on foot, fronted by the President, the Committee, the Officials, two of the founding Plymouth Pioneers (Messrs Goodanew and Reynolds) and various other Society luminaries, and all following in the wake of the Devonport Borough Band.

The walk from the old HQ in Treville Street to the new one in Frankfort Street was lined by thousands of people and there appears to have been a more general procession that took a circuitous route through the Three Towns.

President of the Society, Mr Millman, on presentation of a silver key from the architect, opened Frankfort Buildings, while the Managing Secretary, Mr Young, who was also given a silver key, opened the main entrance on Courtenay Street.

These niceties having been duly observed, the assembled throng made their way upstairs to the great hall. Measuring 86 feet long, 42 feet wide and 38 feet high and capable of accommodating 1,000 people, this was where Snell, the architect, and the principal speakers - Messrs Millman, Young, Bryant and Vaughan, addressed the crowd in-between a variety of musical selections.

At 4pm the first of four sittings for tea was held in St Andrew's Hall (each one catering for 600!) and then at 5.30pm there was a light, popular Concert in the Guildhall, an event which was immediately followed by a Grand Concert and Public Meeting, at the same venue.

Souvenir programme and entertainment arrangements from 21 February 1894.

The New Central Co-operative Buildings incorporated 'Seven Superb Shops' on the ground floor: Glass, China, etc; Boots and Shoes; Tailoring, Outfitting and Ready-made; two General Draperies; a Butchery and a Grocery. Some of these brought new employment opportunities, some saw staff from the three rented Co-operative premises in Cornwall Street move across as No's 3, 15 and 16 Cornwall Street were all closed earlier that week.

The Society's Administration Staff and their General Offices also moved into the new premises, moving up from Treville Street, although, despite the grand scale of the new development there was still not enough space to accommodate the library and newsroom that had been operating above the butcher's shop at No.3 Cornwall Street. However, 15 and 16 Frankfort Street, which had been purchased back in 1890, but which hadn't been included in the redevelopment package, now had space, and a few weeks after the opening of the Central Premises, another, much smaller, procession took place, on 17 March, as the General Committee, together with the Education Committee and various members made the short walk from Cornwall Street to the first floor of No.15 Frankfort Street, where the Library had been rehoused.

Left: The New Central Co-operative Buildings. Above; Back row: Trounch, Sidey, Hartnoll, McHardy, Goodanew, Gard. Middle: Huxham, Pryor, Densumbe, Carwithen, Burton, Cottom, Rogers. Front row: Ford, Young, Millman, Braund, Snell, Trevan, Adams.

The refashioned Treville Street premises.

The Empire Expands

The moving out of the admin offices from Treville Street, facilitated the redevelopment of No's 42 and 43 so that architecturally they could be refashioned in the style of No.44, overall creating the illusion that it had all been built as one block.

Similarly, in April 1896, Henry Snell was instructed to prepare plans for the second phase of the Frankfort Street premises, following the decision to demolish No's 15 and 16 Frankfort Street and hot on the heels of the Society's purchase, January 1896, of a large parcel of land at the back of the new buildings. Known as Frankfort Mews, in Frankfort Lane, this new site allowed for the creation of a drapery warehouse.

Every aspect of the society's enterprise was now being looked at with a view to cutting out the middle man as much as was humanly possible, and as the additional Frankfort Street sites were being cleared a resolution was approved by the Monthly Members Meeting *'that we build the adjoining block ourselves'*.

The Society had spent a lot of money on building projects over the last few years and clearly they felt that they had paid over the odds. The situation had been highlighted the previous summer: having bought a freehold property in Laira - the Plymouth boundary had just been expanded to include that community and there had been numerous requests to establish a Co-op grocery store there - advertisements had been placed looking for tenders to convert 2 Fraddon Villas into such a premises. The tenders that came in, however, were all deemed to be excessive and so the Committee decided that the time had now come to start doing their own property conversion and maintenance work.

John Trevan was tasked with the undertaking and, together with a small team operating out of a loft conversion above stables in Week Street (off Old Town Street), the newly constituted Works Department got the job done. And well done too, one imagines, because after some minor conversion and repair work, we find, in less than twelve months, this same Works Department is being entrusted with the job of completing the Central Premises.

A leading joiner and a leading mason were also appointed and low and behold, two years later, on 27 September 1899, the work was finished and there was another major opening for the Plymouth Co-operative Society to celebrate. This time, however, there were more than eighty vehicles in the procession an increase of thirty-seven in just five years - *'success had succeeded success, and nothing succeeds like success,'* observed Society historian William Watkins in 1920.

1896: A freehold premises in Laira was bought and converted.

Once again the Plymouth and Devonport Borough Bands led sections of the procession, there were the customary key presentations, a tour around the Three Towns and a high tea, this time taken in the main hall of the new Central Premises. The Society's band performed on this occasion and during an impromptu toast John Trevan, the Manager of the Works Department, noted that the new building and foundations had cost £12,950, with a further £2,200 worth of fitting out.

As an aside in his commentary, Watkins added that the work had been carried out *'without the troubles and anxieties associated with the completion of the first block'*, although he makes no mention of what those troubles and anxieties were. Presumably though that is why the Works Department was founded in the first place. Whatever the reason, here was another section of the Society destined to thrive. It really seemed that, notwithstanding the schooner saga, Plymouth Co-operative could do no wrong.

The General Office in Frankfort Buildings

At the evening function in the hall, Charles Goodanew and John Webb, two of the four surviving Plymouth pioneers, both took the stage, with 85-year-old Goodanew among those making a speech. It must have been a heady moment for the old man, although not exactly one of the first offshoots of the Movement that had started in Rochdale, the Plymouth Society was now among the top performing Co-operatives in the country. Doubtless it was a very magical evening for both men.

The 1890s had been a particularly active decade for the society, not only had the splendid new Central Premises been built and then extended, but the Society had steadily extended their presence around the Three Towns.

St Budeaux, then a separate community, had opted not to start their own Co-operative, electing instead to support the Plymouth Society, and so were truly delighted when, late in 1895, the Committee acquired Stuart House in Trelawney Road, and swiftly set about converting the premises to a grocer's and a butcher's shop ... with that all important newsroom above. The building had a long, 80- foot, frontage and was well placed in relation to the railway station servicing St Budeaux.

The new premises opened in January 1896; later that same year No.1 South Cecil Avenue (later 56 Salisbury Road), St Jude's, was bought and opened as a grocery and butchery just a week before Christmas. Then, in October 1898, two freehold plots in Embankment Road, opposite South Devon Place, another rapidly expanding part of eastern Plymouth, were purchased, and once again developed by the Society as a grocery and a butchery.

The latter opened for business at the end of June 1899 with Thomas Reynolds, another of the surviving pioneers, being appointed manager. Reynolds had previously been running the earlier Co-op butchery in the area, in St Jude's Road, however, this had been unable to keep up with the volume of trade - it was closed after the Embankment Road premises was opened. The grocery, meanwhile, was opened six months later, in December, the manager there, Samuel Braine, who at almost half the age of Reynolds, had started working for the Society as a fourteen-year-old, nearly twenty years earlier.

Within weeks of Embankment Road opening, the Society bought a property in Bishop's Place, West Hoe, which they then fitted out as a grocery store.

Top: Embankment Road. Bottom: Salisbury Road

Other Developments

Not all of the Society's late-Victorian investments centred on retail outlets however. On 1 August 1896 a freehold property and some 16,000 square feet of land in Week Street (the old Norley Brewery) was purchased at a cost of over £5,500 – a major sum – in order to extend the Society's stables and to establish a Saddlery Department. With the number of vehicles owned by the society increasing annually and with all but the handcarts being horse-drawn, there was clearly a need to have decent and adequate stabling.

The Plymouth Society had gone from being a tiny co-operative looking to supply its members with small quantities of unadulterated flour to one of the biggest fresh bread providers in the area, if not the biggest, with a flour loft capable of holding 2,500 sacks of flour - enough for six weeks' output.

Hence the calamity on 26 March 1896 when *'the Bakery in Vennel Street took fire and became a total wreck'*. *'This caused considerable loss of trade for some days,'* according the report in the 1910 account of Co-operation in the Three Towns, published in the Congress Souvenir handbook, *'but not,'* the account went on, *'to the extent that some wished.'*

The implication here being that while around 19,000 local Co-operative members and their families might have been inconvenienced by the situation the other two hundred or so independent bakers operating in and around the Three Towns, had a welcome boost to their trade.

Their *'joy'* was to be short-lived, however, as not only was the Vennel Street operation fully insured, ten unused ovens in other parts of town were found and brought into use and all the staff were kept employed. By early May the cake-making ovens in the south part of the bakehouse were back in commission and on 6 and 7 May almost 3,000 lb of cake were baked. Then, on the last day of that month the Society bought a large freehold neighbouring property in Vennel Street, which they promptly demolished and took the opportunity to make the rebuilt bakery even bigger.

The following month the Society purchased six new, Perkins, draw-plate bread ovens to replace those lost in the fire and a year later the Bakery Sub-Committee invited members to come and inspect the new premises.

At that point there were around 50 people employed at the Bakery: 25 baking journeymen, three apprentices, one stoker, one general hand, several 'strappers', seven packers, eleven deliverers and a manager.

Once again this was a far cry from 40 years earlier when the infant society had hesitated to appoint their first full-time employee. Now there were over 400 people on the payroll: around a fifth of them worked in the fifteen or so Plymouth Co-operative Grocery stores around the Three Towns, about 10% worked in the dozen or so butcher's shops, around a quarter were in drapery or tailoring, while over fifty worked in the footwear factory (where they made, on average, 500 pairs of boots or shoes per week).

In total there was little more than 5% of the workforce overseeing everything in the general office and administration centre, while the number working out in the field was about to rise with the purchase, in 1898, of twenty-three acres of land at Laira. The original plan was to provide gainful employment for the growing Works Department on the one hand and houses for sale or rent to the members on the other.

In the event, delays in obtaining planning consent saw the project held up for four years. However it was never intended to develop the whole site and in the meantime work began straight away on the greater part of the plots being used as market gardens, for the supply of fresh vegetables.

Laira Nursery.

Poole Farm at this time was also being used partly for produce, with thirteen acres devoted to oats, two to potatoes, two and a half to mangold-wurzel (beet) and one and a half to cabbage. Of the rest, 15 acres was grass (hay), while 27 cows, 20 pigs and 250 chickens occupied the remainder together with an indeterminate number of rabbits.

Just as the bakery now had its own sub-committee, so too did the farming operation, and, in the summer of 1898, the Farm Sub-Committee paid a visit to Poole Farm. As the distinguished group moved from one field to the next, they happened upon three 'gentlemen' who were engaged in the unsolicited sport of removing 'Co-operative bunnies' with the aid of a ferret and a terrier.

Although, perhaps, more than a match for the Co-operators, the poachers determined that discretion was the better part of valour and elected to engage the Committeemen and the farm foreman in an impromptu sprinting match. Not surprisingly the Co-op men were a little out of training and soon gave up the chase. They did, however, manage to take the terrier and the ferret and associated netting. Attempts to persuade the 'bow-wow' to lead them to the culprits' home, however, were less successful and so the dog was released, while the fate of the ferret went unrecorded.

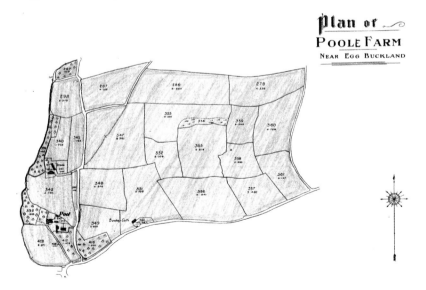

The story was one of many of the more lighthearted items reported in the Society's *Monthly Record* which the Plymouth Co-operators were now issuing free of charge to 5,000 members (which in turn represented around a quarter of the total membership and doubtless took account of households with more than one member and those members who chose not to subscribe to the periodical).

Through the *Record* members were kept abreast of all developments, financial information and little news stories, like the story of Mr WJ Gilbert, a recently appointed Director of the Society.

Gilbert, a 32-year-old accountant in the Dockyard (who had married the daughter of an old and loyal Co-operator), noticed some unsold meat in the Laira shop late one Saturday afternoon and instructed a Co-operative dairy employee to take the meat in his trap - his two-wheeled horse-drawn carriage - to the shop in Courtenay Street where it would be sold. The dairyman, however, refused on the grounds that he only took orders from his own sub-committee. The same gentleman also claimed that Mr Gilbert had invited the butcher to go to a place which *'is certainly not in Europe'*.

In the event the meat was spoilt and the dairyman had to reimburse the Society.

New Roles and Changing Faces

The citing of the relevant sub-committee above, is a reference to the initiative taken the previous year when the decision was made to create a number of sub-committees, to help oversee the growing burden of work.

These were:
Finance: *President, Secretary, Millman & Roberts*
Butchery, Dairy and Farm: Messrs. *Millett & Sidey*
Drapery, Tailoring, Coal, Oil and China: *Hartnoll & Roberts*
Grocery: *Uglow & Vernon*
Bakery and Bootmaking: *Braund & Welland*
Building Loans: *Hardy, Braund, Millett, Uglow & Vernon*
Property not used in trade: *Hartnoll, Roberts, Sidey & Welland*
Stables: *Millman, Braund, Hartnoll, McHardy, Millett & Uglow*
Works: *The President and Full Committee.*

The composition and arrangement of the various sub-committees gives some indication of the importance attached to each activity.

Albert Edward Wonnacott was born in Devonport in the 1860s: he joined the Plymouth Co-operative Society as Boy in the bread room, in November 1880, later becoming a member of the office staff - he was appointed Cashier in 1892, Treasurer in 1899 and General Secretary in April 1900.

Full page ad from the Monthly Record

There were further changes in October 1898, when Joseph Young, who had been managing secretary for just over twenty-two years, was compelled to resign on the grounds of ill-health. The Committee recommended that the Membership pay half Mr Young's salary for a further twelve months, and in the meantime the Assistant General Manager, Henry Heddon, was made General Secretary, Albert Wonnacott was appointed Treasurer and Herbert Millman became Chief Cashier.

As it transpired 34-year old Heddon was to spend just over a year in office, for he died a week before Christmas the following year, the funeral taking place in Ford Park Cemetery on Christmas Eve.

The following April, Albert Wonnacott became the new General Secretary and Herbert Millman was elevated to Assistant General Secretary and Treasurer.

Meanwhile, back in October of 1898, two other initiatives saw Arthur Browne and Ernest Hambley become Departmental Heads, the former, as Grocery Manager and Buyer, the latter, as Butchery Manager and Buyer.

Confidence was undoubtedly running high around the committee table, however, and towards the end of 1898 the Monthly Record started carrying full-page advertisements, the first ever being in the September issue - it was to publicise the Educational Department's forthcoming winter classes. The December edition, meanwhile, promoted Christmas gifts and the China Department.

Moving In For The Kill

With fourteen butcher's shops now spread across Plymouth, Stonehouse and Devonport this department was coming to play an increasingly large part in the Society's trading operations. Consequently, in November 1899 the purchase was completed of a property in Water Lane, Stonehouse, with the idea of converting the building into a slaughter house.

Immediately adjacent to Stonehouse Pool – opposite the Rectory rugby football ground – this was primarily an industrial area and its location made it a very convenient spot from which to supply the Society's growing number of outlets across the Three Towns.

Adding Further Fuel To Their Cause

Another story and another Saturday at the close of business and the Treasurer of the Co-operative Coal Association, after collecting the day's taking from the wharf office, was walking by the side of the canal when he suddenly lurched and fell into four feet of mud and water. The treasurer, it seems, was partial to a drop of whiskey and on this occasion it had got the better of him. Happily the tide was out and he was fished out, money and all, by some men from the store who had heard his cries for help and had come to his rescue armed with ropes and lanterns.

It was around this time that the Devonport Coal Association, which had long been trading as a Co-operative in its own right, started seriously to lose out to the Plymouth Co-operative as members were lured by the attractive 'Divi' available. The Devonport concern had been formed back in 1837 to sell coal to its members at prices below those charged by existing local merchants - and had peaked at over 1,000 members in the 1880s. However, in the late 1880s, the Plymouth Society had rented the Eagle Stores at North Quay to help relieve the pressure on the Phoenix Store on the Barbican.

The Eagle *'being open to the sky, and the coals being likely in the event of rain falling, to get wet, we had the great space roofed at a considerable cost, but the result has justified the outlay, and we possess one of the largest and best stores for coal to be found in the town, or the neighbourhood'* (Webb).

Doubtless it wasn't just the Devonport Coal Association who lost out to the Plymouth Co-operative's coal operation. There were over thirty other coal merchants operating in the Three Towns at that time and more than a hundred coal and wood dealers and they would all have been envious of the Society's wonderful facilities and their fleet of eleven coal trollies.

The jealousy factor was fired up further a few years later when, in December 1903, the Society acquired Furneaux's firewood at Pottery Road, Morice Town. The purchase included sawing and chopping machinery capable of producing 50,000 bundles of firewood a week and the wood was to be sold by the Coal Department and was obtainable from the Society's grocery branches.

Girl Power

Another major event to take place before the close of the nineteenth century was the hosting of the Women's Co-operative Guild Annual Meeting (afterwards known as the Annual Congress) in Plymouth in July 1899. Held in the large hall of the new premises, the event attracted 217 delegates. One notable feature of the proceedings were the meetings addressed by Miss Margaret McMillan on 'First Years of Childhood'. Among the other papers and addresses was one entitled 'Women on Management and Educational Committees'.

Miss Adams was then the Sectional Secretary of the Plymouth Guild, she had also been the first Western representative on the Central Committee (1894-97) and had been President of the Guild for the year 1895-6.

The Plymouth Guild, which had started in 1886 with 24 members had now grown to embrace a membership of 100, and, in conjunction with the Devonport branch, which started in 1893 with nine ladies and now numbered nearly 70, they undertook the work of distributing the Society's quarterly grants to its sick and poor members.

The Guild's income, primarily generated by subscription, was supplemented by their annual 'Sale of Work' and enabled them to sponsor delegates attending Annual Meetings and Conferences and also served to increase their charitable donations.

Born in the year the Plymouth Co-operative Society was born - 1860 - Margaret McMillan was one of the special guests at the 1899 Women's Guild Annual Meeting in the Society's new premises. Like her sister Rachel she was actively involved in politics and schools. She had already written several books and pamphlets including 'Child Labour and the Half Time System' (1896). Her book 'Early Childhood' was published in 1900.

Committee and Officers of the Devonport Branch of the Women's Guild.

1899 Co-operative Ladies Plymouth Guild

These Co-operative Ladies also organised a lively social programme: concerts and social evenings in the winter, excursions in the summer, but the most successful aspect of their endeavours was the fostering of a Children's Choir, which was trained by two of the members.

Many of the ladies were involved with the Education Department, which, at that time held classes in: Principles of Co-operation, Industrial History, Economics, Co-operative and Commercial Book-keeping, Shorthand, Swimming and Dress-making, in addition to Elementary Co-operative Classes for Children, and the Orchestral Band and Choir.

Also under their auspices was the Circulating Library of over 7,000 books and various bits of equipment, all of which were available for loan: they included; Magic Lanterns, Opera and Field Glasses, a Telescope, Microscope, Kaleidoscope, and Stereoscope.

With well over 20,000 members and more than 550 employees, these educational facilities were extremely valuable to the poorly educated and ill-equipped population who constituted the bulk of society ... and the majority of the society's membership. However, it was always a disappointment that interest, while strong, was never as strong as was hoped for.

Although still comparatively young as an organisation, the Women's Guilds worked tirelessly, as did many women generally for the Society. Almost 20% of the Society's workforce was female, and around a third of them were shop assistants. Tailoresses made up the next largest group, then cashiers, bootmakers, dressmakers and milliners, and dairy-workers.

Still deemed to be very much the weaker sex when it came to pay and equality, there was nevertheless a slow cultural change taking place and on the first day of the new century, the 'Seats for Shop Assistants Act' was passed, the terms of which required that one seat for every three female shop assistants had to be installed behind the counter.

Children's Choir and Junior Students.

The Hoe Promenade as it appeared in the Women's Guild Souvenir handbook of July 1899

CHAPTER 5: ARMADA SPIRIT INVOKED

On the same day that the Seats for Shop Assistants Act was passed - 1 January 1900 - the Sale of Food and Drugs Act also became law as the Government sought more rigorous regulations relating to dairy produce - butter, margarine, cheese and milk.

Accurate labelling and even product branding was still very much in its infancy, particularly across basic fresh foodstuff and it wasn't until 1902 that the Grocery Department started its own packaging. And the first food-stuff to get the treatment? It was the green pea. Wrapped with the Society's own label, neat-looking boxes of peas were sent out to the Society's grocery stores with a price tag of tuppence ha'penny.

At that point branding did not bear the Society's name as they chose instead to label their self-packaged items 'Hand in Hand' a reference to the early motif of the Co-operative movement - working together to improve the lot of the working man.

However, not everyone appreciated the sentiment, or the success of the Movement.

Co-operatives around the country were increasingly attracting hostility from certain elements within society, most notably that section of society that had been the butt of Napoleon's disparaging dismissal of Britain as a 'Nation of Shopkeepers'.

Economist Adam Smith had coined the phrase, and the lower-middle classes had come to espouse it, and abuse it, and now along had come the Co-operative Movement to usurp their status. Certain greedy, exploitative businessmen simply did not think that fair trade was fair, at least as far as they were concerned.

It was perhaps inevitable that any organisation that achieved the sort of success that Co-operative Societies were attaining around the country, would foment some sort of adverse reaction. While the population was expanding and Britain was prospering there was, of course, always going to be a bigger pie for everyone to get a piece of. However, in certain areas the Co-operators were doing so well that other businesses were bound to have their noses put out of joint.

As the twentieth century dawned the successes for the Plymouth Society showed no signs of slowing down. Statistics released in 1901 showed that there were 26 Co-operative Retail Societies showing an annual turnover in excess of £300,000 (comfortably around £30 million today - to give some idea of scale, it was announced at the same time that wages for dairymen delivering milk had just gone up from 18 shillings to 24 shillings a week (that's from 90p to £1.20 a week!).

Top of the league was Leeds with £1,474,507 then came Edinburgh, Bolton, Barnsley, Newcastle and Aberdeen – then Plymouth, whose sales had eased past the £500,000 mark. It was a remarkable achievement for the Society which, just three years earlier had been in 14th place. And still Plymouth and its Co-op were expanding, in every direction.

Monthly Record from June 1901, featuring the Fleet Street stores, Keyham.

Bricks and Mortar

HJA Wilkins Chairman of the Works Sub Committee joined the Plymouth Society in 1886.

Federation Road, Laira

Despite a good deal of bureaucratic procrastination on the part of the local authority to grant permission, the Society soon felt confident enough to start work on the Laira Building Estate.

1 January 1902 saw 60-year-old Charles Vaughan, the oldest member of the General Committee (he'd joined the Society in 1869) cut the first sod in front of some 200 spectators, including various committeemen and officials, among them HJ Wilkins, Chairman of the Works Sub-Committee who gave full expression to his frustration:

'Various obstacles,' he said, 'have been placed in the way of developing this estate by those whom the electors have put in place as their representatives on the town council. It's no good mincing matters. Time after time we have submitted plans to the committee of the council, and always some objection or other has been raised. For that, it is the electorate who are responsible.

'The time has come when we should embrace the opportunity of putting men on the council who will do what the electors want them to do. Had it not been for three years of delay, this site could have been covered with hundreds of suitable homes for working men and their families.

'If men would only realise their power, many of the disadvantages under which we now labour could be wiped away.'

It was a theme to which many would return over the next few years.

Initially only four-roomed houses were built, with the idea of introducing larger ones if required. 'At present time the demand for a house in that area is not great'.

However, less than a fortnight later, contracts were signed to purchase 'Block 6' of the Pounds Estate, a site made up of 28 house plots on the south side of Rosslyn Park Road - the cost, fractionally under £100 a plot.

A few months later, 'Block 4' of the Estate was bought for just under £800 - on this site it was proposed that the favoured pairing of a Grocery and Butchery be built at the junction of Peverell Park Road and Weston Park Road.

The recent opening of the tramway along Peverell Park Road had opened up the whole of the Pounds Estate and there some 2,000 homes in all were proposed for the area.

By January 1903 half of those being built by the Works Department had been completed and six of them had already been sold.

Members were being offered these 'substantial, well-built houses at a reasonable price. The society advances 97.5% of the purchase money to members at a moderate rate of interest, and easy terms of repayment of principal.'

Rosslyn Park Road, part of the new Peverell Estate.

The Pounds Park/Peverell Estate was expanding at a phenomenal rate around this time and in July 1903 the Society purchased a further 26 housing plots in Rosslyn Park Road on the other side of the road.

By 1909 it was reported that all the houses on the south side had been finished and work was to commence on the other side to achieve a 'complete little Co-operative Colony'.

All that was needed to buy one of these properties was a member to pay a deposit of £15 to £20 (depending on the number of rooms) and the Society would advance a mortgage based on the balance, the repayments being two shillings and fourpence (approx 12p) a week for each £100 advanced.

Since the mortgage arrangement had been first introduced 28 years earlier, some 760 members had bought houses and many had already paid off their loans.

Clearly not many of these houses to date had been built by the Works Department but progress in Peverell was particularly bright and in October of 1903 the new premises on the junction of Peverell Park Road and Weston Park Road were opened.

The whole of the structural work and the fitting out had been done by the Works Department: 'The elevation is very effective, with its coloured glazed bricks, and Portland stone cornices up to the first floor, and Portland cement piers and moulding with sunk panels filled out with pebble work for the portion above. Other notable features are its turret with vane, and the flag-staff over the main front. The whole of the shop fronts are made of teak and glazed with polished plate glass. The floor in the grocery is composed of concrete and wood blocks, and the fittings are of pitched pine and mahogany. All weighing-up of goods will be done in the Store on the first floor, and a lift is fitted to bring the goods direct into the shop.

'In the Butchery the floors are tiled and the walls to a height of about 10ft. are covered with glazed tiles of a fine design. The counters are also tiled, the tops being polished Sicillian marble. All the running gear, etc., is made of steel. The shop is fitted with an improved cold chamber.'

'The whole of the premises are lit by the electric light, the supply being taken from the Corporation.'

Pounds Stores at the junction of Peverell Park Road and Weston Park Road - note the overhead electric cables for the tram.

IMPORTANT NOTICE!

OPENING OF

24TH GROCERY BRANCH

- AT -

17, York Street,

PLYMOUTH.

The Grocery Committee have much pleasure in calling the attention of Members generally (and particularly those living in the vicinity of York Street,) to the above extension, which . . will take place . .

IN THE COURSE OF A FEW WEEKS.

Further Particulars Shortly.

The 23rd Grocery and 16th Butchery opens at Station Road, Keyham. These new stores 'are the outcome of watchfulness on the part of the management.' 'It was early surmised that the Keyham District would rapidly increase, and this surmise proved correct.'
'It will be noticed that our photograph (of the opening ceremony 9 September 1901) shows the Grocery only. The Butchery is at the other corner of the terrace. The fittings in the Grocery are of pitchpine, counter tops of polished mahogany, and the floor wood blocks on concrete. The Committee decided to spare no expense and the Works Department acted accordingly.

Boom Time

It was a particularly impressive new addition to the Society's portfolio and occupying such a prominent position on the new tram-route it was bound to be noticed.

There could be no denying it, the Co-op were absolutely in the right place at the right time and they were doing absolutely the right thing.

Never before had Plymouth expanded at the rate it was growing in the late-nineteenth century and never before had any one retail organisation been in a position to build brand new state-of-the-art stores with all mod cons each time a new estate was laid out.

There were businesses, chain stores, that had multiple branches dotted around the country, but they tended to be specialist non-food operators like John Menzies and WH Smith who had plenty of bookstalls in railway towns and on station platforms (the former predominantly in Scotland).

But as the new century dawned Sainsbury's empire was still in it's infancy and still mainly concentrated around London: the American chain Woolworth's didn't open in England until 1909: William Murdoch Morrison had only just started his own business, up North, in Bradford, in 1899: TE Stockwell and Jacob Cohen (who would trade as TESCO from the former's initials and the first two letters of the later's surname), didn't meet up until 1924: Marks & Spencer meanwhile had 36 branches by 1900, but most those were in market halls in the north of England.

So the path was clear, here and elsewhere for the Co-op to clean up, their shiny bright new shops, lit by electricity, a far cry from the dingy gas or oil-lit places they had started out in and that some traders were still operating out of. Small wonder that they prospered, and of course, the more successful they became the better off were their members.

Trading figures for the third quarter of 1902 were sufficient to generate a dividend payment of two shillings and eight pence in the pound, the highest since the Society had started, what is more, during October 1902 more than 660 new members joined the Plymouth Society, another record - these were very good times indeed.

Reaction

Small wonder that those who saw themselves losing out, here and elsewhere, to what had become the nation's most powerful collection of retailers, started to mount a rearguard action, albeit a course of action that would ultimately be doomed, partly on account of the negativity of their approach and partly on account of the strength of, and the support for, the Co-operative Movement (even the late Queen Victoria - she died in 1901 - had endorsed the Movement).

In April 1902 the Co-operative Wholesale Society held a 'Great Exhibition' in the Drill Hall at Millbay. The General and Educational Committees were both involved and the whole event proved a tremendous success: it 'must have been visited, during the three days it was open, by half the population of the Three Towns, judging by its crowded state each day'.

But that only served to fuel the mutterings amongst the private trade which had begun around the turn of the century; anti-Co-operative propaganda was published, manufacturers threatened to stop supplying Co-operative Societies and, private retailers made threats to the 'divi'.

At first it seemed little more than bluff and bluster, but then, in August 1902, the self-styled Traders Defence Association of England and Wales resolved that its members would 'pledge themselves not to trade with any manufacturer, wholesaler, or retailer, who is directly connected with Co-operative Stores, or any firm or persons who deal with the said Societies.'

On 1 January 1903 an advertisement appeared in the local press seeking 'a steady young man as driver: good character: acquainted with the Three Towns: Members of the Co-operative Society need not apply.'

The advertiser gave only a box number: 'what a pity he lacks the courage to give his address', commented the Co-op's Monthly Record.

A circular from the Co-operative Union about the problems being experienced with private traders in St Helen's was discussed in a special meeting and it was agreed to give a shilling per member to the Co-operative Defence Fund.

On 21 January 1903 a large Anti-Co-operative Movement, demonstration was staged in the Guildhall; the local organiser was a former minister of the Gospel of Love and Brotherhood, FW Pascoe, and among the speakers, apparently, was Robert Walker – 'the gentleman who organised the traders against the Scottish Co-operators'.

'He is,' said the Monthly Record, 'a champion of lost causes ... he and his friends who desire to smash the Co-op; who desire to prevent municipalities from catering for the public, that a few individuals may become rich – poisonous water supplies, overworked and underpaid workmen, notwithstanding – he and his friends may just as well give up this ridiculous agitation as proceed any further ...'

Co-operation in Scotland was, however, more robust than ever before and Mr Walker's anti-Co-operative actions, it was suggested, had assisted, 'quite innocently, no doubt, in the good work'.

One consequence here was that the Education Committee saw fit 'as a counterblast' to 'publish a large poster and a four-page pamphlet giving the facts and figures concerning the Society'. Thus it was, the month following the anti-Co-op demonstration some 550 new members joined the Society - the Walker effect had apparently back-fired on him here too.

Significantly, though, the anti-Co-operative Movement threatened the very basis of Co-operation and a subsequent Monthly Record piece, by 'Tom Pinch' asked just when Co-operators were going to realise that political representation was the way forward, particularly as there were those already elected who 'make no secret of their hostility towards us; whose avowed object is, on their own declaration, to smash the Plymouth Co-op.'

Great therefore was the rejoicing when two members, John Pryor and Albert Stroud were elected auditor of the Borough of Devonport and Labour Representation Councillor for the Tamar Ward, respectively. The grant to the Labour Representation Association was immediately increased to £25 a year.

John Pryor, Co-op Member was elected auditor for the borough of Devonport, in 1902

Albert Stroud, Co-op Member, elected Councillor on the Labour Representation ticket, for Tamar Ward, Devonport, 1902.

Inside the new abattoir at Stonehouse.

Bigger and Better

As each new Grocery and Butchery was opened, so extra demands were placed on the supply chain generally and with that in mind the Society looked to further develop their farming, warehousing, transport and production capabilities accordingly.

The move into farming had been slower than wished, however in the summer of 1900 they virtually doubled their capacity when they reached a two-year tenancy agreement to lease the 94-acre Wiverton Farm, Plympton, and exactly three years later, in August 1903, they bought the adjoining Hareston Farm from the executors of Dr JH Eccles.

Hareston gave the society an extra 150 acres of farmland (as well as a quaint old mansion house, six cottages and various other buildings). With Wiverton also in the mix it meant they now had sufficient land to accommodate more than 100 milking cows.

The move also added to the working potential of the slaughterhouse they had fashioned at Water Lane, Stonehouse. The new abattoir had been opened in November 1900. Charles Vaughan, of the Butchery Committee had had the dubious honour of slaughtering the first bullock, his colleague, WJ Gilbert, the second. Neither gentlemen used the fearsome pole-axe (as sported here in the publicity shot taken in the abattoir), both rather performing the task with a hand-gun.

The holding pens at Stonehouse were capable of detaining a mixture of eighty-two bullocks and sheep at any one time. However, it's interesting to note, that when the Society opened their new Butchery branch at 47 Treville Street, in February 1904, this particular outlet was to sell a cheaper class of imported meat from the Colonies.

That didn't particularly ease the pressure on the new abattoir, however, and in November 1902 a large block of freehold property adjoining the premises in High Street and Water Lane was purchased for a fat-melting unit and to meet refrigeration demands, as well as providing a better marshalling area for the animals.

Around this time the Committee decided that henceforth, wherever possible they would ensure that any new grocery shop they opened should have a Butchery branch adjacent, and after purchasing a freehold of premises in Bishop's Place, West Hoe, alongside their existing grocery, in March 1903, and then another in Compton, alongside their grocery there, they bought two more properties in Stonehouse, to allow them to further extend the slaughterhouse.

The Society was clearly looking to become increasingly efficient as well as increasingly self-sufficient, and it was to that end that in February of the previous year, 1902, the Committee had invested in some three and a half acres of freehold land – and a cottage – at the junction of Montpelier Road and Beauchamp Road, Peverell, with the intention of erecting a modern bakery and stables on the site.

Remarkably, it was only six years since the fire at the Society's bakery at Vennel Street had seen a significant expansion of that operation. Furthermore, it was only a year or so ago that the Grocery Warehouse was transferred from Vennel Street to North Quay, at the beginning of the year, then in September, No's 3-5 Green Street were bought, both moves designed to allow for further expansion of the existing bakery.

However, the plans for Peverell were altogether more impressive and, in the event, the development went hand in hand with the proposals for another major new building, a Grocery Warehouse on North Quay.

Wednesday, 7 October 1903, saw the foundations stones laid for both structures. The festivities began with luncheon at 11.15am, following which, the Committee, officers and guests travelled by wagonette to North Quay where Mr Marsh of the Grocery Committee placed a bottle containing the *Co-operative News, Monthly Record*, a balance sheet and a number of local papers, beneath the foundation stone.

The four-storey development, once again designed by the Society architect Henry Snell, was to have a frontage of 100 feet. Faced with limestone and brickwork, the design allowed for a floor-space of half an acre and would be able to house 5,000 tons of stock.

The quayside allowed space for vehicular traffic, a railway siding and waterside loading facilities.

The formalities concluded everyone piled back into the wagonettes and made the two to three-mile journey up to the new edge of town at Peverell, where Mr Lapthorn of the Bakery Committee laid the foundation stone of the 160 ft long building.

The proposals included an extensive stabling block and housing accommodation for the manager and selected staff. After the official speeches, founder member Charles Goodanew, now aged 89, spoke of the Society's early days and how, with some difficulty, he had persuaded a few working men to band together for their mutual advantage. He said that their capital had been but a few shillings and that it was astonishing, but gratifying to see such remarkable developments from their small efforts.

At 3pm the Society's increasingly impressive fleet of vehicles (there were now 140 where four years earlier there had been just 80-odd and ten, 50), moved off on a tour of the Three Towns. Punctuated by three bands – the Co-operative's own, and the Plymouth and Devonport Borough Bands – the procession had no real equivalent in the whole of Devon and Cornwall and would have served as an excellent advertisement for the Society.

A large meeting in the Corn Exchange by Plymouth Market, concluded the day's activities and there can have been but few Co-operators who were not proud of their achievement as they made their way home that night.

Above: The Monthly Record from January 1902 featuring Stonehouse Butchery. Below left: One of the Society's procession vehicles.

While all these major development and redevelopments were going on, one more modest enterprise that started around this time was the establishment by the Works Committee of a Funeral Service.

In the April 1902 edition of the Monthly Record the following notice appeared:

The Works Department are now
CARRYING OUT FUNERALS
In all its details
The charges are strictly moderate
Orders should be given direct to the
Works Department, Week Street

The arrangement made perfect sense as carpenters and joiners generally tended to be coffin makers. Indeed about half of the undertakers then operating in the Three Towns – and there were more than seventy – were also listed as carpenters and joiners. More significantly perhaps from the Co-operative perspective, a few of the bigger non-food businesses in Plymouth – Popham and Radford, and Spooners – had the potential to move into this market, as they already made much of their own furniture. Thus the idea of extending the Works' Department offer to include all aspects of the funeral business was a logical one.

Ironically, a spate of significant deaths followed the news. That same month James Goodanew (son of Charles) died at the age of 50. He had been a member of the Education Committee for several years as well as being the swimming class teacher.

The following year, and just a few weeks after he had spoken at the foundation stone ceremony at Peverell, Charles Goodanew himself died after a short illness. Some 2,000 members and employees assembled around his grave at the funeral service in Ford Park.

Just a few months later, March 1904, Herbert Millman resigned as Society Treasurer and Assistant General Secretary, and was succeeded by 32-year-old Edward Bolitho. Sadly Mr Bolitho died later that same year and once again a large gathering assembled at Ford Park.

However, there was to be an even bigger gathering a couple of weeks later, when Joseph Young, the former Managing Secretary, Chairman and General Manager, died at the age of 66.

Young had seen the Plymouth Society grow tenfold, both in terms of members and turnover in his years at the helm; he had also held prominent positions in the National Movement and there were few societies in the South Western Section not indebted to him for assistance and advice.

A service was held in Mutley Baptist Church and at his graveside in Ford Park Cemetery an address was given by the Senior Director of the Society, Charles Vaughan.

Less than a year after Joseph Young took leave of this mortal coil, the man who had originally challenged for his post as General Manager, 76-year-old John Webb, another founding father, also passed away.

Webb was most heavily involved at a time when such endeavours carried little reward, save the knowledge that the foundations were standing firm and that the Society was growing. More literate than most of his fellow founders, he is also certainly owed a more hallowed place in the Plymouth Co-operative success story than posterity, to date, has accorded him.

The same could not be said, however, for the 'Grand Old Man' of the Co-operative Movement generally George Jacob Holyoake, who died in January 1906, aged 88. Rightly regarded as being a saviour of the working classes, it was Holyoake's History of the Rochdale Pioneers that inspired Goodanew and Webb and their fellow founders into forming the Plymouth Mutual & Industrial Society 46 years earlier.

Having noted that the Society at this juncture made the decision to enter the undertaking industry, it is equally worth noting that the Society also did their bit to try and keep its members in good health; to wit, in the absence of a national health service, most hospitals in those days, except the workhouse infirmary, were run on a voluntary basis. In practice that often meant that patrons or people making generous donations could 'recommend' poor sufferers by handing out 'papers' that entitled the recipient to free or assisted treatment.

Thus it was that, from time to time, the *Monthly Record* would have a line or two to the effect that *'the Society's Librarian has a few Ear and Throat Hospital papers he will be glad to dispose of to members in need of medical treatment'*.

Lies, Damned Lies

One issue that would undoubtedly have had all the original Co-operative Pioneers and Founding Fathers turning in their proverbial graves concerned the scurrilous lies put about by the private traders hell bent on crushing the Co-operative Movement.

Arising out of half-baked protests cited earlier, in February 1905, the so-called Traders' Publishing Association Ltd in conjunction with the Argus Printing Company Limited, printed a newspaper called *The Tradesman and Shopkeeper*. Circulated within the Plymouth area, the paper alleged that the Plymouth Mutual and Industrial Co-operative Society was in the throes of bankruptcy.

They further alleged that: the building of the Bakery at Peverell had stopped: that the new Grocery Warehouse at North Quay, which was due to open the following month, was going to be sold off: that the Society's December 1904 balance sheet was faulty and that members were withdrawing their share capital.

The allegations were totally without foundation, and the Society successfully sued for libel at the High Court of Justice in London, on 2 & 3 April 1906. However, it was observed in the meeting held after the case had been heard, that, *'up to the time the rumours began flying about, it was always considered that the society was as solid as a rock.'* But, *'instead of being satisfied with this state of affairs, a lot of members became frightened by the babble of people who pretended they knew, but did not, and drew out their money, the very thing our opponents desired'* (WJ Vernon).

It is difficult now fully to appreciate the shockwaves that these malicious rumours sent through the Movement as other Co-operatives were also being targeted but not all of them had the wherewithal to respond as effectively as Plymouth.

The Plymouth Society had enlisted the services of three-times Mayor of Plymouth, solicitor John Thomas Bond (of the firm Square, Bridgeman, Bond and Pearce), to represent them and he was *'more than anyone else'*, credited with carrying through the trial to such a successful conclusion.

Above: Tavistock Street premises.
Below: The store at Old Road, Laira

The relief at that meeting held in the Main Hall of the Central Premises was almost tangible, it was packed to capacity with *'fully a thousand members present'*.

Mr Bond then addressed the assembled host: *'after the first day it was clear that the case was won … the society's books had been overhauled to their very deepest, and when it was proved that the accountant's independent valuation shewed the actual assets over liabilities to be £106,998, the Judge's remark, "that he only wished he was half as bankrupt as the Plymouth Mutual Co-operative Society" could be very well understood.'*

It further transpired that a week before the case was due to be heard, the counsel for the opposition had returned his brief and refused to have anything to do with the case.

Summing up the case for the jury Mr Justice Lawrence commented on the way that the Society had been libelled: *'Fair comment,'* he said, *'had been pleaded, but it was not fair to make your own facts and comment upon them. The paper was run in the interests of the small trader, its whole business seemed to be to call attention to various co-operative societies. It had instituted a 'War Chest' for the purpose of fighting this action. £49 had been collected in one week: a shriek of joy went up when the fund reached £600. Waving his hand in the direction of the benches where the lawyers were sitting, his Lordship added, "£600 won't go far down there".'*

'Here' he continued, *'was a society composed of working people, who had banded themselves together to buy their goods by themselves in order to get them cheaper; the society was managed by people elected by themselves, and he thought such action was to be approved. The law had given societies of this kind a legal position, and he thought they were entitled to be supported by newspapers, and not attacked as they had been.*

'The learned judge also condoned the use of strong language. The defendants had complained that they had been called liar, damned liars, and Robert Walkers. All he could say was that, seeing the attacks that had been made upon them, co-operators would have been justified had they used even stronger language.'

It took the Jury just half an hour to reach their verdict. They awarded damages against the Traders' Publishing Association of £4,000 and against the Argus Printing Company of £1,000.

In the event The Traders' Publishing Association, which had falsely accused the Plymouth Society of being bankrupt, itself went into liquidation, however a year later the General Secretary of the Co-operative Union, Mr JC Gray, arrived in Plymouth midway through a quarterly meeting.

Having been introduced to the assembly, Mr Gray said a few words and made reference to the historic libel case: *'Plymouth fought alone, but in fighting for itself had fought for the whole Co-operative Movement and killed the opposition, nothing but punishment in a criminal court would satisfy such cases'* and at that point he handed over a cheque from the Co-operative Union Defence Fund. The cheque was for £3,499.8s.8d. which covered the vast majority of the Jury's damages award from the Traders' Publishing Association, and Mr Gray said that it came with the best wishes of the rest of the Co-operative Movement for the Plymouth Society's future.

Mr Vernon, replying for the Society, humorously reminded Mr Gray that it was Plymouth boys to a large extent who defeated the Spanish Armada, and, if given the opportunity, *'would beat creation'*.

Never Mind The Rumours What About The Reality?

While clearly there had been some easily worried members, even the casual observer would have been hard pressed to see any merit in the lies circulated about the Society.

Exactly one month after the offending paper had hit the streets, the Society celebrated the opening of the impressive new purpose-built, four-storey warehouse on North Quay.

The ground and first floors were devoted to the bulk storage of groceries, but the top two floors were used for the mixing and packaging of baking flours, custard and blancmange powders, spices, sauces, peas and beans - even Persian sherbert and health salts – all to be sold in the Grocery stores with the Society's new home brand Hand-in-Hand.

The Packing Department at North Quay.

Fifteen young women were initially employed in this work, but so successful was it that within two years there were about 25 ladies in the packing section.

The following year, on Wednesday, 9 May 1906, the bakery building (on which it had been claimed, work had been halted), was opened amid great pomp and ceremony. Whereas the North Quay opening had come just a month after the false allegations had been published, this opening came a month after the case had been won in the High Court, consequently the Society took the opportunity to really push the boat out.

This time the grand procession was made up of 161 vans, trollies, floats etc., some of them highly decorated – an impressive increase of around 20 vehicles since the laying of the foundation stone a little over two and a half years earlier.

As previously, the Devonport Borough Band, the Plymouth Borough Band and the Society's own ensemble led the march through the principal thoroughfares of the Three Towns and upon arrival at the new Peverell premises, Messrs Vaughan and Wilkins of the Bakery Committee officially opened the building. Each was presented with a gold key and once the doors had been thrown open the assembled crowd, estimated to be more than 5,000, were invited to inspect the inner workings. Before the day was out it was estimated that fully 10,000 people had had a look around the new premises. In the evening there was a public meeting and concert and such was the demand that hundreds had to be turned away. Thomas Reynolds, the last surviving pioneer, was among the speakers.

Of course the opening of this major new facility meant that the old bakery was now redundant ... but not for long. A number of suggestions were put forward for utilising the old Vennel Street property and the matter was promptly sorted by the Boot Sub-Committee who instructed the Works Manager, Ernest Carwithen, to fit up the erstwhile bread room and flour loft as a boot warehouse. The work was completed early in 1907.

Figures for that year aren't readily available, but the Boot Department was clearly doing very well - just a few years earlier it had been reported that 10,000 pairs of boots had been sold in just one quarter and furthermore that almost half of them (4,542) had been *of the Society's own make'*.

Top: North Quay Warehouse. Above: The New Bakery at Peverell.

Inside the new bakery at Peverell.

Taking It To The Streets

A new pair of working men's hob-nailed boots could be bought for just under five shillings, almost 20% of an average weekly wage. For some it was more of an issue than others, but generally most working men were heavy on their shoes, as were all working horses and by January 1907 the society had more horse power than ever before - hence the decision to build an all-new stable block at Peverell, adjoining the bakery.

It wasn't just a question of delivering produce from the abattoir, bakery, boot factory, farm or warehouse to one or other of their many outlets either. To meet the demand from members where there was no handy Co-op shop or just to provide a regular service for different neighbourhoods, door-to-door Dairy and Bakery, delivery vans had already been operating for some years.

Then, in March 1903, the Society had introduced a new service - the horse-drawn greengrocery van. The first of these vehicles was designed by joiner and builder, John Spry of Station Road, Devonport and orders were instantly placed with him for even larger models. By the end of the year the Greengrocery Department already had twelve such vans on the road and a further four were on order, in anticipation of being required.

Significantly at the beginning of that year there was no such thing as the Plymouth Co-operative Greengrocery Department, its earlier incarnation had simply been the 'Potato Department'. The change reflected the Society's increasing growing capacity across their extended farmlands and market garden facilities.

The move also led to another new initiative: on 30 December that year, 1903, the Society acquired a sizeable freehold property off Sutton Road, Coxside, that they might relocate the Works Department from their now quite cramped quarters in Week Street. Eighteen months later they moved the Firewood Factory from Devonport to the new Alma Yard site at Coxside and around the same time decided to establish a Wheelwright and Coachbuilding section.

Why pay someone else to manufacture your carts and carriages when you had the wherewithal to do it yourself?

94   *Top: Grocery cart is loaded ready to leave. Bottom: The new stables at Peverell.*

On the road: at St Michael Avenue, Keyham.

Top: Inside the dairy. Right: You provide the container, the Society, represented here by Charlie Gerry, provides the measuring jug. Below: The first steam lorry ... the Society starts to look beyond the horse.

The Greengrocery delivery van operation was, however, still small beer when compared to the Dairy Department, who, around this time, were serving around 12,000 families in the Three Towns each day. When you consider the average family size around that time that would have represented a significant percentage of the local population – comfortably somewhere between a quarter and a third.

Some 68 Co-op milkmen were, between them, responsible for the deliveries, each with an average of 172 families on each of their rounds.

The milk was apparently delivered daily in sealed churns to the dairy shops - from specified, and contracted local farms (including Poole, Hareston and Wiverton - the Society's own farms) and then, after inspection, poured into churns on the delivery carts for door to door selling. This would be done by the milkman ladling the milk into a measuring jug and then ladling the same into the customers' own jug or container – with rarely a bottle in sight!

Often Greengrocery or Dairy vans would have a roundsman and a boy working the round. Young lads, fourteen or younger (with parental consent) would knock on doors and take orders while the roundsman stayed with cart, partly to prevent pilfering and partly to stop the horse going off on his own although most of the milk was delivered on hand barrows. Some of the Grocery branches also employed boys to deliver weekly parcels to anyone living within a reasonable distance – this way the Society were able to reach further and further afield with each branch that opened.

One must assume that delivery boys were also using bicycles, for the Ironmongery Department were selling them in 1907; guaranteed for five years, with best quality tyres and two-rim brakes – yours for £5.

In the summer of 1908 there was an exciting new development as the Society road-tested its first horse-less carriage – a steam wagon – supplied by Robey & Co. of Lincoln, registration number FE 443. Purporting to be capable of carrying a five-ton load, the wagon was severely tested in its first month and attempting to transport five tons of building materials to the Society's farm at Wiverton the motor was strained and required costly repairs. Thereafter the capacity was capped at four tons – much to the frustration of the Committee.

Whatever Next?

As the Plymouth & Mutual Co-operative Society rapidly approached its 50th anniversary, members must have wondered what more they could do.

By early 1908 the Society had started selling pianos. Prices ranged from 18 to 29 guineas – a substantial sum considering the wages for men were still around the one pound a week mark, whilst the pay rate for a female cash clerk in the butchery shops that year was fixed at five shillings a week for the first year, seven for the second, nine for the third and eleven shillings a week thereafter with a shilling a week bonus for every extra £25 worth of trade.

Another new territory taken on by the Society at this time was jewellery. For some time now, Butland and Son of Old Town Street had been happy to credit the 'divi' account of any Co-op member making a purchase in his shop, however the arrangement came to an abrupt halt in March 1908 when the Society opened its own Jewellery and Watch section within the Drapery Department.

The following month the Works Department was instructed to build a bigger Grocery store at 13/14 Courtenay Street and to create a restaurant above it. The existing Grocery had become too small and once it had moved out the new Jewellery and Fancy Goods section of the Drapery moved in.

The new restaurant was an instant success; opened at 8.30am on Saturday, 17 April 1909, and it was estimated that over 1200 people passed through its doors before closing time at 10pm. With a separate tea room adjoining the restaurant, a hot dinner could be bought for 6d, a three-course lunch for 1/6d, and tea and cake for a little less. Wedding cakes could be made to order at 5/- a time.

The Society's capabilities in the bread, cake and confectionary direction had taken a major step forward the previous year when the leasehold of the Great Western Flour Mill, also known as Risdon's Mill in Millbay Road, had been acquired for the the 'most satisfactory', though not inconsiderable, sum of £6,000.

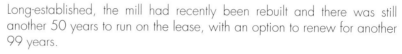

Inside the Restaurant

Top: No trouble at Mill just yet.
Below: The Drapery warehouse.

Long-established, the mill had recently been rebuilt and there was still another 50 years to run on the lease, with an option to renew for another 99 years.

For some years this had been the principal source of the Society's flour supply but for some time the mill had lain idle following the death of Richard Risdon, the head of the firm. The business had been put onto the market but had failed to reach the reserve price, consequently the Society had been able to make an offer on the premises and eventually the offer made was accepted.

It was good news all round for the sale not only secured the ongoing supply of quality flour for the Society, it also meant that jobs were saved for the 38 employees and manager of the mill, who thereafter became employees of the Plymouth Mutual & Industrial Co-operative Society.

That same year, 1908, saw another firm more linked with the Plymouth

Society, as, in February the first edition of the *Monthly Record*, to be printed by The Plymouth Printers Limited, hit the shelves. All previous issues had been printed by private printers, the new contractors, however, were themselves Co-operators.

Formed in 1899, The Plymouth Printers Limited were a *'local Co-operative Productive Society'* and being handed the task of printing 10,000 copies a month of a magazine that didn't need to make a profit – copies were distributed free to the Society membership – would have been very welcome.

There could be no denying it now, the Plymouth Co-operative had truly come of age and was a force to be reckoned with. With over 1,200 employees it was one of the larger, if not the largest employer in the Three Towns outside of any Government-funded organisation, and certainly with its emphasis on

education, self-improvement and, in pure business terms – self-sufficiency – it was a model organisation in every respect. Small wonder that it had risen to be the fifth best performing Co-operative in the Country.

This truly was the 'Caring Sharing' Co-op as the 'divi' was there for all members and there were now the best part of 40,000 of them across the Three Towns. Furthermore, in 1908 suggestions were put forward to help ease the local unemployment situation as a proposal was made that £50 be put aside for this every quarter. LG Williams also suggested that, as a means of creating employment, idle land at Laira might be turned into gardens (a veiled reference to the fact that the society had still not got planning permission to develop the Little Efford Estate).

The Society were also assisting the Social Democratic Association who were providing free meals for children of the unemployed. Other organisations benefitting from grants from the Education Committee included: the Labour Representation Association, the Kitto Institute for Working Lads, The Three Towns Housing Association, Worker's Educational Association and the Swimming Associations of Plymouth and Devonport.

The Women's Guild also had an important part to play and much useful work was done by the teaching of Co-operative Book Keeping, Dressmaking, Shorthand, First Aid and Home Nursing ... and by the payment of half-fees to students attending the new Technical Schools.

Of all the Society's classroom work, the Children's Classes in Co-operation were undoubtedly the most successful. Begun at the turn of the century, going into the 1909-10 session, there were more than 1,700 students enrolled.

A liberal distribution of prizes and an annual summer outing to a large extent, helped with the recruitment, *'but no-one blames the Committee for the means they employ to get hold of the children and most of them become diligent little students'* (Burton 1909).

With the national organisation about to stage their 42nd Annual Co-operative Congress in Plymouth – on the occasion of the local Society's 50th anniversary – the future had never looked brighter.

Princes Street store, as it appeared on the cover of the Monthly Record in 1907.

J Hayne Pillar taking a class.

Mutley Plain at the dawn of the twentieth century.

CHAPTER 6: JUBILEE TIME

The 1,600 Congressional visitors to Plymouth that Whitsun - 1910 - would have each been issued with a copy of an impressive 250-page Souvenir Handbook *'with the Reception Committee's compliments'*. The book contained a potted (90-page) History of the Three Towns by the long-serving Society Librarian, Edward Burton, a member of the Reception Committee, and no less a comprehensive account (running to some 50 pages) on the History of Co-operation in the Three Towns, by the same author.

Within the latter were contained current statistics on the state of the Plymouth Society, the figures made impressive reading:

'At the close of the year 1909 the Society possessed the following places of business: 26 Grocery shops, 22 Butcheries, 7 Boot shops, 1 large and 7 small Boot Factories, 9 Dairy Branches, 6 Drapery, Furnishing, and Ironmongery Departments, 2 Tailoring and Outfitting Branches, a Bakery, a Flour Mill, 2 Farms (330 acres), 5 Dressmaking and Millinery Departments, China and Glass Stores, Oil and Firewood Stores, 2 Coal Stores, Firewood Factory, Greengrocery Department, Market Gardens, Grocery and Packing Warehouse, Drapery Warehouse, Works Department, Stables, and Saddlery Department, Restaurant, and an Abattoir, practically the whole of which is freehold property.'

Department	£ Trade	Staff	Outlets	£ Output
Grocery	245,135	219	26	10,084
Butchery	108,069	103	22	
Bakery		56	1	81,853
Mill		26	1	91,221
Bread Room	81,381	47	1	
Dairy	68,469	112	9	
Boots and Shoes	27,556	25	7	
Boot Factories		55	8	8,375
Drapery & Furnishing	63,214	160	6	
Tailoring & Outfitting	27,620	89	2	
Greengrocery	21,694	47	vans 17	
Coal	55,007	70	2	
Oil	10,664	16	1	
China and Glass	2,288	5	1	
Restaurant	7 months 1,693	8	1	
Works Department	work done 14,695	109	1	
Total	747,505	1147	106	

1910 Co-operative Congress Souvenir

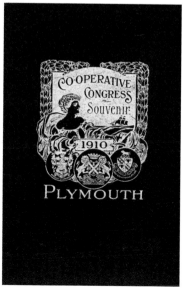

Based on those figures it would seem, on the face of it, notwithstanding the overheads, it was the food that produced the best return with fuel in second place and tailoring, drapery, china and ironmongery very much in the next league down. The works department was not strictly comparable, while in terms of output, the bakery was clearly ahead of the field.

To put some meat on those statistics, as it were, we also learned that the Butchery Department in the previous year had slaughtered 2,086 bullocks, 3,458 sheep, 1,894 lambs and some 6,812 pigs.

The Dairy Department, meanwhile, had produced over half a million gallons of raw milk, 150,000 gallons of 'scald' (sterilised) milk, almost 100,000 lbs of cream, more than 300,000 lbs of butter, and some 567,927 eggs.

Overall the picture was extremely impressive with the annual turnover now approaching three-quarters of a million pounds, at a time when you could buy a Co-op steak-and-kidney pasty for tuppence (less than a penny today)!

Looking at the figures during the 50-year period over which the Plymouth Society had now been trading it's interesting to note that the turnover per member was consistently around the £15 to £20 mark, per year, while the increase in member numbers was consistently up from one decade to the next (the final figure was not for the full ten-year period). Consequently the turnover was growing at a remarkably constant rate.

Year	Members	£ Sales	£ Profits	£ Share Capital	£ Reserve Fund	£ Education Fund
1860	90	98	41	81	..	9
1870	568	11431	644	1817	31	16
1880	5154	99318	12850	23671	2088	304
1890	13972	212113	33380	94696	10221	691
1900	25653	452090	76611	264339	26921	1522
1909	37184	730879	117743	432011	72182	2195

No wonder the Plymouth Committee men were proud of their achievements and chose to fill the first sixteen pages or so of the handbook with group and individual portraits of themselves, including one that was very obviously intended to be a pastiche of the famous photograph of the original Rochdale Pioneer committee (opposite). Theirs was now the third biggest society in the country, in terms of membership, with the fifth highest turnover.

The Plymouth Congress, like its predecessor, was a great success. HJA Wilkins, the first Plymouth man to sit on the CWS Board, served as the President of the Congress, while a fellow 'graduate' of the local Education Committee classes, William Watkins, delivered the Inaugural Address.

As well as the usual round of talks and papers, the visiting delegates, many of whom were housed with members locally, were treated to evening concerts by the Society's Orchestral Band and Adult Choir, as well as a revisiting of the excursion to Land's End. Three trains transported the travelling contingent to Penzance and thereafter a selection of motor buses, wagonettes, and 'other vehicles ancient and modern' completed the journey.

The only shadow to be cast over the proceedings was the death of King Edward VII on Friday 6 May which put paid to the proposed Jubilee Procession through the Three Towns on the first day of the Congress.

'The opportunity it would have provided to demonstrate more fully to Co-operators from other places what the resources of the Society were, was therefore lost.'

The event was rescheduled for the August Bank Holiday Monday. Once again massed bands and a vast array of vehicles - some 200 of them - congregated at Friary Station and set off through the principal thoroughfares of Plymouth, Stonehouse and Devonport.

Thomas Reynolds, the last surviving Plymouth Pioneer, travelled with the Directors in the first of nine wagonettes packed with the Society's principal players. Tea was provided for 300 of the dignitaries in the Society's main hall in the Central Premises and Mr Reynolds, who was two weeks shy of his 79th birthday, addressed the congregation.

The General Committee, 1910. Back row: J Marks, J Hayne Pillar, AN Stroud, AW Grigg, T Gidley, WG Finch. (Assistant Secretary) Front row, seated: WJ Vernon, E Truscott, AE Wonnacott (General Secretary), WG Millman (President), HJ Lacey (Committee Secretary), J McHardy.

This page: Jubilee Celebrations in
Central Park.
Below: Jubilee Plate.

Such a major anniversary wasn't allowed to pass that easily, however and also that August several children's Sports Days were held: one at the Rectory Ground on 6 August that attracted 1,100 children; one a week later at Home Park that was attended by 2,600 young people and finally, a fortnight later, by which time word had clearly spread, some 4,600 youngsters joined in the Jubilee Celebrations at South Devon Place.

Professor Howell's Band played *'an excellent selection of popular airs'*; Professor Johns enthralled all with his conjuring skills, while Professors Lawrence and Bickford had everyone roaring with laughter at their Punch and Judy show.

'I sincerely hope that great institution, Punch and Judy, will never fade,' wrote the *Monthly Record's* man on the scene, Tom Pinch: *'There is nothing that I know of more cleanly funny for children. Oh, those smiles! And especially when Mr Punch (artful scamp that he is!) hanged the hangman instead of quietly consenting himself to be hanged ... Reversing the order of things seems to appeal to youngsters.'*

The Committee, incidentally, had *'decided that those attending should be over seven and under fourteen years old. The writer of these notes however, came across a number of little dots who really looked to be just over five; whilst on the other hand he made himself acquainted with several very fine specimens of boys and girls* **under** *fourteen.'*

Whatever the entertainment there can be little doubt that the *'bagful of good things'* did much to lure the younger generation. *'A Congress Tart, a Beef Pie, a large Currant Bun, a small Lemon Bun, and a portion of Jam Sandwich,'* was made available to all, with *'a large mug (which the children kept) of Lime Juice or Lemonade'* and on the last occasion this was augmented with *'a bag of Nuts, with squares of CWS Chocolate thrown in'*.

A member of the General Committee, addressing a little party of about 40, who were sitting on the grass cracking nuts, said: *'How nice would it be boys and girls, if we could have an outing like this every other week.'*

'Yes', they replied in chorus. Then one of the number enquired as to when the next outing would take place. *'In about ten years' time,'* he replied.

Later in the year there was also a series of Old Folks' Socials and Teas, held across the Three Towns, which catered for more modest numbers. To cap all these events a Founder's Tablet was hung in the Large Hall in the Central Premises.

One of the more enduring features of the Society's Jubilee Year was undoubtedly the opening, just two weeks before Christmas 1910, of the 'Jubilee' stores at the top of Peverell Park Road. Several hundred spectators turned out to see what now became the Society's 27th grocery, 23rd butchery, and 11th dairy.

The northern part of town was the prime growth area at this time. With the Bakery and Stables only recently completed, some 66,000 square feet of land was purchased at Langstone Field, Peverell, for the construction of a major laundry facility which duly opened in November 1911. Seven hundred and eighty people applied to work at the new premises.

With new houses going up every year this was becoming an increasingly populous area: Hyde Park School had opened in 1904 for the local children and the new parish of St Gabriel was formally created on the day the church was consecrated, 26 July 1910.

Once again the Society had seen a market and made a bid to compete: the Plymouth Steam Laundry, established back in 1885, had moved a little earlier, to Hyde Park Road (later Weston Park Road and still known then primarily as 'The High Road'). This facility was close to the Co-operative Society's new stores at the other end of Peverell Park Road and it claimed to be the largest and best equipped laundry in the West of England. In town there was also the Central Steam Laundry and the Millbay Laundry, plus maybe a dozen or so others - laundry was big business. And so the Society weren't afraid to step in and set up shop 'at the highest point in the Three Towns thereby commanding the purest air, essential to the health of the employees and the successful carrying out of the industry.'

Within no time at all they were cleaning, amongst other things, in excess of 30,000 shirt collars a week. The work was not without its problems however and the first manager did not last long; but after this, and a few other initial glitches had been ironed out, the Laundry soon became a lively part of the Society's offer.

Co-op United AFC 1913-14, Winners Devon Wednesday League and Devon Wednesday Cup. Back: E Maddaford, E Parkin, W Scoble, C Davies, S Symons. Middle: G May, B Williams, W Blatchford, H Sincock, S Tanser, R Kirkwood, A Phillips. Front: A Crocker, P Steed, E Memory, J Hosking, E Davy, W Cummings.

The New Laundry

Co-op United?

One of the difficulties arising out of the new Langstone Road Laundry concerned the status of the women working there. Ten shillings a week, it was argued, was not enough to keep female laundry workers respectable. The Committee, for their part, explained that this was just a starting wage and cited the instance of one young lady, aged seventeen, who had asked for a job and had offered to work for just four shillings a week.

Curiously enough, the Committee had come under fire the previous month for deciding to only employ men who were trade unionists for the task of unloading coal at North Quay, but eventually the membership accepted the idea. The whole question of Union Membership, however, was about to come to a very ugly head.

Initially all had seemed relatively fine, indeed back in July 1906, at a meeting of the Amalgamated Union of Co-operative Employees, a decision had been taken to start a Football Club - the Co-op United - with membership open to all Co-operative employees. A field had been found at Oreston and the team had joined the Second Division of the Devon Wednesday League with the blessing of the Education Committee who gave them a football with the words 'Good Luck' stamped on it.

However the Amalgamated Union of Co-operative Employees (AUCE) was not recognised by the Trade Union Movement and this was to cause a headache a few years later when the local branch of the Dockers and General Workers Union submitted a wage claim of an extra three shillings a week, and the AUCE submitted a separate claim for an extra *five* shillings a week, but nevertheless tried to involve itself in the Docker's Union talks.

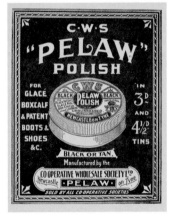

One interesting innovation around this time was the fixing of an 'All Co-operative Week' during which only co-operatively produced goods were to be exhibited in shop windows.

In the course of events Co-operatve coal-storemen and loaders, greengrocery, grocery, and drapery storemen and drivers all went out on strike, along with stablemen and a number of shop and clerical workers who came out in sympathy. The situation gathered much press, and lasted many weeks.

Eventually, in November 1916, a settlement was reached between the Society and the Dockers' Union and the following month's members' meeting decided that henceforth all new employees should be a member of a recognised Trade Union.

Trouble At Mill

Another area of enterprise that had attracted adverse criticism around this time was the ailing Flour Mill at Millbay. Quite what the situation behind the troubled business was, is unclear. Certainly when the Society had bought the former Risdon's Mill four years before it had seemed like an excellent move, but perhaps the signs had already been there, after all the business had failed to meet its reserve price and the initial reluctance to accept the Co-op's lower price had eventually evaporated.

Whatever the bigger picture, the bottom line was that the Mill was operating at a continuing loss, a loss that many were unhappy with when announced in October 1912 and which precipitated the closure of the Mill less than two years later, in 1914.

This was a comparatively quiet time for the Society and apart from the purchase of a freehold property in William Street, Morice Town, which was soon afterwards opened as a new Grocery branch, it meant that the last twelve months of William Millman's 33-year tenure as President of the Society were remarkably subdued. Not that that in any way detracted from Millman's extraordinary record.

'A man of irreproachable character and strong will, he served the society faithfully and well' said his successor William Watkins, a Director since 1902, who chaired his first meeting in Millman's seat, in January 1914.

Millman's departure was not the only one and six other new faces joined the General Committee at the beginning of 1914 and almost immediately the new regime made its impact.

Between June and October seven freehold properties in Raleigh Street were purchased (21-27 inclusive), and by Christmas Eve a further seven buildings in Courtenay Street (6a -12) had been added to the Society's portfolio, rendering virtually the whole of that island block – bordered by Frankfort Street, Raleigh Street and Courtenay Street – Co-operative property. The idea was to build a new major store adjacent to and to relieve, the now-cramped Central Premises ... for the time being, however, the events of August 1914 were to put these ideas on hold.

War, What Is It Good For?

The threat of war had been in the air for some time before the actual declaration of hostilities on 4 August 1914. One notable consequence of the anticipated event on the domestic front had been the panic buying of food. Across the country shelves were cleared. The Co-op held their prices firm: less scrupulous private traders didn't, and as the demand went up so did their prices. Some even bought from the Co-op to resell to the public at an inflated price.

As some lines disappeared, so the Management Committee took it upon themselves to issue a direct appeal to the membership through the August edition of the *Monthly Record*:

'Fellow Members - We have done all that was possible, under extraordinary conditions, to meet your food-stuff requirements, and as the conditions have changed from day to day, it has become necessary to make an appeal to you to adapt yourselves to these conditions.

'We believe it is your desire that the Society should exercise a steadying influence on prices of food-stuffs in the locality. Our efforts have been directed to that end, but you will materially assist us by so arranging your requirements that our supplies may be extended over the longest possible period.

'There is a loyalty which can best express itself at the present time by refraining from complaints, accepting the present position as one calling forth unselfish conduct and a generous recognition of the fact that your Committee and staff generally have done their best under trying circumstances. We beg to thank you for your forbearance in many matters during the past few days, and we further appeal to you to show to the public the realities embodied in our motto: "Each for all and all for each" – The Committee.'

The appeal was well-received. Generally speaking members did their bit and when called upon voted £1,000 for the local War Distress Fund as well as creating a fund of their own for members and employees.

Pride And Prejudice

Nationally the British Co-operative Movement was better placed than any other organisation to help the Government and therefore the Country at this time of need. A food ship sent over to Dublin the previous September when industrial action had severely compromised food supplies there, had already demonstrated this point. Now came an even greater emergency.

Within weeks of war being declared the Co-operative Wholesale Society were churning out 10,000 suits a day for the army. They had stockpiled some 70,000 blankets and were looking to meet the Government's requirements at as close to cost price as was possible.

It was clear that many private traders were looking to exploit the situation to the maximum, but the Co-operative Society, as a whole remained committed to their principals. While private traders were buying huge quantities of food to sell on at a much higher price, the Co-op sought to control supply.

Advocating rationing, they instituted their own system, and as the CWS took care in supplying its retail societies, they in turn were careful in the supply chain to their members ... and very well it did them too, at least as far as the great British public was concerned. Faced with inflated prices almost everywhere else, people flocked to their Co-op.

In October 1914 alone, 716 new members joined the Plymouth Society, and as the war limped on and conditions were exacerbated so the Co-op adapted and thrived: during May 1917 a record number of new members joined the Society - 1,417.

The Government, however, appeared to take no notice of this self-sacrificing patriotism, for them it was business as usual. If anything it appeared that they were happy to let private commerce use the situation to their own advantage and even, covertly, to let them have a chance to do the Co-op down. When rationing was introduced for sugar, the Co-op didn't even get a place on the commission controlling the supply, despite the fact that the Co-op was both the largest wholesaler – and retailer – of sugar in the Country. Locally, even with rationing, *'no less than 132,000 people buy their sugar from the Society every week'* (JW Fletcher 1920).

Mutley Plain: Plymouth Co-operative Society – Are You A Member?

Hudson Ewbanke Kearley,
1st Viscount Devonport.
MP for Devonport 1892-1910.
Made his fortune in the grocery
trade, great rival of Sir Thomas Lipton.
Appointed Food Controller by Asquith
in 1916.

Early removal lorries.

Nor was there representation on the Wheat or Coal Commissions when they were set up. Furthermore the rationing system when implemented saw goods distributed according to the number of pre-war customers a store had, which meant that many of the new, and old, Co-op customers had to fall back on private traders for their rations. This situation was of course aggravated by the fact that, with no declared membership records of their own, private traders could - and did - exaggerate their pre-war figures, while the Co-op Movement, with its trading figures and membership statistics readily available, could not and generally speaking, would not, be so economical with the truth.

Plymouth, however, was one of the first Societies in the country to institute rationing - *'potatoes being the first commodity thus dealt with during that period when it was practically the sole provider of potatoes locally'* (C White, 1920).

White, writing in the Diamond Jubilee 'Special' Record, continues: *'The submarine menace brought about the National Control of Food, and the setting up of the Local Food Control Committees, and it will be remembered what a strenuous fight had to be made before the consumers could get anything approaching fair representation thereon.'*

The situation wasn't helped by the fact that the Government had appointed Lord Devonport, *'a wholesale grocer and competitor of the Co-op'* (Birchall 1995) as Food Controller.

Up and down the country war-relief committees were set up and Co-op members, whose societies had given generously to these bodies, were excluded from sitting. Similarly, military service tribunals were packed with private traders, who seemingly took delight in sending Co-op workers out to the front, while somehow exempting their own employees:

'One society lost 102 out of its workforce of 104, while surrounding shopkeepers were keeping their sons out of uniform. Some army officers sent in to oversee the process had naively explained that the Co-op was an unfair competitor in any case and should be closed down' (Birchall).

In the Three Towns, by the end of 1915, some 209 Co-op workers were serving out of 363 who were then eligible to be called up. To compensate, more women were taken on. Three months later the number had risen to around 300. In the Laundry all the van drivers had been called up and 53 wash-house women had been moved to munitions, leaving the department in a very difficult and precarious position, causing many complaints - bad work, lost items, etc.

By the summer of 1916 the number of those called up had risen to 350 and by May 1917 that number had doubled. There were now 700 employees serving in the Armed Forces, with the Society making up the difference to families of the shortfall between what the Services were paying and what the employees had been paid before they were called up.

All these measures took their toll on the Society's resources, but none compromised their integrity, and membership rose dramatically. From around 40,000 members in 1913, the roll had risen around 50% to almost 60,000 by 1918. The number of staff employed by the Society had gone up by a similar percentage from 1,521 to 2,400. Trade meanwhile had gone from just over three quarters of a million pounds, to over two million.

Part of this was due to a degree to increased prices, but primarily it was down to the tremendous increase in membership and to the Committee grasping the situation and, honourably, taking the opportunity to manage the circumstances to everyone's advantage (apart, perhaps, from that of certain private traders).

The first innovation, just weeks after the war had started, came in September 1914, when, in the wake of so many of the Society's horses being requisitioned for military purposes, a Transport Department was formed, under Mr Gilmore. Pinwells Yard off Vauxhall Street, and a site at Sutton Wharf, were both acquired in 1915 to garage the new fleet of motor vehicles. In the meantime another large site at Peverell (off Recreation Road) was bought with a view to utilising it for one department or another - Transport Maintenance would be one of them.

1915 turned out to be very much a bumper year for property purchases. Most (but still not quite all) of the missing bits of the Central island block - the Frankfort Street section, No's 21-25, - were added in April. In September the business premises of Graves & Sons - the oldest and largest furnishing business in town - comprising five neighbouring properties in Fore Street, Devonport, and 38 York Street and 70 St Aubyn Street (on the corner of Fore Street) were bought, with fixtures and stock, and re-opened as the Fore Street Emporium. Other properties bought from Graces included a building down on Stonehouse Creek where the Society started a sausage factory, and later a kitchen.

Before the year was out a dozen or so additional properties had been acquired, in Mutley, Cattedown, Ford, Greenbank and Stonehouse which between them spawned four new groceries, two butchers' shops, three confectionery shops, a greengrocers' and a dairy.

Small wonder, then, that the turnover that year topped the one-and-a-quarter million mark for the first time and that the 'divi' was particularly healthy.

In 1916 the acquisitions policy was maintained at a similar pace as premises were bought and converted in Stoke, Devonport, Laira, Lipson, St Budeaux and the Barbican.

The appetite for joining the Society with members, new and old, benefitting both from the fair pricing and the 'divi' was fast becoming all-consuming. The main problem in these difficult times was, how to keep the supply chain going.

With transportation by sea becoming increasingly difficult, and expensive - shipping companies increased the cost of bringing coal down from Blythe to Plymouth tenfold - the Society decided to get its own coal-carrying steam-ship. To that end, in November 1915 they bought the *Levenwood* from the Meteor Steamship Company for £26,250 - almost as much as they'd paid for all the property they'd acquired that year.

Renamed the *Charles Goodanew* in honour of the Plymouth Society's founder, the ship was soon (1916) requisitioned by the Admiralty for War Service - operating in the North Sea and carrying stores to Scapa Flow. In that capacity she made many successful trips, but then, on the morning of 17 April 1917, proceeding north from Aberdeen in rough seas, she struck a mine in the Moray Firth and was lost with all hands but two - an officer and a crewman.

The Society was compensated by the Admiralty, remarkably receiving some £20,000 more than they had paid: however the widows of the lost crew received very little in the way of compensation.

With the death toll rising daily the Three Towns, with their Services connections, were also home to several impromptu hospitals (Hyde Park and Salisbury Road Schools and various churches were converted to these ends) for wounded soldiers and sailors. On 23 February 1916 the Ford Women's Guild invited fifty such servicemen to a tea and entertainment in Ford Hall. The Peverell Guild did the same with 60 soldiers, on 11 March in Frankfort Street Hall, and on St Valentine's Day the Plymouth Guild dined and entertained 150 men.

Salisbury Road Baptist Church serves as a hospital for the wounded.

Loading coal from the SS Charles Goodanew

Down On The Farm

The following month, March 1916, saw the Society consider another basic commodity that they were having trouble sourcing in sufficient quantity – milk. *'The milk supply was one of the greatest difficulties the Society had to contend with, and circumstances well-known to the members compelled us to go further afield for supplies.'*

There was evidently *'a ring of local milk suppliers'* who were, presumably, refusing to trade with the Co-op in order to try and keep the prices high. Whatever the circumstances, *'well-known'* at the time, it would appear that two solutions presented themselves: one to find a source further afield, which in this instance turned out to be west Cornwall (Penryn); the other to develop their own means of production locally.

The establishment of a Milk Collecting Station at Penryn, while undoubtedly facilitated by improvements in the transport network, had an interesting spin-off in that there was *'a strong desire being expressed from Penryn and from Falmouth, where there is a small Society, one of the oldest in Cornwall, that the resources of the Plymouth Society should be applied for the benefit of taking over, and working as a branch of Plymouth, the existing Society.'*

Meanwhile, the purchase of additional farms, created an asset *'unique in the history of the Movement'* ... the Holiday Home. March 1916 saw the first of these purchases as two, large, South Hams farming estates now came under Co-operative ownership:

Above: The earlier Hareston Farm, purchased in 1903. Top of the page: Netton Farm.

Membland - made up of Lambside Farm (192 acres), Caulston (384), Stoke House (14) and Netton (376) and Whympston - comprising Whympston itself (240 acres), Stubston (142), Little Modbury (103) and Stoliford (75).

All told, the new acquisitions more than quadrupled the Society's farm holdings adding a massive 1,500 acres at a cost of around £45,000 – that's roughly what the Society received as compensation for the *SS Charles Goodanew*!

There was more to come however, and in April 1917 two further farms were purchased: Preston (196 acres) in the parish of Ermington, and Scobbiscombe (560 acres) in the parish of Kingston.

These were big steps to take, but were *'the direct outcome of the difficulty experienced and the absolute necessity to provide as far as practicable for our own needs.'* Furthermore, *'it can now be claimed that our Society has a firm hold on the source of all wealth and production, viz.: The Land'* (WJ Lapthorn, 1920).

Mr TEW Dobson became Farms Departmental Manager, on a salary of £200 per annum, plus accommodation (Lambside Farm), plus - coal, light, milk, butter, eggs (poultry was another new departure) and vegetables.

Notwithstanding the exigencies of war, the purchase of Whympston Farm included a large manor house which was deemed to be ripe for conversion to a holiday home for Co-operative Members. Stoke House was also included, and, on 22 July 1916, the Holiday Homes were officially opened. Miss E Bradshaw was appointed matron (her salary just £50 per annum plus board and laundry), and for one pound a week (or around ten shillings for children) members could spend a week in residence.

The tariff included bed and four meals a day, plus indoor, outdoor games and pastimes, including tennis, cricket, bowls and bagatelle. Within the building there was also a large dining room, a drawing room and a music and reading room. Around 35 guests could be accommodated at any one time.

Stoke House was on a slightly smaller scale and didn't include full board.

Whympstone House - The Society's Holiday Home.

Around the same time the Society invested in a charabanc body which they fitted on to one of their own chassis and the vehicle was used to convey guests to and from the Holiday Homes, as well as providing daily outing trips to the Homes ... return fare - 2/6d (12p).

That September the Society held its first Summer School at Whympston. Inaugurated by Professor Hall, adviser of studies to the movement. This proved a great success and gave grounds for considerable optimism, although it wasn't long before Stoke House was *'required for the ordinary purposes of the Society'*.

The first Summer School at Whympstone, 1919.

Jam Today

Another unanticipated consequence of war was the creation of a Jam Factory.

'As a wartime emergency measure to conserve the fruit in this district, a temporary jam factory was erected and jam-making commenced. A permanent factory is now being constructed at an approximate cost of £25,000 plus machinery, which will enable the whole of our large membership to be supplied with our own production' (Lapthorn 1920).

The temporary Jam Factory had been set up in Treville Street, in September 1915, and despite initial problems and wartime difficulties, had proved a success. *'Little did we imagine at the time what a great service it was to render both from the National as well as the local standpoint.'*

'In April 1918, the Food Controller, because there was a danger of the fruit crop in the Tamar Valley not being utilised on account of the lack of transport, requested the Society to undertake the collection and preserving of the fruit. This was readily agreed to, and, to undertake this task, a temporary Jam Factory had to be expeditiously erected at Peverell and a motor system of collection organised' (White, 1920).

It is worth mentioning here that the Food Controller now was no longer Lord Devonport, who had resigned in 1917, not all that long after announcing to a shocked Parliament that the German U-boat campaign had accounted for two million tons of shipping and that *'the country had only three or four weeks'* food in stock.

The new man in charge was Lord Rhondda, who was altogether more supportive of the Co-operative Movement.

This was only to be welcomed as a positive attitude from the Government was long overdue. The antipathy towards the Movement as a whole had turned into blatant vindictiveness in the wake of Chancellor of the Exchequer's Finance Bill of 1915, when a move was made to tax all the profits made in excess of the pre-war standard. This was done primarily to penalise those unscrupulous private traders who had made fortunes at the consumer's expense. *'But his scheme was incomplete in that it did not appropriate the whole of the excess but allowed the plunderers of the public to run off with a portion of their spoil. And it was worse than incomplete since, under pressure from the enemies of the movement, he was induced to distort his bill so as to include Co-operative Societies. although it had been admitted by previous chancellors that they did not make profits' (William Watkins, 1920).*

'It was rightly regarded as the first successful attempt on the part of the profit-making interests in the country to utilise Parliament for the purpose of damaging the Movement and retarding its development', he added.

The Plymouth Society was handed a bill in excess of £40,000. Almost alone in the Movement, they refused to pay. Meanwhile others *'paid up and looked pleasant'*.

William Watkins, as President, accompanied by Mr Prince, ventured up to London to put the Society's case. After a great deal of debate, it eventually became apparent that these private interests *'in their misplaced zeal, had overstepped themselves, and a modification of the terms of the imposition had to be made'*.

The Plymouth Society kept their £40,000 and in the process earned the respect of the many other Societies, within the Movement, who were then allowed to reclaim the amounts they had paid. But scars ran deep and across the country there could not have been a more effective call-to-arms for the Co-op, whose entry into the political arena, in order that they might be better able to represent themselves in future, was now only a matter of time.

In the meantime there was a more gradual recognition of the fact that by keeping their prices low, the Co-op had forced other traders to keep their prices at a reasonable level or risk losing even more custom: *'thus it was rightly claimed that the operations of the Society in this respect benefit the whole body of consumers, members and non-members alike'*.

Small wonder that during the five years leading up to the end of 1918, covering those war years, membership increased by over 18,000 compared to just 5,000 in the otherwise respectably successful ten-year period prior to that.

The Co-op had done so much good work during that period, not just in keeping prices low for those who could afford it, but also for those for whom getting food, at any price, could be a problem. Once again, to quote the words of the President:

'Following the unenterprising, if not unpatriotic, refusal of the Plymouth City Council to carry out the desires of the Ministry of Food and establish National Kitchens in the town for the benefit of those who found it difficult to obtain food, the Society determined to open two such kitchens on its own account on property it had acquired for other purposes in Notte Street and at Stonehouse. This it did, and the kitchens, although run at a loss to the Society, undoubtedly served the purpose for which their opening was intended while the great scarcity of food prevailed.'

In the six months up to the beginning of April 1918 it was calculated that some 56,000 meals were provided, mainly for children, at Notte Street and Valletort Place and, in the same time period, it was noted that over 10,000 rabbits were caught on the Society's farms. It is not clear if a relationship between the two statistics was being inferred, but certainly rabbit stew was more popular then than it is now.

A Fishy Notion

Another move in 1918 saw the Society take the lease on Halton Quay on the River Tamar. The previous owner had been conscripted into the Army and now the Co-op found itself with a convenient quayside right in the middle of a local market garden area, an excellent base from which to ship out fresh fruit and vegetables. The Quay already had an existing coal, oil and corn business, which the Society undertook to continue, as well as a salmon fishery, which availed the Committee of the opportunity to set up a fishmongers within the Courtenay Street premises - thereby conferring on the Plymouth Society the distinction of being the first in the Movement to open such a 'fishery'.

Of course the combination of transport difficulties during wartime and the acquisition of Halton Quay meant that the Society were again looking for water transport and within a week or so of purchase of the lease of the latter they bought the barge *GWB* (later rechristened *PCS* - Plymouth Co-operative Society).

The abbreviated form of the old name Plymouth Mutual and Industrial Co-operative Society had been introduced, incidentally, back in 1916 and interestingly enough, there was even a suggestion that it should be called Plymco. However the Plymouth Co-operative Society it became and the first vessel to bear that name was a three-masted schooner that the Society bought in July 1917 (following the requisition of *Charles Goodanew*). Previously known as the *Elizabeth Alice*, this *PCS* made several successful wartime trips across the Channel before being sold off when major repairs were needed. She was replaced by a similar vessel, the *MA James*.

To the above, the Society added the *Prima Donna*, a fishing boat capable of being fitted with a motor engine, the rationale here being that this would help supply the newly established Fish Department without incurring the *'heavy toll exacted alike from fishermen and consumers by the fish-dealing middlemen.*

'Bought largely as an experiment, it is to be hoped that the Prima Donna *will enable the Society to obtain a fish-catching experience and so prove the predecessor of a numerous fleet of fishing boats putting out from Plymouth and owned by the people to obtain food for the people which shall be untaxed by unnecessary profits paid to unnecessary people. With this hope and with sincere wishes for its realisation, the consideration of the yet unnamed Shipping Department may be left for the time'* (Watkins).

In the event little came of the move - *'the venture failed through lack of net income'* (Barton 2005).

Increased Horse Power

If the war had forced the Plymouth Co-operators into looking at alternative transport, it was a move that proved both timely and profitable, although not in an obvious way.

'The Traffic Department of the Society is, comparatively speaking, a new department,' wrote WJ Lapthorn in 1920. *'It is not directly profit making, except that it reduces charges to the respective departments by concentration on efficiency by an organised control over the traffic of all departments.'*

'Previous to the war,' Lapthorn continued, *'we were content with horse transport, with few exceptions, but the exigencies at the commencement of the war, when horses were commandeered by the nation, compelled the Society to rely more on mechanical transport, which was a very wise step, and during the railway strike were an asset to the Society and the nation. Our power vehicles were travelling for commodities as far away as Bristol and in the opposite direction, to Penryn, and, in the former instance carrying food or fish for the general public, which otherwise would have decayed and been lost to the consuming public, and, in the latter, bringing milk to our membership, and also saved another important and perishable article of consumption from being lost.'*

With no facilities to freeze or even properly refrigerate food stuffs the significance of being able to move it around the country relatively quickly can easily be appreciated: not everything could be readily transported by rail. And even there the Society made major investments: buying 20 railway trucks in 1916 to bring down coal from South Wales, then another 38 the following summer to pick up coal at the pit heads. A further seven were added to the Coal Department that December and, at the same time, land was leased at Friary Station for coal storage. By the end of the war the Society was running 100 of its own trucks and renting another 70 besides.

By this time the Society had decided that hiring road transport no longer made good sense and so started buying up a variety of vehicles of their own. This too had its down side: *'Our first haphazard system of having*

Above: The three-masted schooner MA James. Top left: The Levenwood aka the Charles Goodanew.

114   *Co-op charabancs at Queen's Gate, Lipson. 'During 1919 orders were placed for some fourteen or fifteen chars-a-bancs. These have since been delivered and have been fully booked for day and longer journeys.' Note the solid tyres and the registration plates CO 2641 and CO 2643 - CO numbers were the first plates to be issued in Plymouth, conveniently personalised for the Co-op!*

all kinds of machines' was soon 'replaced by a gradual standardisation on two or three reliable types of machines, with spare parts in stock.' This meant that 'a speedy repair in case of temporary breakdown could be effected by our own engineering staff at the Garage on North Quay.'

Lapthorn, writing in 1920 then added: 'A very important adjunct of this department is the "Char-a-banc" which provides for the recreation of our vast membership during the spring and summer seasons, and keeps the prices at reasonable limits and enables our membership to see the beauties of nature in two or three counties of the South West of England famous for its natural beauty as well as being a profit for the Society.'

All this was not to suggest that the age of the horse was over, far from it, horse-drawn door-to-door delivery vans 'are as essential now as ever' and at the end of the war the number of working horses had actually increased 'in the aggregate', to 135, with another 80 in service on the farms.

However, the indications were clear and in a paper produced for the 'First Co-operative Trades and Business Conferences' in 1921, RW Royle – the traffic manager for the CWS – wrote: 'A comparison of the merits of the motor vehicle as against the horse-drawn vehicle would obviously lie in favour of the former under certain conditions.'

He then added: 'It is impossible to make a general comparison between horse and motor on account of the fact that horses could not travel the distances easily covered by motors, but there are still some instances where the horse can retain its usefulness with economy.

'The capital cost of the horse and its vehicle may be anything up to £200, in addition to which there is the wage of the driver; but in the case of the motor vehicle, the cost may be upwards of £1,000 and in addition there are the wages of both the driver and his mate. As the wages of the motor driver alone exceed those of the driver of the horse lorry, it is obvious that not only is more capital standing idle, but that a great wages bill is accruing.'

Maintenance was another time-consuming issue with these early motors: 'If on return of a vehicle to the garage at the end of the day, the vehicle shows signs of requiring mechanical adjustment, it should have attention

The Motor Char-a-Banc.

Many societies have realised that the passenger-carrying vehicle provides a source of revenue, in addition to providing members with a means of seeing the country. The motor coach or char-a-banc furnishes a cheap method of seeing the country, and that this mode of travelling has become very popular is proved by the large number of machines on the road to-day. These vehicles are made with a carrying capacity of anything from 14 to 30 persons. It will be seen from the following tables that the running costs are practically the same as for the ordinary commercial vehicle, and, therefore, if passengers are charged the same rate per mile as per passenger train a very good margin of profit is left, and what is more important, members of societies are able to travel by their own coaches as and when they please. There are numerous societies which are in a position to supply actual data as to running costs and revenue earned. The following table of running costs will enable one to form a good idea as to the value of these machines as an investment:—

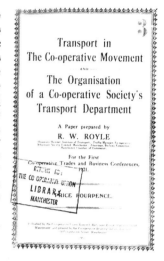

Transport in The Co-operative Movement AND The Organisation of a Co-operative Society's Transport Department

A Paper prepared by R. W. ROYLE

For the First Co-operative Trades and Business Conferences, 1921.

THE CO-OPERATIVE UNION LIBRARY MANCHESTER

PRICE FOURPENCE.

APPROXIMATE RUNNING COSTS OF 40-H.P. 30-SEATER CHAR-A-BANC.

Taking an average of 100 working days per annum at 100 miles per day.

	£	s.	d.
Cost of Vehicle £1500 0 0			
Driver's Wage at 76s. per week	198	0	0
Petrol at 2s. 1d. per gallon	148	16	2
Tyres at 1d. per mile, guaranteed 12,000 miles	41	13	4
Lubricating Oil at 4s. 6d. per gallon	3	15	0
Repairs per annum	50	0	0
Insurance	50	0	0
Interest at 6 per cent per annum on £1,500	90	0	0
Depreciation at 20 per cent on Chassis (£970)	194	0	0
„ 25 per cent on Body (£530)	132	10	0
Motor Tax	60	0	0
Total cost per annum	£968	14	6
Cost per mile .... 1s. 11d. approximately.			

NOTE.—Driver's Wage is charged at a full year's rate, although he would only actually be on the vehicle 100 days.

Assuming the vehicle carried 28 passengers per journey, at 1½d. per head per mile, the income would amount to £1,750. Deduct 25 per cent for empty seats—leaving a gross profit of £403 15s. 6d. from which must be deducted cost of advertising, garage, and establishment charges.

Approximate consumption of petrol: 7 miles per gallon.

PCS Charabancs in Guildhall Square.

From the Co-operative Society's Transport Department.

immediately and not be left until the morning, as time must be given each morning for a general look over the chassis. Strict attention must be paid to lubrication. Efficient lubrication is the key to success in the running of a motor vehicle, and the garage foreman, or whoever may be in charge, should see that this is carried out.'

There was also the issue of fuel and a storage tank for petrol was considered 'an essential instalment of every (Co-operative) garage.

'It is a very good practice to insist on the tanks of all vehicles being filled immediately after the day's work, so that the drivers are left free next morning to attend to the starting of their engines.'

In terms of design and location Royle suggested that 'the garage should be as near the commencement and termination of the day's work as possible. There should be an entrance and exit at opposite ends of the building so as to obviate any necessity for reversing and turning vehicles in the garage, which only means lost time and occasional accidents.'

'Plenty of headroom and natural light are essential. If artificial light is needed a number of small lights over the gangways between the vehicles are much better than a few big lamps, which only throw shadows.'

1921 Fernley Hockin PCS charabanc driver

A selection from the Sundries Department including Chinese Soy, Curry Powder, Caramel and Pimento.

Similarly, in the construction of warehouses in the future, Royle suggested that; 'the street space available, having regard to the possible number of openings required for loading and unloading lorries, should be one of the first considerations,' adding, 'in many cases it would be a sound investment to alter existing buildings to cope with present-day traffic.'

Meanwhile, another significant spin-off for the increasingly motorised Society was the 'peaceful penetration into country districts'.

From the enhanced packing department at the Central Stores and Warehouse on North Quay goods were sent out around the area: 'Throughout the day the scene is a busy one, here are the Society's heavy steam lorries delivering loads of provender, collected from the railway depots and docks, whilst another fleet of up-to-date motors and vans is being dispatched with supplies to feed the branches which spread to all parts of the town' ... and beyond.

In April 1918 the Society acquired properties in Newton Ferrers (1 Newton Hill) and Modbury (36-37 Church Street) which they swiftly converted to Groceries. 'Our country Order Department is, in this respect, serving a very useful purpose, delivering to country districts (where as yet we have no branches) parcels of groceries by motor van, and spreading Co-operative propaganda, and preparing people for our coming.'

Oddly enough, however, before the war, the Society had decided against taking over the Plympton Society (founded in 1890) which was suffering on account of not being able to offer as good a dividend as Plymouth and therefore many of their members were using Plymouth stores.

And ever more stores there were. By the time the Society came to celebrate its Jubilee, in 1920, it had over 130 retail outlets including: 37 Grocery stores, 25 Butchers, 20 Dairy branches, a dozen Baker's and Confectioners, seven Boot and Shoe shops and 23 Greengrocer's. As well as the various Draperies, Tailors, Coal, Coke, Oil and Fish departments, nine Farms and ... 'to be opened soon' a Tobacconist and a Chemist.

It had been a trying time; 49 of Society's serving employees had paid the ultimate price in war, but overall the Society had come through the ordeal in style, with its head held high.

The Society's Grocery Packing Department. Note the boxes of Co-operative Wholesale Biscuits - Milk and Aladdin varieties, plus Doctor Eales, infant biscuits and the boxes of Huntley & Palmers on the counter.

The Legacy of War

Jam, confectionery, pickles and sauces (the Sundries Department originally grew out of a perceived potential wartime need for Concentrated Foods and Dried Vegetables) were a few of the other unanticipated by-products of the War for the Plymouth Society, and there was also a move into mineral water:

'As we are aware, many people consider that the excessive amount of alcoholic beverages consumed would be reduced to more normal proportions if really satisfactory non-alcoholic drinks were available to the public. In that direction the Society is endeavouring to do its share.'

However perhaps more significant in some respects than any of the issues surrounding retailing, production and transport, was the whole question of representation.

It was during the 1914-18 war that, locally and nationally, the Society became painfully aware that it wasn't well represented in the corridors of power. Furthermore, the Excess Tax saga had highlighted the extent to which some people were prepared to go, to do damage to the Movement.

At the Annual Congress in 1917 (held in Swansea) a decision was made to enter the political arena with the creation of the Co-operative Party. There had been similar suggestions in the past, and a Parliamentary Committee had been set up back in 1880, but the prevailing opinion had always argued against direct involvement. Consequently faith had been placed in a number of Co-op-friendly Liberal MPs and that great Liberal Co-operator Edward Owen Greening, who believed that entry into politics would alienate a great many members of the Movement who were Conservative voters.

The decision to form a party of their own however was taken, although it might not have amounted to much had not the Prime Minister, David Lloyd George, subsequently refused to meet the Parliamentary Committee - apparently opting to see the Jockey Club instead.

An emergency Congress was called, tempers were high, Greening withdrew his opposition and a resolution was passed, it read:

'This conference desires to place on record its indignation at the contempt with which the current Prime Minister has treated British Co-operators, not only in refusing to receive the deputation appointed to place the grievance of the Movement before him, but also at his failure to take any steps, after repeated appeals, to recognise the existence or usefulness of the Co-operative Movement in the present national crisis.'

This was no minor boast, the Society nationally had played a huge part in helping to feed the nation without exploiting the man in the street. Thus it was that at the General Election of 1918 ten Co-operative candidates stood and one, Alfred Waterson, was duly elected to represent that hot-bed of Co-operation, Kettering. In Plymouth a slightly earlier manifestation of the bubbling political unrest was the launch, in January 1917, of a weekly paper called the *Plymouth Co-operator*, edited by the progressive, Thomas Mercer.

The formation locally of the Labour and Co-operative Representation Party had, to a certain extent, pre-empted the national response, which embraced an electoral agreement with the Labour Party. However, there were clear divisions within the Plymouth Society and just a few months after the end of the war, the 'progressive' Plymouth Co-operator was stopped, officially as part of a cost-cutting exercise, but in reality it reflected the ascendency of the 'blues' on the Management Committee.

Not long before that the forthright propagandist, Mercer, had also been relieved of his editorial duties on the *Monthly Record*, another little triumph for the conservative faction. Then, in April 1919, at the election of Officers, President Watkins was unseated and replaced by the markedly less progressive J Hayne Pillar.

Interestingly enough it was also around that time, March 1919, that the monthly meeting was called upon to consider Lady Astor's application to join the Society. Lady Astor was the wife of the Conservative MP for Plymouth Sutton (a distinction she would herself hold before the year was out) and one prominent member of the Ladies' Guild claimed that Lady Astor *'meant to capture the Movement for party purposes'*. Moving that Lady Astor be accepted as a Co-operative member, Mr FW Ireland said that if 60,000 members were afraid of one individual then they were a pretty poor lot.

Jam And Cream

Certainly as Plymouth and the nation settled back into peacetime the local Committee had little to fear; they were running the biggest business in the area, and it was getting bigger on a daily basis.

The new store at Newton Ferrers was opened in February 1920. In June the Modbury ventures started trading and that same month two shops and a bungalow were bought in Yealmpton. Further investments in Devonport and St Judes were also made and new units opened in Embankment Road, Old Town Street and Exeter Street.

This was the Society's diamond jubilee year and they were intending to celebrate in style. On 4 August, at the height of the British summer a red-letter day was diaried to mark the laying of the foundation stone for the brand new Preserve Works at Peverell and the opening of the new Radnor Dairy in town.

Once again there was a massive rolling-stock procession: assembling in two sections, where most of their vehicles were housed, at Peverell and North Quay, they came together at St Jude's around 3pm and processed through Ebrington Street, Old Town Street, Frankfort Street, Union Street, King Street and Milehouse, ending up at Peverell.

Taking fully half an hour to pass any point and marshalled by mounted police, the parade was made up of over 100 horse-drawn vehicles, and some eighteen motor steamers and lorries, on top of the fifteen or so charabancs full of Society VIPs. A source of wonder for the thousands who turned out in the miserable summer drizzle to line the streets.

Afterwards there was a grand tea in a large hall in Frankfort Street and then, three days later, on the Saturday, over 12,000 people, most of them children, made their way to Home Park for a massive celebration. Bands, minstrel parties, acrobats, clowns and the inevitable Punch & Judy provided non-stop entertainment and a seemingly endless supply of sweets, buns, toffees and chocolates added to the attraction.

However the dark skies that clouded the August 4 celebrations were about to get a whole lot darker.

CENTRAL DAIRY DEPOT

Top: 4 August in the summer rain, President Hayne-Pillar is presented with a silver trowel inscribed 'Plymouth Co-operative Society Limited - Diamond Jubilee 1920'. Below: just hours later the President opens the new Radnor Dairy.

Horses still predominate at Peverell.

CHAPTER 7: THE NOT-SO-ROARING TWENTIES

The trading figures for the half-year ending 5 March 1921 were down for the first time since the Society started trading.

'The truth is,' ran an article in the Co-op's Monthly Record, 'that the economic consequences of the war and of the peace are now becoming visible. Unemployment, the slump in trade, lower wages and falling dividends are all direct results of war, and there is not likely to be any real improvement in the economic situation for some time to come ... Nearly two million workers are either unemployed or are working part-time ... Many societies will soon find it necessary to reduce their working expenses.'

The President, Hayne-Pillar, in his opening remarks to the Special General Meeting convened on 31 March, explained the situation in a little more depth:

'In order to understand the position, it is necessary to recall the circumstances that existed during the war and for eighteen months after the Armistice. We had experienced a great demand for all classes of goods until the middle of 1920, as the demands for clothing, etc., for the returning service men, and the expenditure of large amounts of war bonus, prize money, etc., kept our trade at a high level. Our stocks had to be maintained to meet these requirements.

'Then suddenly the bubble of inflated trade burst; financial stringency caused the stocks of many manufacturers and retailers to be thrown on the market at greatly reduced prices ... Some of the items affecting the trade are those just mentioned, but certainly not the least important is the greatly reduced earnings in this town, due to the Dockyard discharges and short time.'

The Three Towns, Plymouth, Stonehouse and Devonport had merged just before the outbreak of war in 1914 and now as one town the area faced severe financial difficulties. There had been 19,000 employed in the Dockyard at the peak of the war, but that very soon dropped by over 3,000 and would fall by a further 4,000 by the mid-twenties.

Largely brought about by the decommissioning of ships, this, in itself, added to the agony as thousands of servicemen, many of whom were local, were also out looking for work. Most of the Society's van and charabanc drivers were ex-servicemen and many others were involved in setting up other coach and charabanc companies, often using refashioned service vehicles. But work-wise it wasn't anything like enough and the situation was only going to get worse.

The March figures saw the 'divi' drop to 1/3d - amongst those areas worst hit - the farms had lost £7,500 and the jam factory nearly £5,000.

Introducing the figures for the period ended 4 June 1921, the newly elected President, Charles White, said that he thought he was safe in asserting that the 'pleasure' he had in presenting the report was purely a courtesy phrase. Sales were down 16.4% on the corresponding period the previous year and the dividend was down to 8d.

'Members have to face the fact that they bought in a dear market and are now selling in a falling market,' said LG Williams.

Arguments over the pricing of stock, the over-valuation of stock, and the propping up of the dividend with money from the reserve funds raged back and forth, but all the while the figures got worse.

Their Names Liveth For Evermore. The memorial tablet to the memory of the employees of the Society who fell in the Great War 1914-1918 was placed beside the main door of the entrance to the General Office.
The carving was done by local sculptor JB Hunt and supplied by the Works Department.

The last quarter of 1921 saw trading figures drop by 30% of the corresponding period the previous year, of which 23% was due to decreased prices … but of course overheads remained largely the same.

Largely, but not entirely, as at the December 1921 meeting members confirmed, despite strong opposition, a 5% reduction in wages for employees. The President also announced a clearance sale.

It was, however, a tough time for the Movement as a whole and indeed the only time that the Co-operative Wholesale Society made a loss was in 1921, when turnover shrank from £105 million to just £65. The actual loss was only £3.5 million and was easily covered by reserves.

Of course, this also meant that the retail societies got the advantage of cheaper prices and thus the consumer gained. However, nationally the Co-op was starting to face serious competition from the likes of Liptons, Home and Colonial (which had had a branch in Plymouth since the end of the nineteenth century), and Maypole, in food and disposables and the so-called 'Bazaar Stores' like Woolworths and Marks & Spencer (both of whom were in Plymouth by the end of the war) and the Domestic Bazaar Company (who had also been in Plymouth since the nineteenth century) who were selling thousands of lines at guaranteed prices, plus major department stores, like Debenhams, which stocked a wide range of clothing and fancy goods. Locally Dingles, Yeo's and Spooners (who would be bought out by Debenhams in the twenties, but would retain their name) represented the major competition in the department store field.

'Taken together, the multiples and bazaar stores had, by 1920, begun to overtake the Co-op, when they both had around 9% of the retail trade' (Birchall).

Derry's Clock with the George Street premises of the Domestic Bazaar Co. behind it.

A Sticky Situation

Meanwhile the Preserve Works at Peverell had not got off to a good start. The plant had ten times the production capacity of the old Vennel Street works but that was far in excess of the trade achieved. Furthermore the majority of the pulped fruit there had been bought in at 1920/21 prices which meant that stock values were seriously overstated and a massive depreciation was required to put it right - £40,000! In fact much of the stock had deteriorated to such an extent that it had to be thrown away.

The factory manager was demoted to foreman and the grocery manager Mr Fletcher, was given overall control.

The Laundry situation, however, was looking much brighter. Now handling 100,000 items a week - including 35,000 starched collars - they had also started dyeing, dry cleaning, bed-cleaning and carpet cleaning. Unlike other areas of the Society's trading around this time, the Laundry's turnover had actually doubled over the previous three years.

It was one of the few sunny spots in an otherwise very gloomy picture. The March 1922 statistics revealed a drop in sales of £628,000 and fall in the trade surplus of nearly £100,000 and the average 'divi' for the year remained at that low point of 8d. Three months later members at the July meeting expressed severe dissatisfaction with that quarter's figures. Eighteen thousand pounds had to be taken from the Reserve Fund to meet the losses and 30,000 pairs of boots and shoes were put on offer at 25% to 50% below cost but it was almost like locking the stable door after the horse had bolted: there should have been more effort made to clear stock when prices first started falling. There were justifiable complaints that propping up stock values to maintain dividend levels was not good policy.

In November there was another Co-operative Shopping Week during which all sorts of bargains were advertised, notably in drapery, tailoring, footwear and furniture. On the last day of the week a procession of rolling stock was trundled out again to help boost the promotion. While at a meeting later that day, the vice-president of the CWS, Plymouth Co-operator, Henry Wilkins, explained how the day of the private trader had passed and how his place had been taken by the Co-operative Movement and the multiple shop. The difference being that whereas the net profits in a Co-operative Society were distributed among the members and remained in the town, in the case of the multiple shops it was taken out of Plymouth and spent elsewhere.

Tightening The Belt

While members had voted President Hayne-Pillar out of office in 1921 when they were perhaps looking for a scapegoat to blame for the financial downturn, in 1922 they voted him back in with a comfortable majority.

The following month, members resolved that all Reading Rooms not on Society premises be closed. A few months later all dressmaking classes were closed down and then at the December meeting it was decided that all employees' bonus payments be suspended until the 'divi' rate was back up to a shilling in the pound (1/20th).

Introduced back in 1877 to replace a commission system, the idea was to provide an annual incentive to staff based on 2.5% of the net profit, however this had increased to 5% in 1918, 8% in 1920, 11% in 1921 and 13% in the first half of 1922. Set against a backdrop of falling 'divi' rates for the members from 1/4d to 8d, such a backlash was inevitable.

Reductions in the Society's net surpluses also meant reductions to the annual grant made to the Education Committee: in 1920 it had been over £5,000, the following year it had dropped by over £800, by 1922 it had dropped below £2,000 and in 1923 it was just £1,370. Some of the space at the new Drake Circus premises was vacated and rented out. There were changes to the Library's opening hours, classes were cut, and the number of pages in the *Monthly Record* were restricted. From September 1923 the issues got thinner, and thinner and the December edition was skipped altogether - the editor himself, JT Robson, being a victim of the cut-backs.

Down on the farm things were particularly tough and, as if to make matters worse, in January 1923, members heard that some 868 incubator chicks had been stolen along with 21 turkeys. However it transpired that although the farm manager had made a full statement to the police, he was in fact merely trying to cover up losses incurred during the hatching season - not surprisingly he was dismissed.

All was not doom and gloom, however, and that same month, at a meeting of Co-operative employees, a proposal was put forward to develop and encourage social, recreational and educational gatherings. A scheme, financed by participating employees, contributing a penny per week, began later in the year.

Painting The Clouds With Sunshine

Depressing trading figures being something of a national phenomenon, the appetite of the Plymouth Society to press on with their programme of expansion went on relatively unabated. Having acquired property at Yelverton at the beginning of 1921, they also invested in Ermington and, with the blessing of the Saltash Society, in Callington.

There were those who argued that it wasn't the best time to be buying more property, however WH Drake, on behalf of the committee, made it clear that the Society had done well with this move. One hundred and fifty new members had enrolled in the first two days and by the end of the third week that figure had risen to 350.

Membership generally had been falling – although this had been partly down to members leaving the area it was largely due to the writing-off of lapsed members.

In 1922 further coal stores were purchased off North Quay, along with another 68 acres of farmland at Membland, and the following year a couple of the outstanding pieces of the Raleigh Street/Courtenay Street jigsaw were added to the island block, as well as another chemist's in Fore Street, Devonport.

Plymouth itself, of course, was still expanding and as work began on the creation of the new Swilly Estate, so the Society opened new branches in North Down Crescent and Swilly Road.

There were bright notes in other areas too as at the election in 1923 Mrs EA Wall, *'a keen worker in the Women's Co-operative Guild movement, who has held various offices, local, district and national,'* became the first woman to be elected to the Plymouth General Committee.

Meanwhile the following year Henry Wilkins, who had himself been elected a member of the General Committee in 1898, was appointed President of the Co-operative Wholesale Society. Plymouth-born Wilkins had been on the CWS board since 1907, having originally joined the Plymouth Society at the same time as that great local Co-operator, William Wilkins.

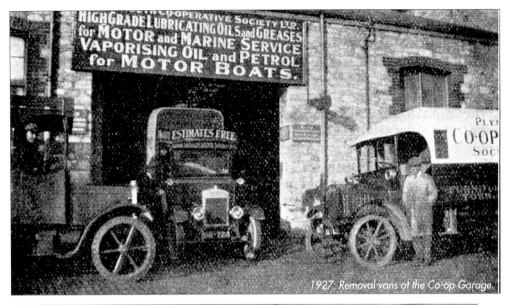
1927: Removal vans at the Co-op Garage.

1928: Peverell Jubilee staff with Doris Tootel cashier centre.

Sadly Wilkins' success was somewhat overshadowed, locally, by his erstwhile colleague's demise. A Labour Councillor for Pennycross then Charles Ward, Watkins was a founder of the Co-operative Party and its first Chairman, from 1919-1924. Indeed he had chaired an interesting meeting in the Courtenay Street premises in January 1923, when another great West Country Co-operator, AV Alexander, one of the first Co-operative MPs (elected in 1922), was guest speaker.

Talking on a topic headed 'Current Affairs', Alexander quoted from a letter sent out by the secretary of the National Traders' Defence League to its constituents, asking for funds for one thing and one thing only - to wage a campaign to get the Government to bring Co-operative surpluses, and Co-operative members' savings brought within the scope of Income Tax.

William Watkins had been President of the Plymouth Society throughout the Great War, since when, 'despite the depression of business, he never lost heart, but believed with all his soul that it was a righteous movement and must, therefore, succeed'.

Happily his optimism was well-founded and the trading figures published just before his death in the summer of 1924, allowed a 'divi' of ten pence - a turnaround at last after several bleak years. The figures up to the year end of March 1925 were better still, showing the first trade, and surplus, increases for four years allowing a further rise of dividend - to one shilling.

There was another sad departure that year too, as the last surviving Plymouth pioneer, Thomas Henry Reynolds, Co-op member No.3 and son-in-law of the principal pioneer Charles Goodanew, died aged 92.

'This great heart lived far beyond the span usually allotted to man, but he ever treasured the ideals with which his name will always be associated, and he rejoiced to see the Society growing from such humble beginnings to the mighty edifice which is now in our midst,' read the report in the Record, which, incidentally was now in the hands of Jos Hill.

Having grown drab in appearance the new-look, brighter, livelier Record was deemed to be much more in keeping with contemporary periodicals.

Farmyard Blues

A letter in the June 1925 *Record* praised, in particular the Society's catering facilities, citing a wedding reception that had been held in the Homeward Bound cafe that had been opened a few years earlier in William Street, Devonport. The service was top notch as was the food and the total cost for 25 people was a reasonable £5 – that's two shillings a head.

Not so impressive was the performance of the Whympstone Estate and related Holiday Home and Summer School. A member's meeting in September 1924 had tried to suggest selling off the estate, but the proposal was turned down. A similar proposal with respect to all of the farm properties, was put forward a few years earlier only for the redoubtable Mr Watkins to say *'faint heart never won fair co-operators'*. Watkins was referencing the successful co-operative farmers in Denmark.

It was clear however that all was not well down on the farm, and the following summer Whympstone was put on the market. Since its purchase in 1916 this estate had lost money year on year. However no bids were forthcoming and so the whole was split into seven parts - only Stoliford exceeded the reserve price.

A little later, in the November 1925 *Record*, a photograph of the farm committee, made up of very senior Committee men (Hayne-Pillar, Lapthorn, Welsford and Hartnoll) appeared, alongside an article by Hartnoll. In it he quoted some alarming statistics from the Co-operative Union that showed that in ten years farms run by the Co-operative Movement had a net deficiency of over £900,000 and that over £200,000 had had to be found from the Movement's trading profits to balance the books.

Hartnoll added that the Co-operative Union were holding an inquest into the situation and he would report back in due course. It was to be a report that Alderman William Welsford would never hear, for he died the following February. Welsford, a Conservative, had joined the Society 50 years earlier and had come to the fore in 1919 when he headed the poll on a 'No Politics' platform.

He was actively interested in housing matters and the area that he lived in has an avenue named after him.

Credit Where Credit's Due

In order to help try to ease the Society's farming problems and to assist in the sale of feeding stuff to the farming community in general, the Society bought land, stabling and 140ft of waterfront at Pomphlett Mill, including the mill itself, a cottage, house and stores. The coal department was thus able to move into agricultural supplies and henceforth became the Fuel and Agriculture Department.

Meanwhile, moving away from farm produce altogether, another familiar topic was raising its tentative head once more - the question of credit for non-food goods. Two consecutive meetings at the beginning of February 1926 saw an exhaustive debate on the question of credit facilities for non-food. However, at the end of it all a 2-1 majority voted in favour of continuing to operate, as they had been since 1860, on a cash-only basis.

Other Co-operative Societies were doing it though, as was the rest of the retail trade generally, so it was no great surprise when the issue was raised again, four months later. HJ 'Harry' Drake, made the point that *'there was evidence that poorer people were being fleeced by the private voucher issuing firms'* and armed with this knowledge he had decided to support the Committee (he had been on it himself a few years earlier) in their move to begin a mutuality club for dry goods and a hire-purchase system for furniture.

This time the proposals were approved by a large majority and the Mutuality Club was started on 1 July 1926. Four hundred and fifty applications were received from people wishing to become a collector, and 39 were appointed. Once a week they were to go round and collect a repayment, equal to one shilling for each pound voucher issued.

It was also around this time, after many earlier attempts that consent was given to the idea of running Sunday charabanc trips for members. The fleet now numbered 23 vehicles, of which 13 were 29-seaters, five were 14-seaters, four were 22-seaters and one was a 33-seater. The previous year, the year the first pneumatic tyres had arrived to steady the ride on these hard-road bone-shakers, over 60,000 passengers had used them, equivalent to every member making at least one trip.

Prizewinners from a 1927 window dressing competition.

The logo of the woodcraft folk.
Below: Removal vans on North Quay.
Bottom: Strike - Read All About It.

Ideal Society

Sixty thousand members represented the involvement of the majority of households in the area: the population of Plymouth around this time was about 220,000 of whom a huge chunk were children - incidentally the Co-operative Movement generally launched a more inclusive approach to young people in 1925 with their initiative 'Woodcraft Folk'.

More and more people were coming to terms with the democratic principals that underpin Co-operation. *'The whole social system, built as it is on self-interest, competition, and capitalism is saturated by falsehood; and no one need be a student of ancient history to discover that a civilisation built on falsehood cannot possibly stand for ever'* ran an article in the Monthly Record in the wake of Stanley Baldwin's election success over the first Labour Prime Minister, Ramsey Macdonald, in 1926.

'Competition makes men rogues,' it continued, the implication being that despite the election result Co-operation was the way forward. Locally, as it transpired, there was a long-standing Co-operative Member in the highest civic seat that year, as Alderman Jimmy Moses was elected Mayor of Plymouth. Traditionally this honour had tended to go to the wealthiest individuals on the Council, those who could best afford to wine and dine their fellow council members and take time out of their working life, but the times they were a-changing.

It's interesting to note that the Society decided to invest £100,000 in Plymouth Corporation at this time. The rate of interest was 5.25%, nevertheless the move caused a few ripples among the membership.

1926 was also marked out as the year of the General Strike, the TUC deciding, on 3 May, to back the miners whose employers wanted to decrease their wages, yet increase their hours. The dispute brought Britain almost to a standstill, literally, until retired drivers, servicemen and others came in to man the trains, trams and other modes of transport. Locally 400 people enrolled in the first hour of recruiting held in the Guildhall.

Not surprisingly there were one or two ugly scenes around town, a tram window was smashed in Old Town Street, where one woman was arrested for throwing eggs at the Police (she was ordered to do a month's hard

labour) and another was fined ten shillings for using obscene language. The General Strike lasted little more that a week (although the miners stayed out until November), but its impact was enormous.

It was just weeks after the strike that the membership decided to reverse the decision on offering credit to members (for non-food items) and then in February 1927 the Plymouth Society was one of 500 local societies to sign up to the National Co-operative Propaganda Campaign (organised by the Co-operative Union and the Co-operative Wholesale Society).

The Campaign started on 5 February, and thousands of leaflets, posters and pamphlets were distributed across the country and window displays were used to maximise the impact. It generated some excellent press:

'Co-operative Trading in Plymouth and throughout the country is at this moment being prominently brought to the public notice by a big propaganda and advertising campaign, and there is little doubt that the figures being disclosed are amazing many people who had little idea of the extent to which this Movement, founded in a modest way as a community of consumers, has developed.

'The co-operative movement is assailed on many sides. It is criticised by the apostles of private trading to whom, of course, it represents a formidable business competitor; it is an occasion for nervousness among politicians; and it had always to contend against the divergence of views and aims among its members, some of whom want cheapness before dividends, and some of whom want to make it a political and industrial weapon to be controlled by one party.

'But, in spite of it all, the progress has been somewhat remarkable as an illustration of the possibilities of working class organisation ... And it is a movement which demands public attention as it is already exercising in the minds of politicians, sociologists and economists ... These combinations tend to economy in management, the elimination of waste, and the opportunity to buy in bulk and to advantage,' the report, published in the *Western Evening Herald*, added *'...it is within the power of the co-operative societies, under wise and statesmanlike direction to exert a very powerful influence upon the conditions by which, in the future, trade shall be conducted and employees treated.'*

In conjunction with all the printed matter, the Plymouth Society also organised a number of talks and demonstrations and at one of these, held at Ford Hall, the Labour MP and ardent Trade Unionist, knowing that he was already preaching to the converted, said: *'It is no use fulminating on platform or soap box against the evils of capitalism, and then to spend your very wages in building up the system you condemn.'*

Another meeting held in the Guildhall was addressed by the MP James Kidd, while a mass meeting for women was conducted in the large hall in the Courtenay Street building, where JT Davis was the principal speaker - Davis was another of the Plymouth Society's local successes, having been elected to the Committee of the CWS board the previous September.

After the disappointing run in the early-twenties, the turnaround continued to gather pace, with the 'divi' as announced in March creeping back up past the shilling mark and membership, no doubt boosted by the February campaign, increasing by nearly 3,000.

A 'big day out' was planned to celebrate International Co-operators Day on 2 July and Lady Astor and Mayor Jimmy Moses were due to speak. In the event Lord Astor and the Deputy Mayor JH Churchward spoke, the latter urging members to celebrate the day by working towards world peace, while Lord Astor highlighted the fact that the Co-operative spirit was needed in all sections of industry.

Alderman Moses, however, was on hand to lend a bit of Council approval on 26 March, when the new pasteurising and bottling plant was opened at the Radnor Dairy. Meanwhile, further National Co-operative approval for Plymouth was confirmed in December that year, when it was announced that next year's Women's Guild Congress would be held in the Guildhall here. Bed and breakfast would be needed for about 900 delegates.

There was something of a fillip for feminine representation announced in the same edition of the *Monthly Record* as it was revealed that a long-standing member of the Women's Guild (Plymouth Branch), Mrs Jacquetta Marshall had become the first woman Alderman in Plymouth (she would later, in 1950, become the first female Lord Mayor)

Right: The Radnor Dairy seen here above Sutton High School and below Sherwell Church

Homeward Bound restaurant in William Street.

The New Library
Is NOW OPEN in
Plymouth Chambers (Second Floor)

127

Time To Consolidate

An increase in trade by over 10% and a steady growth in membership brought the dividend up to 1/3d, sevenpence up on the dark days of a few years earlier, and as the first quarter's figures for 1928 were published so the 'divi' held firm, although it was interesting to note that the Works Department sales yielded a dividend of a shilling, while the Agricultural Department 'divi' was a paultry fourpence.

This consistent positive run ushered in sufficient feeling of well being to bring Hayne-Pillar back to the Presidency after yet another interlude and with him a number of his fellow 'Blues'.

It would appear that consolidation rather than expansion was the watchword, however, and the *Record* was full of refinement stories; there were new machines and alterations at the bakery which when commissioned, in June 1929, rendered the Peverell Bakery the *'most modern type, unexcelled by any in the Kingdom'* ... and capable of baking enough loaves to feed the entire population of Plymouth.

The butchery was also something to be proud of; the Medical Officer for Health having stated that there was only one clean and proper slaughterhouse in Plymouth and that was the property of the Plymouth Co-operative Society.

Meanwhile the introduction of new lighting in the tailoring and outfitting departments now meant that there was *'no need to carry your cloth pattern to the doorway to be certain whether it is blue or grey'*.

And then there was the new Library and Reading Room at the Plymouth Chambers, Drake Circus. With over 8,000 books it had a borrowing membership of 2,304, which was undoubtedly impressive given the fact that a few hundred yards up the hill, Plymouth's own Municipal Library had now been open for nearly twenty years.

In terms of retail outlets, however, the activity over the last year or so had been comparatively modest. A bigger grocery had been opened at Laira, a branch was opened in Randwick Park Road in Plymstock and there were new groceries in Pasley Street, Devonport and at Crownhill.

All in all this brought the portfolio tally to: 48 grocer's, 28 butcher's, 14 confectioner's, 13 greengocer's, 8 dairies, 8 shoe-shops, 4 draper's, 4 tailor's and outfitters, 3 ironmonger's, 2 each of furniture stores, china shops, chemists and tobacconists. Memberships of which could be bought into simply on payment of a shilling joining fee - alternatively you could shop at the Co-op without being a member and the dividend on your spending would be distributed across the rest of those who were members, in relation to their spending.

No wonder the membership continued to rise, along with the 'divi' as the overall economy strengthened.

On The Road Again

In the summer of 1929 all twenty-three of the Society's charabancs were wheeled out for the annual Grocery Department jolly. The vehicles assembled at 7.30 in the morning and after negotiating Tavistock and Liskeard arrived at Falmouth where members of the party elected variously to bathe, snooze or explore the town. Tea was taken in Truro and the travellers were afforded the chance of a trip to the Cathedral and a listen to the town band. By the time the trippers arrived back in Plymouth it was almost midnight.

This was very much the golden age of the charabanc and before the year was out a new garage for the entire fleet was being constructed at North Quay. International Co-operators Day, 1931, witnessed another trundling out of the Society's rolling stock, now numbered at 120 vehicles, many of which were still horse-drawn.

With the Society generally and within society as a whole, there was still a place for the horse. Ten years on from Royle's report on Road Transport for the Co-operative Societies, the Traffic Manager of Leeds Industrial Co-operative Society, JS Holloway, prepared a similar report, this time for the Eleventh Co-operative Trades and Business Conferences, 1931.

'There is no doubt,' he wrote, *'the petrol machine holds the premier position in mechanical transport, and so far as the heavier types are concerned there are many points in its favour.'*

However Holloway was clearly a champion of the horse: *'there is no doubt*

that under certain conditions the horse can compete successfully with the motor, and I now propose to indicate how it can be determined as to when those conditions are favourable to the employment of horse vehicles.'

He then went to great lengths, employing a variety of statistical formula and equations, to argue that horse transport held an advantage *'where the distance to be travelled is a comparatively short one, where the streets are narrow and congested, or where the condition of the road is bad'.*

Holloway further recognised that the electric vehicle too, now had a place: *'under favourable conditions, (it) has certain advantages over the petrol motor, in relation to cleanliness and simplicity of construction, but the factors which militate against its use for ordinary work are: Its restricted mileage, the heavy cost of batteries both for replacement and maintenance, its very moderate speed, especially in hilly districts, and, above all, the lack of facilities for battery charging at mid-day and during the night.'*

The good news in relation to motor vehicles appeared to be their improved reliability. In Holloway's own garage, he was employing one mechanic for every ten vehicles ... *'and as we do all our own maintenance work, I think this may be taken as a fair indication of any society's requirements so far as staff is concerned when mechanics are employed.'*

As for the life expectancy of the vehicles: *'In our case all rolling stock is depreciated according to rule at the rate of 15% per annum, and this practically compels us to fix the life of a motor at not less than seven years. We find that in relation to the lighter type it is advisable to dispose at the end of the seventh year, but that heavier lorries can reasonably be carried for a longer period.'*

Motors under one ton	34s. per day.	Saturday,	20s.
One-ton motor and mate	45s. ,,	,,	25s.
Thirty-cwt. motor and mate	50s. ,,	,,	27s. 6d.
Two-ton motor and mate	55s. ,,	,,	30s.
Three-ton motor and mate	65s. ,,	,,	35s.
Four-ton motor and mate	75s. ,,	,,	40s.
Horse	20s. ,,	,,	10s.

Meanwhile the water-based fleet was about to be expanded with the purchase of a barge - the *M.M.R.* - seemingly a snip at £50. Clocking-in at a little under 23 tons, the *M.M.R.* was not quite in the same league as the Co-operative Wholesale Society's newest vessel, the *SS Progress*, which arrived in Millbay Docks, on her maiden voyage, with 900 tons of coal for the Plymouth Society, on 1 March 1931.

Figures from a contemporary traffic review.

Note the fact that in 1922 motorcycles outnumbered any of the other mechanically propelled vehicle categories, note also the fact that among the white population there were proportionally more vehicle owners in significant parts of the Commonwealth than there were in Great Britain itself, although the British were well ahead of the rest of Europe.

Year.	H.P. Class.	Motor Cycles.	Goods Vehicles.	Motor Hackneys.	All Mechanically Propelled Vehicles (Excluding Tram-cars and Trade Licenses).
1922...	314,769	377,943	150,995	77,614	952,474
1923...	383,525	430,138	173,363	85,965	1,105,657
1924...	473,528	495,579	203,156	94,153	1,299,824
1925...	579,901	571,552	224,287	98,833	1,509,786
1926...	676,207	629,648	248,367	99,077	1,689,722
1927...	778,056	671,620	275,831	95,676	1,858,794
1928...	877,277	690,672	294,190	93,429	1,995,827
1929...	970,275	705,025	318,253	95,798	2,130,628
1930...	1,042,258	698,878	334,237	98,865	2,217,609

4. No one can predict with certainty for how long, and to what extent, the total will go on increasing. Some authorities think this country's motor traffic must be near saturation point. They might change their minds if they spent a few days in New York or other big American cities; they may be influenced, too, by the following figures :—

Country.	Persons per Motor Vehicle.	Country	Persons per Motor Vehicle.
U.S.A.	4.9	Union of S. Africa (All)	62.4
New Zealand (White)	9.1	Great Britain	34
,, ,, (All)	9.6	France	37.4
Canada	9.1	Belgium	70.1
Australia	13.2	Germany	117.2
Union of S. Africa (White)	13.9	Italy	215.5

St Andrew Street circa 1925

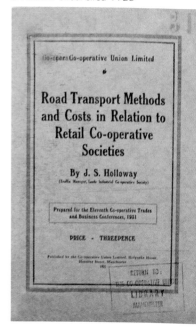

Unsportsman's Like Behaviour

Unity Park: Wonnacott and Hayne-Pillar lead the official party.

There was a degree of irony in the air in 1931, the year the Plymouth Society paid £2,500 for five acres of land at Efford for use as an employees' sports ground. First and foremost a football pitch, there were plans for cricket, putting and tennis to be played there and a competition was launched to find a suitable name for the premises.

In the first week alone, 800 employees paid their penny joining fee and, on 3 September 1931, AE Wonnacott kicked off the first match for Co-op United at the new ground. However, the official opening of what, by then, had become known as 'Unity Park' came the following May, when General Secretary Wonnacott, accompanied by President Hayne-Pillar and some 2,000 employees and friends enjoyed an afternoon of organised activities which ran through until 7pm, after which there was a Celebration Ball in the Guildhall.

Not everyone within the Society embraced the notion of sporting fair-play though and, earlier in the year, three employees were discharged after irregularities were discovered in the accounts department - two of them were later convicted at the Devon Assizes.

A few years later several more employees were shown the door in connection with the suspected forging of checks – dividend tokens – notably in the dairy and greengrocery departments.

Unfortunately it wasn't just internally that the Co-op were experiencing a degree of foul play. In August 1931 the *Monthly Record* noted that: *'The economic crisis which led to the formation of what has been called a 'National' Government, revealed the fact that certain interests in the country do not scruple to use a national emergency as a cover for anti–Co-operative campaigns.'*

The report noted how the Co-operative's competitors together with the capitalist press were pushing Parliament for the imposition of special and inequitable taxes on Co-operative Societies and how, fortunately, to date, the Chancellor of the Exchequer - at that time Philip Snowden - had ignored the 'advice'.

However with unemployment reaching new heights and the Government under increasing pressure, it was an issue that was not going to go away easily. Thus

Co-op Athletic AFC League Winners 1932-33 Back row: J Wheeler, G Lane, W Foster, S Brown, V Scamp, T Newton, A Harris. Middle: D Burt, W Soper, H Netting, E Ponsford, P Pearce, F Ferris, C Oakes. Front: K Pengelly, R Stribling, H Randall, W Eastcott, W Horan, F Squires.

Plymouth Co-operative Society Limited

MONTHLY RECORD

No. 511 [No. 59 New Series].   JULY,   1932

THE PAVILION AT UNITY PARK

FOR THE

PLYMOUTH CO-OPERATIVE EMPLOYEES' SPORTS
ASSOCIATION.

Unity Park: The Official Opening. General Secretary Wonnacott (hatless) had President Hayne-Pillar on his left.   Inset: Raising the flag.

131

GROCERY STORE, INCLUDING PROVISIONS, CONFECTIONERY, SWEETS, AND GREEN FRUIT DISPLAY STAND.

Top: A typical Co-operative interior from the mid-thirties.
Bottom: Inside the Laundry at Peverell.

it was that in February 1933 the Government published their Enquiry Report into the 'Taxation of Co-operative Societies', the main proposal of which was that Societies should be taxed on any trading surplus not allocated as dividend to members. Henceforth any surplus retained within the Society - as, for example, reserve funds - should be subject to income tax under Schedule 'D' - i.e. trading profits. Previously Co-operative Societies had only been liable to Income Tax under Schedule 'A' - income from property; or Schedule 'C' - investment income.

Both the Co-operative Union and the various local Societies launched campaigns against the proposals arguing that all surpluses were a product of the basic principal of mutuality and therefore should not be considered to be trading profits. At a special meeting of members held in Plymouth in March 1933 there was cross party support for trying to persuade the Chancellor not to accept the recommendations contained in the report:

'This Special Meeting, representing a membership of 74,000, having considered the report of the Committee appointed by the Chancellor of the Exchequer to inquire into the present position of co-operative societies in relation to income-tax, strongly condemns the recommendations submitted therein, which would destroy the established principle of mutuality, are inequitable, and would, if adopted, result in great injustice being inflicted upon Co-operative Societies and their members, a large section of whom are drawn from the poorest section of the Community.'

'The meeting calls the attention of the Government to the fact that to pass legislation on the lines of the committee's report would be to make false use of the Income Tax Acts, and would make taxes chargeable not according to the origin and nature of the funds, but according to the use to which they were put.'

Nationally the petition was backed by 3.3 million Co-operators, nevertheless, the following month the Chancellor announced that discussions were proceeding; but he also added that *'in the opinion of the Government the matter cannot be allowed to rest where it is, and some provision would be inserted in the Finance Bill.'*

Ultimately the protests were to little avail, indeed in July 1937 the Chancellor, Sir John Simon, proposed to further increase the taxation on Co-operative

Societies. The Committee duly sent a telegram to the local cluster of MPs - Lady Astor, Leslie Hore-Belisha, Col Guest, Mr Rathbone, Mr Patrick and Major Rayner – but none of them supported AV Alexander's amendment.

The proposed tax, which had become known as the National Defence Contribution – why would any true Briton not want to contribute? – thus passed into law and a leaflet was drawn up and distributed to Co-op members to explain the circumstances.

Certainly the circumstances, internationally, were not looking good. Nazism had been on the rise for many years but at the dawn of the thirties the menace had barely been recognised by Co-operators in Germany, let alone in England. However, by October 1933 we find *'grave disquiet'* being expressed in the *Monthly Record* about the position of the Co-operative Movement in Germany under Nazi rule and, by 1936, Co-operative conferences and schools had become increasingly concerned about the rise of Fascism in Germany and Italy and this doubtless was a major topic at the International Exhibition in Brussels in 1935.

It was becoming increasingly difficult to ignore the international situation, and certainly, where they could help, the movement was doing its bit. Members of the Plymouth Society were particularly supportive of the Co-operative Union's initiative, the 'Milk Token for Spain' appeal, for the *'starving women and children'* enduring hardship in the Spanish Civil War.

In Britain, with something like 22% of the milk trade, the Co-op were able to keep prices comparatively consumer-friendly, even in the tough climate of the mid-thirties. They could exert similar influence with regard to bread and tea too, however such successes did not endear them to the private traders and the national press was generally hostile to the Movement. Hence the decision back in 1929 for the Movement to buy their own weekly newspaper, the *Reynold's Illustrated News* (*Reynold's News* from 1936). This did not stop the private traders seeking to set up price rings where they could and it wasn't long before they realised that one of the booming, new technologies offered just such an opportunity.

The wireless had been one of the great innovations after the Great War: *'The twentieth century is the period of the motor car and wireless,'* said JT Davis (a CWS Director) at a Co-operative weekend summer school in the

large hall in Courtenay Street in May 1932. *'The world today is a very small place,'* he added, *'we can listen-in to other countries and can fly to Australia in about ten days.'*

Indeed it was such a small place that wireless manufacturers across the board could get together and refuse to supply the Co-op because they believed that the Co-op's dividend undermined their fixed prices. All set makers were coerced into joining and GEC even abandoned an order for making and supplying radio sets to the Co-op when they were already half way through that order. And then, when the Co-op went off and started to make their own wireless sets - appropriately named the Defiant - the Society were barred from exhibiting at the Radio Manufacturer's Show at Olympia.

Meanwhile *The Grocer* magazine, that organ of small independents shops, and one of the most venomous towards the Movement, even succeeded in getting a programme about the Co-operative Movement dropped from the BBC's radio schedule on the grounds that the Co-op was adversely affecting high-street trade and furthermore that its principles of mutuality and equality were little better than Bolshevism.

Gramophone players and other new electrical goods were swiftly added to the list of products that manufacturers sought to deny supplying to the Co-op. Chemist's suppliers were similarly targeted and in 1935 the *Monthly Record* noted a letter from the Newsagents' Union stating that retail newsagents would not allow Co-operative Societies to enter the news agency business, even if Societies were to purchase existing newsagents businesses. Furthermore, pressure would be placed on wholesale agents to prevent them from supplying Co-operative Societies.

There was also a proposal from the National Chamber of Trade to promote a bill designed to ensure that no new shops would be opened unless and until the need for such a shop was proved to the satisfaction of the licensing authority. Another move on the part of the private trader was to block the Co-op with their consumer-friendly approach to pricing.

As the Depression deepened, so the Society was increasingly picked on. There were even stories about how employees of private companies were sacked when it was discovered that they had a family member working for the Co-op. Dreadful discrimination executed in a Canute-like manner.

The Co-op decided to manufacture their own radios when no-one else would supply them.

Ten-Year Plan

Having captured an impressive 11% of the British retail market and having out-performed various multiples with regard to staples such as bread, milk and coal, there is an argument that suggests that the Co-op nationally perhaps failed to tackle the non-food market as aggressively as it might have done. Apart from basic clothing lines, boots and shoes and household goods, it had fallen behind somewhat. Which is not to say that it wasn't doing very well, however it perhaps could have been doing even better.

At the beginning of the twenties, Sidney and Beatrice Webb undertook a thorough investigation into the Movement, and others followed later, and, at the end of it all *'the researchers agreed that at its best the Movement could be outstanding, but at its worst, it could be parochial, unimaginative, complacent and badly managed'* (Birchall).

The Co-operative Union was reorganised in 1932, and a more powerful Executive Committee was set in control. Four years later the Society set up a Research and Statistics Department of its own and that same year launched a 'Ten Year Plan' to enable societies to celebrate the Rochdale Centenary with demonstrable increases in trade and membership.

In Plymouth the January *Record* announced that 1936 would be a year of big events for the Co-operative Movement and it would mark the real start of the Ten-Year Plan.

A problem for Plymouth however was that growth at anything like the same level as the late-nineteenth century or even early-twentieth century was always going to be difficult due to the dramatic slowdown in the growth of the Three Towns and, the wider area, generally.

In 1861 the population of Plymouth, Devonport and Stonehouse had been around 127,000, by 1931 that had increased by 100,000 - most of it in Plymouth itself and most of that (over 60,000) coming in the last two decades of the nineteenth century. In this climate the Plymouth Co-operators had found it easy to move into each new area as it was built: Ford, Greenbank, Prince Rock, Lipson, Laira, Peverell, Swilly and, in 1937/38, West Park (as the new branches in Higher St Budeaux were to become known).

The new facilities - grocery, butchery, confectionery shop and greengrocer's - were opened at West Park in March 1938, and, together with the new units at the Jubillee stores site at Peverell, further added to the Society's penetration in the area. There were now well over 100 Co-operative stores of one kind or another around the area, most of them grocer's and butcher's shops.

Most Plymothians had a Co-op within easy walking distance and for those venturing in town, the new Furnishing Emporium at least demonstrated that the Plymouth Co-op was making a serious attempt to take at least part of its non-food trading that bit further.

Located on part of that island site of Courtenay Street and Raleigh Street, the new building had been erected by the Work's Department and fitted out by the CWS and was claimed to be one of the finest furnishing stores in the West Country. As well as the usual staircases the new building had an 'electric passenger lift' to convey customers from one floor to the next.

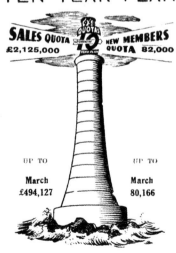

Wednesday, 16 November 1932, Mr WJ Lapthorn at the opening of the new Courtenay Street Furniture Emporium.

The impressive facade of the Co-op Central Premises dominates the foreground, with the roof of the new Furniture Emporium right in the middle of the picture at the bottom, on the other side of Courtenay Street.

1938 Book your holiday now!

P. C. S.
"ALL IN"
MOTOR COACH TOURS, 1938.

Tour No. 1.	3 Days WYE VALLEY.	£3 12s. 6d.	
	June 1st, 15th and 29th.	"All in."	
Tour No. 2.	5 Days BLACKPOOL.	£6 0s. 0d.	
	Sept. 5th, 19th and 26th.	"All in."	
Tour No. 3.	6 Days LLANDUDNO.	£7 12s. 6d. "All in."	
	June 20th, July 18th, Aug. 2nd and 22nd, Sept. 12th.		
Tour No. 4.	6 Days SOUTH COAST.	£7 12s. 6d.	
	June 27th, July 25th, Aug. 2nd and 29th.	"All in."	
Tour No. 5.	8 Days ENGLISH LAKES.	£10 10s. 0d.	
	June 25th, July 23rd, Aug. 6th and 27th.	"All in."	
Tour No. 6.	14 Days SCOTTISH.	£18 10s. 0d.	
	June 11th, July 9th, Aug. 20th.	"All in."	

The "All in" fares include Bed, Breakfast, Lunch, Dinner and Hotel Gratuities.

A limited number of tickets will be issued for each Tour, and early booking is necessary to enable us to reserve Hotel accommodation.

Full details and Booklets may be obtained from

P.C.S. BOOKING OFFICE, Courtenay Street.
Phone 2800.

As that part of the Movement with the greatest national profile, the CWS were ever on the lookout for ways to increase the commercial impact of the Society, even if they may not have been perceived as pursuing this policy aggressively enough. As the 1930s unfolded it was becoming increasingly apparent that other multiples were making substantial inroads into the market place, among them Woolworth's with their 'bazaar' approach to retailing.

In 1935 the CWS floated the idea of various existing Co-operative Societies opening similar bazaar-style outlets, in conjunction with the CWS themselves, and, indeed, the Paignton Society did set up such a joint effort, around this time, on a 50/50 basis.

Meanwhile the Plymouth Society continued to experiment with new ventures of their own:

At the November 1935 meeting it was announced that the Butchery Department had appointed Mr H Docker as a *'small goods man'* to develop a trade in sausages, meat puddings, pork pies, cooked meats, etc. The experiment thrived and before long a Small Goods Factory had opened alongside the Butchery Warehouse at Peverell. By the summer of 1939 a Co-operative Pork Shop had been opened in Old Town Street.

Reflecting the move away from the Depression and towards greater leisure time and spending power, the Society opened their first Ladies' Hairdressing Salon, just in time for Christmas 1938, in Frankfort Street. Miss E Perkins was appointed 'Assistant in Charge' and was put on a weekly wage of three pounds plus commission. A basic shampoo and set cost 2/6d, while prices for a full perm started around 12/6d.

Another new departure, also indicating the increased economic power of the working man, was the opening of a Travel Office next door to the Hairdressing Salon. Offering 'All In' tours (which included *'bed, breakfast, lunch, dinner and all hotel gratuities'*) the first season's deals included trips to Scotland, Wales and the Lake District (8 days for 10 guineas).

The frequency and availability of these trips gives us some idea of the size of motor coach fleet the Society now had at its disposal, although early booking was always advised.

It was all a far cry from those dim distant days when the Plymouth Pioneers had met on Christmas Day and that day had been about the limit of the working man's annual holiday allowance. Now, in addition to the Plymouth Society's own excursions, we find the Education Committee teaming up with the CWS Excursion Department and the Workers Travel Association offering holidays at home and abroad. The Wheatsheaf holiday guide in the mid-thirties, contained over 5,000 addresses at some 300 holiday resorts.

The Movement was growing and so too was the CWS as another announcement - in 1934 - informed members that the CWS was setting up a new subsidiary, The CWS Retail Co-operative Society Limited, which was later (1957) destined to become the CRS - Co-operative Retail Services.

These were good times for the Society locally ... and nationally.

As the thirties came to a close the British Co-operative Movement had some eight and a half million members and a turnover of some £272 million. This was generated by over 1,100 independent Co-operative Societies who between them controlled around 24,000 shops. Overall the Co-operative Movement had something like 11% of the total retail trade and that included approximately 10% of the meat trade, 16% of the everyday household stores, 20% of the sugar, tea and cheese sales, 23% of all groceries and provisions, over a quarter of all the milk sold in the country and a whopping 40% of the UK butter market.

Meanwhile, on mainland Europe, by mid-1939 - in Germany, Italy, Spain, Austria and Czechoslovakia - the Fascists had made their attitude to this democratic, and essentially working-class organisation perfectly clear ... they had destroyed it! Indeed on Hitler's birthday the Nazi's gave him a million deutschmarks (£50,000) from Co-operative funds.

However with war between England and Germany looking increasingly likely, it seemed as though this time the Co-operative Movement in Great Britain, with nine Co-operative MPs and hundreds of local Councillors, would not have quite such a hard time gaining the ear of the central, and local, Government.

Inset: 1936 removal van. Above: Pre-war Plymouth City Centre.

Looking from the Guildhall roof, across to the back of the Central Premises, the new emporium in Courtenay Street to the left and the Regent Cinema to the right.

CHAPTER 8: IT CAME TO OUR DOOR

The *Western Evening Herald* didn't normally publish on a Sunday, but they did on 3 September 1939 and the reason was all too evident from the headline:

WE ARE AT WAR

Premier Says 'We Are Fighting Against Evil Things'

The Prime Minister, Neville Chamberlain, had made the solemn announcement on the BBC's Home Service at 11.15am that morning and his broadcast had been swiftly followed by the news that there might be air raids on London sooner rather than later. Plans were soon put in place to start evacuating children from the big cities, with the West Country among the prime destinations for these vulnerable young travellers. Plymouth was considered to be in a safe place, well beyond the range of the Luftwaffe.

Nevertheless, precautions against hostilities were being effected throughout the region and even though there was once again an expectation 'that it would all be over by Christmas', there was a serious note of caution sounded at the Plymouth Society's September meeting. Stressing the need to comply with the Civil Defence Act, the President, WJ Gilbert, pointed out that it was now an offence for anyone to purchase more than the accustomed week's supply of any kind of food and, furthermore, it was also an offence to sell quantities in excess.

The President also reassured members that steps had been taken to safeguard essential records and documents in the event of air raid damage. However, despite the potential seriousness of the situation there was still a degree of levity in the air. The first edition of the *Plymouth Co-operative Journal* to be published after the declaration included 'the Co-op Manager's Song':

'Our tame poet broke loose from his moorings last week, and burst forth into unrationed song, as follows:

We've camouflaged the roof-tops, and put sand bags round the door;
We've made our gas-proof shelter, and propped the walls and floor;
We've darkened all the windows and we've formed a first aid corps,
And we're going to keep on smiling, and we're going to win the war.

Young Tom has joined the Army, and young Jack is on the sea;
The clerks go out at midnight and come home at half-past three;
It's not a pleasure jaunt though - they're all in the ARP.
Like all of us, they do their bit: we mean to win you see.

So if your order's rather late in coming to your door,
Or if you get two pounds of butter when you ordered four,
Or if the Stores is dark at night, just sing with us once more;
We're going to keep on smiling, for we're going to win the war.'

The loss of the Devonport-manned *HMS Courageous* two weeks after the war started, quickly introduced a more sober note. Sunk by a German U-boat in the South-West approaches, the carrier went down in just twenty minutes and over 500 of her 1,200 crew were lost. Many Plymouth families were directly touched by the losses.

In November the *Journal* noted: 'It is now two months since this country declared war on Germany, and any idea that it was going to be an affair of short duration is gradually being dispelled in people's minds. The prospect appears to be that it is likely to be a matter of years, which implies that we have to steel ourselves to endure for a long time, bearing the difficulties and trials which come to us with courage and fortitude.'

Above: Drake Circus, then advertising Bovril not Guinness, and on the right the newly acquired Plymouth Co-operative premises.
Below: The same view looking from the opposite direction, looking down into Old Town Street.

Conferences were cancelled, evening classes struggled, thanks to the combined effects of the blackout and petrol rationing, and food rationing loomed as the Government advised people to try and make it 'Christmas as usual'.

The December *Journal* published the result of a competition to find a recipe for 'Christmas pudding under War Rationing,' and two weeks after Christmas butter, bacon and sugar were all rationed. Meanwhile, in marked contrast to the 1914-18 War, maximum retail prices were set for these items, as well as for lard, potatoes, eggs, dried fruits, tinned salmon, condensed milk, herrings and kippers. The public were also advised to register with butchers in readiness for the rationing and pricing of meat.

In the event, meat rationing was introduced on 11 March 1940; every adult and child over the age of six was entitled to an allowance of 1s.10d (children under six 11d). Sausages, pasties, pies, corned beef, kidneys, liver, poultry and game were excluded. Diabetics were allowed to exchange sugar coupons for meat coupons.

Mindful of the implications of rationing and the desirability of being relatively self-sufficient, the Plymouth Society bought a large dutch barn at Lambside Farm for storing food. Furthermore some 300 acres of the Society's farmland were ploughed up for the planting of vegetables.

Earlier the Society had purchased land, buildings, machinery and vehicles at Kelly Bray for use by the Fuel and Agriculture Department, plus another 23 acres of land at Kingston, near Modbury, which were added to Scobbiscombe Farm.

Now, so much of that farmland that had caused concern a few years earlier was coming into its own, as was the Co-op generally.

'With 155 factories the CWS was easily the largest consumers' self supply organisation in the world. On the food production side, for instance, it had ten flour-mills, nine farms, five bacon works, four aerated-water factories, four preserve works, four abattoirs, four packing factories, three butter factories, three soap works, three milk products factories, two glass factories, two biscuit works, and a margarine factory.

'On the non-food side it had nine cabinet and upholstery factories, seven footwear factories, six printworks, six clothing and five shirt factories, three cotton and three woollen mills, a colliery and railway wagon works.'

As the war progressed a Co-op jute works in Scotland started turning out millions of sandbags; in Manchester a Co-operative shopfitting concern started making parts for gliders; a quilt factory made flying suits, and a cycle works turned to manufacturing wheelchairs for injured servicemen.

Additionally the Co-op's various clothing factories, all told made some two million battledresses for the Army plus a further half a million for the RAF, not forgetting the millions of pairs of boots that the Society had been churning out since before the war had started.

The fact that the Movement as a whole was based on the principal of mutual aid saw it gain considerable advantages over the private sector. The degree of flexibility in production, the range of production and the special relationship between the wholesale and retail operations gave the organisation a degree of strength unmatched by any of their competitors.

Business Almost As Usual

Locally life went on almost as usual: anticipating further rationing, members were advised not to leave it too late to buy clothes and in March 1940 the long-awaited new emporium in Fore Street, Devonport was opened.

Officiating at the event, the President said, in his opening remarks: *'The recent trade increases are an indication that Devonport as a great naval, military and dockyard centre, is not commercially derelict, but contains great resources of trade and commerce.'*

But it was wartime, and Devonport had always prospered during wartime. Indeed its heyday had been at the turn of the eighteenth and nineteenth century, during the protracted Napoleonic Wars, when the town had been a virtual money-go-round, but that had dried up spectacularly in the 1820s. In the 1920s there had been a similar downturn after the Services and the Dockyard laid off thousands of men at the close of the Great War.

To compound the problem, there could be little doubt that after the amalgamation of the Three Towns at the beginning of the 1914-18 War, the commercial focus had moved away from Devonport towards Plymouth. The increased activity in the Dockyard and the commissioning and manning of new warships revived the fortunes of the ailing community, but there would always be a question mark over its post-war future.

As it transpired the prosperous new emporium – embracing a drapery, furnishing department, hardware, china, footwear, tailoring, a chemist, tobacconist, optician and so on – had barely celebrated its first anniversary when it was reduced to rubble and the heart of the Devonport community was ripped out … and not replaced.

But no-one could have anticipated that on the opening day, 16 March 1940. Although that same month the President had to announce, at the monthly meeting, the deaths of two employees from the grocery department - Messrs J Loughlin and R Poyntz - the first two casualties among staff called up for national service.

Just a few weeks later the Germans pushed into France and by the end of May Plymouth was no longer a remote target.

The imposing Central Premises, viewed from Frankfort Street, the Western Morning News building (left) was opened on 1 December 1938

The first air-raid siren warning sounded on the last day of June 1940: the alert lasted an hour, but there was no incident. The celebrations for International Co-operators' Day scheduled for the following week, on 6 July, were cancelled for fear of air raids and possible loss of life. Prophetically, on that very day, just before noon, the first enemy bombs were dropped on the City. Three explosive devices were launched and a man, woman and child were killed on the Corporation's Housing Estate at Swilly.

Plymouth was not the first city to be in the firing line, however, notwithstanding that fact and despite further incidents occurring throughout the summer months and into the autumn, the potential gravity of the situation was still not fully appreciated.

In the October edition of the *Journal* there was an advertisement for the Furnishing Department with the headline:

Air Raids in Comfort
Sit or Sleep in your Shelter, Warm and Comfortable, on a
'Co-op' Two-Tier Bunk Bed
A Settee by Day, Double-Bed by Night
Priced at £3.7s.6d

The following month, in an article written in decidedly questionable taste, there was an attack on the newly imposed Purchase Tax: *'"Life is dear", said the people of Britain as they plunged into shelters when large-scale bombing began.' That was three months ago. '"Life is dearer," say the people of Britain, as they plunge into new, heavy and unnecessary expense, now that the Purchase Tax has begun. Like the German Luftwaffe, the Purchase Tax means to make things harder for everyone in the country. And like the Luftwaffe, the Purchase Tax succeeds in hitting the home hardest of all.'*

While men and women at the front were risking their lives for our freedom, so those at home were left worrying about rising inflation (prices had risen 20% since the start of the war) and Purchase Tax. Co-operators appeared to be no different to the Private Sector as they fretted over such matters, and, of course, the level of dividend. The 'divi' thanks to – the increased income-tax assessment, to help with the National Defence Contribution; the Excess Profits Tax; ARP expenditure; the effect of rationing; the dislocation of home and overseas transport; the Price of Goods Act; the paper shortage and

the payment of war bonuses to employees – was not surprisingly struggling to stay at pre-war levels.

Christmas 1940 saw a brief respite from the air raids, but three days later Plymouth experienced its 242nd 'alert' and one of the worst incidents of the war to date in the City. Eleven people were killed, a dozen seriously injured and over 300 houses badly damaged, with 17 being completed destroyed, including a few in Wilton Street, just two doors from the Co-operative store there.

The following month saw a devastating bombing raid on Coventry and the destruction of their city centre. Suddenly the value of insurance of property against war risks seemed eminently sensible. However while the Plymouth Co-operators looked on and admired the way their counterparts coped, they little imagined that their turn was to come.

A week before their January interim meeting *'the members of number one committee met in the board room with the managers of the grocery and bakery departments and the General Secretary, when we heard the wail of the siren followed by gun-fire. We decided to adjourn to the basement of the central premises, and remained there for three hours until the 'All Clear' was sounded.'*

Wilton Street, a bomb wrecks houses just two doors from the Co-operative premises.

'During that time, repeated attempts to persuade the young telephone operator to come down were made by the General Secretary, Mr Blackburn, and ourselves. The young heroine refused - she said: "This is my job, I just remain here until the 'All Clear'".

'It is strange that it did not occur to anyone of us that a direct hit on the central buildings would have probably killed us - whether in the basement or any other part of the building. It was the beginning of many terrifying experiences. And so through January, February, and March we went from one nerve-racking experience to another' (Gilbert).

On 20 March 1941, their Majesties, King George VI and Queen Elizabeth visited Plymouth for a tour of the Dockyard and an inspection of the Civil Defence and Voluntary Services in the Guildhall Square.

The King and Queen, who had toured the city and seen the damage done in the earlier raids, left with the message of an air-raid warden still fresh in their minds – 'We are keeping our chins up'. Little did they or the people know of the awful experience which was to be theirs within a few hours. The Queen had replied to that warden's words by saying: 'Well done. It is only by keeping our chins up, as we are doing, that we shall win the war'.

The Royal couple left Plymouth from North Road Station at 6.30pm by which time squadrons of 150 Heinkel and Junkers bombers, loaded with high explosives and incendiary bombs, were already on their way to the city. Less than two hours later the air-raid sirens sounded – a familiar sound perhaps, but still a stomach-turning experience – there had been, on average, at least one a day since the previous June. It was a clear night, the moon was in its last quarter when, at 8.39pm 'the inferno was let loose on the eastern (Plymouth) end of the city ... the devastating attack went on without any weakening for about four hours. It was well after midnight before the attack died out' (Twyford).

Altogether some 159 tonnes of high explosives and 31,000 incendiary devices fell on the City Centre. The following night Plymouth suffered again. The emergency services were still hard at work from the previous night's devastation when another two-hour onslaught was unleashed, this time with even more fire power.

The resultant fires themselves were the main problem as the majority of those buildings that were lost might well have been saved had it not been for the incompatibility of the fire-fighting equipment of those Fire Brigades from outside the Three Towns that rushed to Plymouth's assistance. They were here, but they couldn't hook up to the local hydrants and consequently were rendered virtually useless amid the mayhem.

The King and Queen visit Plymouth on 20 March 1941. A few hours after their train left Plymouth Station, the Luftwaffe launched their biggest raid on the city to date (right).

144 *Servicemen arrive to clear up the debris as the Western Morning News building is one of the lone survivors in this part of Frankfort Street. The Central Premises are burnt out.*

Plymouth suffered, and so did its largest retail employer and business, and nowhere was the situation better described than in the national *Co-operative News* published shortly afterwards.

DEVASTATION OF WORLD WAR II

A MEMORABLE INTERVIEW CARRYING ON AFTER THE BLITZ

CO-OPERATIVE NEWS 28th June, 1941

HUGE BLOCKS OF PLYMOUTH PREMISES DESTROYED
BUT SERVICE IS MAINTAINED

'Plymouth has been badly battered by "blitzes". Successive heavy raids within a comparatively short period did much damage to shopping and commercial buildings, and destroyed or damaged many homes.

'One of the biggest sufferers among the principal traders of the city was the Plymouth Society. Warehouses, huge blocks of trading premises, offices and shops were in turn gutted and reduced to debris by fire and high explosives as the Nazi bombers repeated their savage attacks.

'After the first severe raid, the emergency committee, along with the principal officials and departmental managers of the society, made plans to overcome the dislocation that had been caused. On the following night another raid prevented the plans from being put into operation. Buildings which it had been intended to use to replace those that had been lost were destroyed. So the officials and managers had to make new plans.

'The general and administrative offices were in part of the principal central buildings in Frankfort Street which were destroyed in an early raid. At the following half-yearly meeting members were informed that a temporary general office had been established in the educational building in Drake Circus. That night, this building and other properties were razed to the ground.

'Since the heavy raids ended, the Society has sustained another serious loss, which has added to the difficulties of the administrative staff. When I visited Plymouth after making an appointment to see the General Secretary,

Mr. E. F. R. Cocks, I learned that the secretary had died the previous day. 'By that time, the administrative staff had been housed in two large houses in Thorn Park and it was in one of these houses that Mr. Gilbert and the committee secretary, Mr. L. G. Williams, told me some of the experiences of the society during the hectic weeks the Nazis were trying to blast the city off the map. So far as buildings are concerned, they caused wholesale devastation, but the people still carried on and the Plymouth Society also carried on.

'As far as it had been possible to do so, the society has restored the facilities that formerly existed. As the normal trading organisation was dislocated by blow after blow, so improvised arrangements were put into operation to maintain services and feed the members.

'In the replacement of stocks, food received priority, and unstinted praise has been given to the C.W.S for the prompt and effective measures adopted to meet all demands made upon them. All departmental managers have testified to the ability and efficiency of the C.W.S. in dealing with every emergency. Officials, departmental managers and staff also earn praise for the manner in which they ignored their own personal troubles and cheerfully faced the task of maintaining the society's services despite what seemed insurmountable difficulties.

'The one bright ray in the dark cloud of troubles the society experienced was that the bakery, dairy, preserve works and laundry were not put out of action, and were able to function normally.

'The society's losses were very heavy, however. What were known as the central premises in Frankfort Street, accommodating drapery, tailoring outfitting, butchery, and florist departments, a large hall, the check office, and the general office, were totally destroyed, apart from the strong-room.

'Another block of property, in which were the rationing offices, mutuality club office, the travel department, pork shop, butchers' cold store, boot and shoe, hairdressing and grocery departments and café, were also destroyed. Other property destroyed, included jewellery, fancy goods, drug and optical departments, co-operative dental association surgery and the drapery warehouse.

'One building that escaped destruction or serious damage, in this area, was a comparatively new emporium for the sale of furniture, soft furnishings, hardware, and china.

'At Devonport the handsome emporium completed in May, 1939, which accommodated tailoring, drapery, boot and shoe, hardware, china, drug and optical departments, and the co-operative dental association was a total loss. A branch store comprising grocery, boot and shoe and welfare departments, and a grocery branch were destroyed, and other branches sustained damage of some kind principally to windows and roofs. Seven motor-coaches and six coal lorries were also lost in the garage fire.

'The society's works department, which did Trojan work in carrying out temporary repairs to various damaged property, undertook the task of getting through the debris and forcing an entrance to the strong room. They had to cut through the concrete and steel grills but they were successful. All the documents, deeds and share ledgers were found to be intact and were safely removed.

'Some months before the heavy raids began, the Committee decided to store important documents and records in the country. The first selection had to be changed as the district was chosen and a strong room was built. The deeds and documents rescued from the central building have since been deposited in this new strong room.

'The precaution of duplicating all essential documents had been taken from the beginning of the war, Mr. Gilbert informed me. This decision was made by an emergency committee then appointed, so that in the event of records being lost they could be built up again in 48 hours. The value of this wise precaution has been proved in recent months.

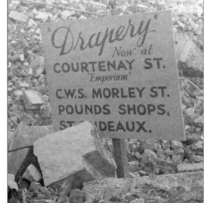

Above: Not all of Courtenay Street escaped. Right: We have moved!

The rubble has gone, and little else remains. No decision had yet been taken on the shell of the Municipal Building.

'There have been numerous instances of the courage and resource of employees, who disregarding personal danger, have endeavoured to save the society's property.

'At the height of one raid, several employees rescued thirty-three horses from a blazing stable and led them through the streets in which bombs were falling and fires were raging, to other accommodation nearly two miles away.

'One of the branches was in a danger area on an evening when a new registration period closed. Although the employees on duty had been warned by firemen, they collected all the counterfoils and registration details before leaving the premises.

'Two or three members of the Committee have had their homes completely destroyed. One of these is the president, Mr. W.J. Gilbert, who was lucky to escape serious injury. When a high explosive bomb destroyed his bungalow and houses in the neighbourhood, he was standing near a shelter and was blown off his feet. Officials and employees have also lost their homes, or had them damaged, and many employees have lost their lives.

'Steps to restore trading facilities in all sections were taken immediately after the raids. In the furnishing emporium, the only large central building that survived the raids, accommodation was found for the general drapery, boot and shoe, drug, optical and tobacco departments.

'So far as the branches are concerned, the policy of the committee has been to use shops under the society's control if, at all possible. For example, a greengrocery shop has been taken over by the grocery department. In other instances, greengrocery and confectionary shops have been converted for use as dry goods departments and the greengrocery, or confectionary, business has been transferred to the nearest grocery shop.

'In addition to the two houses purchased for the administrative offices in Thorn Park, accommodation for other sections of the office staff have been provided in a building in North Road.

'Two additional boot and shoe shops have been obtained, many private enterprise boot and shoe shops were destroyed and the society has now almost a monopoly of this business, and the trade is growing at a remarkable rate. In a recent week there was an increase of 60 per cent, compared with a corresponding week a year ago. These shops have been so busy at certain periods that it has been necessary to limit the number of customers entering at one time.

'Trade in other dry goods departments had fallen considerably, however, due to evacuation. The removal of the children has particularly affected the bread and milk trade. The sales were unaffected immediately after the raids, but since the evacuation of the children they have shown big decreases. The milk sales have dropped by one thousand five hundred gallons a day. In regard to bread, the effects are not so noticeable because the society is baking bread for several private bakers whose premises have been damaged or destroyed.

'Mr. Gilbert and Mr. Williams paid high tribute to the CWS for their magnificent assistance. "Day and night, by rail and road, supplies arrived for the main food departments from the Bristol depot and the London branch" said Mr. Gilbert . "Supplies were so promptly sent that, from the consumers" standpoint the loss of the grocery warehouse was unnoticed. The CWS saleroom in Morley Street was placed at our disposal. We used the first floor for part of our drapery department and Mr. Burdett, Grocery Manager, was allowed to use a portion of the saleroom at his office'. When the central grocery department was destroyed, the CWS allowed the use of part of the Summerland Place furnishing depot as a grocery branch.

'The loss of so many trading premises has naturally caused some redundancy to the staff, and the Committee have been compelled to discharge a number of temporary staff, who were employed to replace the men called up in

Looking through the space formerly occupied by the Central Premises.

148   *Fore Street, where the Society's newly built emporium, which had occupied half of the stretch between the remains of the post box on the right and the corner building in the middle distance had, overnight, been reduced to rubble in the April 'blitzes' focused on Devonport.*

the Forces. A few of the employees have reached the optional retiring age under the pensions scheme and that has also eased the labour situation.

'Throughout the period when temporary dislocations were frequent, the members retained their confidence in the Society. The membership total has been almost unaffected; but it is apparent that all the members are not trading with the Society at present, although they have retained their membership. The effects of the evacuation are indicated in the drop in sales of 16%, although rationing and the general restriction of supplies has had some influence on this reduction.

'In their report to the half-year ended 1st March this year presented to the members' meeting in April, the committee said it had been possible to reconstruct departmental estimates, and they recommended a dividend of 1s. in the £ on general trade and 4d. in the £ on agricultural department sales for the 1st quarter of the half-year.

'In view of the destruction of the check-office records of purchases for the March quarter, the committee stated that dividend would be calculated on the basis of members' purchases for the corresponding quarter of 1940; but those members who could produce their climax check to show they had made higher purchases in the recent quarter could have their accounts adjusted.

'Dividend payments were delayed after the third "blitz", and the method of paying was changed. In present conditions the usual method of confining the payments to a fortnight and using a large hall for the purpose was impossible. Therefore, the period of dividend paying has been extended. According to their number, the members go to the offices in North Road on certain specified days. For example, those members whose numbers range from 1 to 15,000 can draw their dividends on Mondays. The remaining numbers are allocated on a similar basis to different days of the week.

'In a statement made to the members' meeting it was reported that the sales for the half-year ended March, 1941, amounted to £1,128,962, compared with £1,193,936 for the corresponding half-year of 1940. Share capital made a total of £2,191,375 against £1,988,882. Loan capital stood at £395,665 (last year £366,048) investments totalled £1,800,656, and reserves amounted to £140,723. The membership figures (83,334) showed a slight decrease on the previous year's total of 84,303.

'Every facility has been provided for the members to obtain their money from the Society and members, who from stress of circumstances due to the "blitz" have been compelled to remove from the city and needed temporary

financial assistance, have availed themselves of the facilities provided for by the society's rules and the arrangements made by the management committee. The remarkable feature of the share capital account, however, is that from 1st March to 31st May, no less a sum than £21, 438 was deposited - an impressive indication of the members' faith in the society in these unhappy times.

'So far as the future is concerned, Mr Gilbert and his colleagues are optimistic. The extensive destruction of property and goods and the dislocation of trade will mean that a substantial loss will have to be borne by the society, in addition to any return made under Government schemes; but the wisdom and foresight of past committees and officials has placed the society in such a strong position that the blows so far received will not affect the financial stability of the society or impair the security of members' savings.

'Educational work has suffered considerable interference as a result of the repeated raids, but the mere fact that some of the organisations are still carrying on is an indication that the members are determined not to be beaten by "blitzes".

'In the period before raids began, there were eighteen women's guilds and one men's guild. The men's guild has ceased to function but there are still fourteen women's guilds meeting, in spite of the fact that they have had to change their meeting rooms so frequently that the educational department has had difficultly in keeping in contact with them.

'Although a large number of children have been evacuated, every effort is being made to keep the junior choir in being. This choir has been a very strong organisation for many years and has gained many successes in the city contests.

'Before the war, the Educational Department used to run twenty children's classes, but the war caused a considerable reduction and great difficulties were experienced last winter in obtaining teachers. Nevertheless, six classes were held, and the Education Committee were hopeful of future prospects when the "blitzes" resulted in the evacuation of children.

'Accommodation problems nearly prevented the annual festival from being held. This event, which is usually held in February and is spread over a week, took place in April this year. It should have been held in the society's hall, but this had been destroyed and a hall was obtained at Devonport. A "Youth Day", a handicrafts competition was spread over four days, and the festival had a tonic effect on the people taking part.

'By the loss of its office and library, the department has been considerably

handicapped in its work. There were about 14,000 books in the library, with an average issue of 1,500 a week. All the books, scenery for the dramatic section, and equipment for ambulance classes, were lost.
'The department had one piece of good fortune. The CWS fireproof filing cabinet, in which the department's records and books were kept, fell from the second storey to the basement when the building was destroyed but the contents with a few exceptions were rescued intact. The educational department is now sharing a building at 83, North Road with some sections of the general office staff.'

Soldiering Through

The problems faced by the Society typified the situation in the city generally. Some businesses were lost altogether, some were partially destroyed, one or two managed to escape - but in the thick of it they were few and far between. Many tried to relocate, to Tavistock Road, North Hill and particularly, Mutley Plain, which having escaped almost unscathed (the Co-op pharmacy at No.51 was among the few casualties), quickly became the new heart of retail activity.

Mutley Plain after the war

A tailoring and outfitting shop was opened at 4-6 Peverell Park Road, next to the grocery branch there. A pharmacy and optical service was set up at Lisson Grove, off Mutley Plain, to replace the damaged premises at 51 Mutley Plain. Meanwhile the general administration staff were rehoused in two properties in Thorn Park, while the general offices and Education Department were moved to North Road in premises (in Caer Baden Terrace) that the Society had acquired twenty years earlier. A Co-operative Youth Group and Club were established there in May 1942.

In the short, term all sorts of buildings had been pressed into action. At one stage the Society temporarily used a Mission Hall as a grocery branch. The padre in charge of the Mission made it clear that he wanted the hall to be returned to him as soon as possible *'in order that the work of God should not be interfered with'* - to which the Grocery Manager, Mr Burdett, said something like .. *'Sir, I think that the provision of food for the people is God's work.'*

Nevertheless the grocery did not stay long, but feeding the people was a serious issue and the Society had no intention of shirking their responsibilities: *'We shall have difficulties, but we are alive, and not all the hordes of hell can beat us, if we do our utmost with kindness and understanding to help the people who have suffered so severely: some of our own staff and friends are among these,'* read one grocery department emergency circular. It continued: *'No routine nor detail must stand in the way of keeping faith with the supplying of foodstuffs to our customers and to people in distress. Many people are in serious distress and need careful, courteous, and sympathetic consideration from us.'*

There were reports of looters, but generally there was an accentuated sense of community and at the end of the year the Presidential New Year Message from the Society was a confident and positive one: *'Once again, we assert our unshaken belief that the future welfare of mankind is linked up with the fundamental principles of security, freedom, liberty - the very basis of a free democracy ...'*

Having said that, the Society decided not to hold elections in 1942, in much the same way that the City Council took the decision at the beginning of the war to appoint Lord Astor as Lord Mayor for the duration of the conflict. There were still changes in personnel at the top, however, as the death of the General Secretary, EFR Cocks, in June 1941, meant a successor had to be found quickly (Cocks was just 51 and there is little doubt that the anxiety and trauma brought about by the blitz hastened his demise).

In what turned out to be a relatively brief interregnum, the former General Secretary, Wonnacott, stepped back into the office, and in November Herbert Twigg was formally appointed to the post.

For obvious reasons sales figures as announced at the April 1942 half-yearly meeting were down, but that year the Society capitalised on the fact that they were more cash-rich than many of their local competitors: they bought an established coal and agricultural business at Launceston: a pharmacy at Yelverton; property in Torpoint for a dairy depot and for receiving laundry and footwear repairs: a drapery and outfitting concern in Kingsbridge: as well as a property in Callington and a few other, more local, purchases.

Add into this the fact that the Society had been successful in tendering to supply the City Council with bread that year and had been asked by the CWS to supply jam to the other Co-operative Societies in Devon and Cornwall and happily the previous half-yearly sales drop was turned into an 8.8% increase.

By the end of 1942 yet more acquisitions had been made in the Mutley/Peverell area as well as a further 84 acres of farmland adjoining Lambside and Caulston Farms. The idea here was to provide additional pasturage for the dairy herd and as production increased so, on the first day of January 1943, the Society opened a Dairy Shop in newly acquired premises in Saltash. Before long pasteurised milk was being supplied to all public schools in that town for the first time ever. The following month a similar purchase was made in Yealmpton so that the Society could supply the dairy needs for Yealmpton and Brixton areas, and then in June, Donkin's milk delivery business at Kingston, near Modbury, was added to the expanding portfolio.

As well as expanding its coverage, the Society was also looking to improve deliveries and was replacing all its milk-barrows with Graiseley electric vehicles. That same month, June 1943, saw Plymouth Corporation decide to compulsorily purchase the Society's market-garden site at Laira - in preparation for proposed post-war housing (this lead to the Committee buying Chittleburn Farm at Brixton the following year).

'Over here' US military vehicles dominate the foreground - note the Co-operative sign on the barn-like building.

Looking To The Future

By this stage, the summer of '43, the document that would come to shape the post-war city - the Plan for Plymouth - was almost finished. The City Engineer, James Paton Watson, and the distinguished Town Planning Consultant, Patrick Abercrombie (he would be knighted in 1945), had been working up the Plan for almost two years and by September 1943 they had completed the task, although publication would not come until April 1944.

Nevertheless there was an easier feeling in the air. There had only been one night-time raid on the city in over eighteen months and that was back in February. The Americans had entered the war, and, in the spring of 1943, Plymouth, taking over the whole of Seaton and Plumer Barracks at Crownhill and Raglan Barracks at Devonport *'... and from then on they became even more familiar in the streets of the city than were our own soldiers'* (Twyford 1945).

Although there was still a long way to go, it now seemed realistic to think that the end may be in sight.

Then, on the night of 14 June 1943, the alert was sounded just after midnight. What followed was, particularly for Plympton, the worst raid of the war: five people were killed and 600 houses damaged, 11 of them completely destroyed. Plymouth too suffered, with a further 13 fatalities and another 3,000 homes damaged or destroyed.

It was estimated that around twenty enemy planes were involved and remarkably four were brought down, including one that crashed in the garden of a house in Stoke that was being used as a hostel for the WRNS (Woman's Royal Naval Service). Incredibly it was the first time an enemy plane had been brought down within the city. None of the crew survived, although three crewmen of another bomber baled out over the city and were captured, one in Alexandra Road, Mutley, another in Lisson Grove and a third between Plympton and Crownhill.

Two months later, again not long after midnight, the City suffered its worst attack since the heavy blitzes of March/April 1941. Forty-one men, women and children were killed, 90 more were seriously injured and a further 70 slightly injured. Like the previous raid, it might have been a whole lot worse had all the bombs actually gone off, mercifully however a high percentage failed to explode. Nevertheless there was extensive damage and the Society itself suffered damage at North Road, Adelaide Street, Manor Street, Lipson Vale and Alexandra Road, Ford.

As it transpired it was to be one of the last raids of the war for Plymouth, the last coming just after five o'clock in the morning of 16 November 1943. Six hundred houses were badly damaged, 40 were completely destroyed and eighteen civilians were killed.

All in all there were some 59 air raids on the City, one for every ten 'alerts' (there were 602 of these). The very last came in April 1944 when more than 30 enemy bombers caused havoc over the waterfront, most notably at Oreston, where 18 were killed, including six in one public air-raid shelter and nine in another. Among them were the wife and two daughters (aged four and twelve) of a Merchant Seaman serving in Alexandria. Plymouth too was hit, with nine fatalities and a direct hit on the Western National Bus Depot at Prince Rock.

Above: An American anti-aircraft gun in position.

Prof. Patrick Abercrombie and Lord Waldorf Astor, Plymouth wartime Lord Mayor

Dusting Off The Ashes

With its army, navy, marine and air force bases - and so many American servicemen based in and around Plymouth - the area had a positive bustle in the lead up to Tuesday, 6 June 1944. The Allied success that day, D-Day, and over the days that followed, virtually signalled the end of the war. As it transpired, however, hostilities in Europe did not formally come to an end until 8 May 1945 - VE Day, and even then there was the issue of Japan, and so it wasn't until 15 August, a week or so after President Truman had given executive orders to drop atomic bombs on Hiroshima and Nagasaki (killing 220,000), that we had an end to the Second World War.

Over 850 pre-war permanent staff had served in the Armed Forces, Civil Defence or in the Munitions Factories. Thirty or so of those in the Armed Services had not come back, the majority of them in the Army, five in the Royal Navy and a few in the RAF. One munitions worker and two Civil Defence members had also lost their lives, as well as four employees who were air-raid victims in Plymouth itself.

From a Co-operative perspective, and a social one, only Hull could claim to have suffered anything like as badly as Plymouth. Certainly, with over 1,200 civilian casualties, Plymouth, per head of population, was the worst hit of all Britain's blitzed cities, including London. Consequently the task of rebuilding was correspondingly daunting.

The Society had its own post-war Development Committee and, at the July 1944 meeting, the first major meeting after the Plan for Plymouth had been published, the President had this to say: *'The future planning of the city, and its reaction on the location of our business premises is quite naturally our chief concern. In this connection, the post-war development committee have applied themselves to examination of certain departmental submissions of a far-reaching character.*

'The proposed new city shopping centre, the approaches thereto, the surrender of blitzed and blighted business areas - to say nothing of the remaining problems included in the Abercrombie-Watson Report, render it imperative that, as a society, we should take our rightful place in the shopping precinct, and that we should make adequate provision for potential Co-operative trade in satellite areas.

'In this connection, it seems desirable to state that as the largest business ratepayer in the city, we hope to submit the society's requirements both for shopping and for warehouse space commensurate with our business commitments to the appropriate authorities.'

The President then went on to recall a statement made by the Society's representatives at their initial meeting with Professor Abercrombie two years earlier; they said: *'The society would regard any attempt in re-development to give preference to either large traders, or small traders, as extremely improper and undesirable. The only proper attitude for a public authority in this matter can be summarised in the phrase: A fair field and no favour.'* He then added that this was still the Society's position in July 1944.

The following March the Society noted with interest that the Council was prepared to allow temporary shops in areas where they were proposing to erect temporary bungalows - prefabs - to meet immediate housing needs. It was also reported that the Society had applied to use a section of the temporary shops that the City Council was intending to erect in the centre while the new city centre was being built.

Clearly the redevelopment question was the biggest issue to confront the Society to date. A large number of the Society's properties came within the Area No.1 that the City Council had scheduled under the Town and Country Planning Act of 1944. This rendered almost the whole of the old city centre for clearance and redevelopment - over 70 acres - a considerable amount of which had been freehold property purchased by the Co-op. Under the new arrangement however, this meant that ownership of all this freehold land on which surviving buildings stood - like the 'new' 1930s Emporium - together with that covered only by rubble, would eventually pass to the City Council, to be re-leased for periods of up to 99 years.

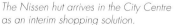
The Nissen hut arrives in the City Centre as an interim shopping solution.

The Society to use one of the new Cornish unit houses for its first Ernesettle branch.

The land affected included, in terms of properties that had been destroyed: the Central Premises, the restaurant block, Courtenay Street jewellery, the Frankfort Lane warehouse, the impressive Drake Circus section, the stables in Week Street, as well as properties in Treville Street, Green Street and Summerland Place.

Then there were all the properties within that area that were still standing: like the Central Furniture Emporium, the hairdressing and grocery office in Cambridge Street, the York Street and Oxford Place block, the boot and the confectionery store in Ebrington Street, the grocery in Treville Street and the CWS property in Morley Street.

All of this was scheduled for clearance as the Council proposed to fulfil the Abercrombie-Watson vision - twipe the slate clean and start from scratch.

'When re-development first began, the chorus of objections was small,' relates Briscoe in his centenary story published less than fifteen years later, *'since comradeship surviving from the days of the air-raid shelters was sufficient to enable people to think in terms of collective well-being rather than their own self-interest. As the re-development proceeded, and standing property as well as war-damaged ruins were removed to make way for the new city, the chorus of objection grew in volume; but the initial drive for a new Plymouth was sufficient to sweep aside most of the objections.'*

'There is,' he added, *'a certain unanswerable logic in a bulldozer!'*

However there were other problems: the arrangements under the War Damage Commission meant that official recompense was essentially at 1939 prices with just a 'small uplift', which was basically not enough to replace like for like. Furthermore, building costs were rising all the time, materials were scarce and the pace of redevelopment was infuriatingly slow, all the time adding to the final cost projections.

Meanwhile, on the rapidly expanding new 'spacious and beautiful' housing estates the local authorities took it upon themselves to build shops and then looked to let them to traders. The problem here was that these purpose-built premises did not always suit the particular purpose; *'Only recently has it been accepted,'* wrote Briscoe in 1960, *'that certain trades need more space than others.'*

He went on to quote one critic who claimed that the council were *'playing at shops'* and furthermore that *'it seemed that if the advice of traders was requested in the planning and siting of shops it was largely ignored.'*

There was another problem too, in as much as there was often a substantial delay between the construction and occupation of the new houses and the erection of shops to serve them, although, in Ernesettle, this was partially solved by the authorities allowing the Society to use one of the new Cornish unit houses for its first Ernesettle branch.

Elsewhere the problem was circumvented by the Society increasing its use of travelling shops. For many, these mobile grocery stores were veritable lifelines. Attractive as the new estates were, with their open spaces and homes with gardens, they were far removed in every sense from the tight, terraced housing with corner shops and community facilities that the displaced population of Plymouth was used to.

'There can be little doubt that much of the reluctance of the "in town" folk to move to the new housing estates was occasioned by the lack of community facilities and, in particular, shopping facilities. The "pioneers" in many of these estates would have had a rough time but for the travelling shops,' wrote Briscoe, adding, *'the society's coach-building department effectively converted a number of coaches into grocery travelling shops, and these became a familiar sight on the estates.'*

The new city housing estate at Efford takes shape as hundreds of pre-fabricated houses are erected to relieve the pressure for accommodation .

Few people on these early post-war estates were car owners. Furthermore most people tended to shop on a day-to-day basis rather than in one large weekly shop, and with the only alternative being to wait for a lengthy bus trip to the nearest established shopping area, it's easy to see why, despite the lure of an indoor bathroom and a fitted kitchen (facilities that many had never enjoyed before), people weren't always in a hurry to move out of town.

But move out they did and of course this too brought it's concerns for the Co-op: *'The Society was finding that many of its older branches in the "in-town" area were no longer as worthwhile as formerly, and adjustments were necessary. Branches that had been erected to do a substantial trade were no longer so important'* (Briscoe).

Notwithstanding all these difficulties the Plymouth Co-operative Society was better placed than most to take on the challenge and the post-war period saw a succession of amalgamations with smaller and neighbouring societies - Lee Moor in 1945 being the first.

Around the same time the establishment of the Admiralty Estate at Lee Mill offered another opportunity for the Co-op to reach a new market. A number of other dairy rounds were also purchased as was a pharmacy business in Wolseley Road, a drapery concern in Albert Road. Meanwhile a new grocery was opened in Blandford Road, Efford.

Generally though, for the Plymouth Co-operative Society, and for the City itself, there was to be no easy slipping back into 'life as normal' once the war had ended, as the process of rehousing the population and reconstructing the shopping centre was, somewhat inevitably, well outside the bounds of what generally passed as 'normal'.

Nevertheless with the war over, the process of demobilisation began and within a month of VJ-Day some sixty employees had returned from active service and been re-instated and the November issue of the Journal was able to extend a warm *'welcome home - to your own society'*. By September the following year some 598 employees had been demobbed and returned to the Society's employment to the great delight of management and customers, who were pleased to see the back of some of the inexperienced temporary staff 'conscripted into shops by the Minister of Labour.

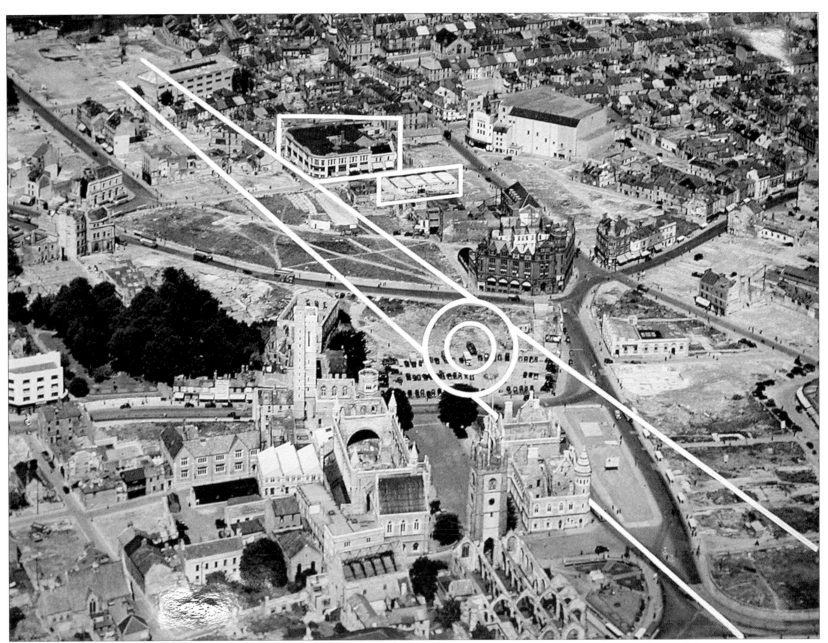

Royal Parade is mapped out, and the surviving Co-operative premises are highlighted.

CHAPTER 9: THE BEST LAID PLANS

While the Society may have been bidding a less than fond farewell to some of their temporary employees, they were inevitably having to make the most of temporary shops. 'Make Do And Mend' was the prevailing philosophy across the City and the Society, while on the one hand making long term plans for the future, were also determined to find short-term solutions for the present.

Temporary shops were erected on the site of the old Central Premises opposite the Odeon to supplement the space available at the Courtenay Street furnishing emporium and before long *a number of pre-fabricated shops made their utilitarian, if ugly, appearance and rendered excellent service to the society for many years* (Briscoe).

Meanwhile, in addition to the obvious planning for a new Central Premises, a variety of other developments were mooted, including: the purchase of property in Albert Road to replace the soon-to-be-demolished store in Ross Street: the enlargement of the employees' sports ground at Efford: the purchase of land for development in Launceston: part of a hotel in Callington - for adaptation to business use; plans for rebuilding the grocery warehouse on North Quay, and plans for development on the land between the bakery and the laundry at Peverell.

Confidence was high and so too, in the wake of servicemen and evacuees returning home, was the dividend - at its lowest ebb the population of the city had dropped to something like 60% of its pre-war level.

Change was in the air and the Society was ready for the challenge. The January 1946 meeting saw the first election of officers since 1940, in what marked another landmark in the return to 'normalcy' as the Amercian President, Warren Harding, had called the situation, Stateside, after the First World War.

However, there had been no damage at home after the Great War, so there were no homes to rebuild, no businesses to re-establish just an economy that needed restoring.

The Second World War had bankrupted Britain, but we had been victorious and the man in uniform as well as the man in the street, had respect for Churchill, our wartime leader. However, it was clear that there needed to

Royal Parade takes shape, early 1947.

Plymouth under snow in the winter of 1947: the Hoe, St Andrew's and the City Centre.

be changes made. Heroes needed homes again, and with imports being reduced to help balance the books, rationing and austerity were still the order of the day, and looked like remaining so for some time to come.

People wanted change, and just as the Labour Party won a landslide victory after VJ Day, with the promises of a welfare state, a free national health service and state ownership of industries like coal and the railways, so the Progressives swept to success in the Society's 1946 election - all told over 20 vacancies were up for consideration and not a single Blue Ticket candidate was successful.

Nationally, Churchill had done the Conservative cause no favours by suggesting that *'no socialist system could be established without a political police ... some form of Gestapo.'* The attempt to taint men like Labour leader Clement Atlee and Ernest Bevin (who'd been the wartime coalition government Labour Minister) with the Nazi slur undoubtedly backfired on the Tories.

Notwithstanding the problems being faced by the Goverment, life for the Plymouth Society was becoming somewhat easier: *'trade was booming, though this was in part a reflection of continuing inflation brought about by "too much money chasing too few goods". Even so, the 7.6% increase in sales represented a real increase as well as one in money values. For 1946 the sales target was £3,000,000'* (Briscoe).

This target was attained, the year-end figures showing an increase of 18.4% over the previous year and the dividend reaching 2/- (it included a 4d 'loyalty bonus'), the highest it had been since the Great War.

With talk of a 'crusade of youth' in the air and the Education Department moving into new premises (the erstwhile Western College at Mutley) the future was looking very rosy.

January 1946 had seen the Society order 100 new motor and electric driven vehicles and later that year eight new charabancs were bought to rebuild the fleet so sadly depleted in the blitz. Curiously enough the Society also won four prizes that Whitsun in the Plymouth Horse Show, but there could be no doubt now that the horse had had its day.

In September '47 the first electrically propelled vehicle was brought into service for the greengrocery department and in 1948 a group of 18 lock up garages - Abbotsfield Garages - were bought to house the butchery fleet of vehicles. The first mobile-butchery vehicle took to the streets on 30 August 1948, its round embracing the Honicknowle, Tamar Way and Ham areas.

Amalgamation

With the coldest winter of the twentieth century prompting a fuel crisis affecting coal - and thus electricity - supplies, the south-west shivered along with the rest of the country in the early part of 1947.

A paper shortage followed, thwarting the publication of a March edition of the Journal. A combined March/April magazine was printed instead. However, before the year was out the *Plymouth Co-operative Journal* ceased to be a fully independent organ and instead became the middle section of the centrally produced *Co-operative Home Magazine*. A number of other Societies had already gone down the same path, on the grounds that it could offer more attractive features.

Derry's Clock, with the Co-op and the Odeon Cinema in the background.

Amalgamation was certainly on the agenda at this time. It had been in March 1947, that after protracted negotiations and one or two failures to achieve the required majority, the engagements of the Plympton Society were successfully transferred to Plymouth, thereby bringing in outlets at Plympton, Hemerdon and Ivybridge.

A few months later, at a conference in Plymouth, the Society's Chief Executive Office, Herbert Twigg spoke on the 'pros' and 'cons' of federal action and amalgamation. Twigg was an ardent advocate of amalgamation arguing that small societies, however willing they were, were unable to offer their members the same range of services and benefits.

Quite clearly the increases in trade at both Lee Moor and Plympton, so soon after coming under the Plymouth Society umbrella, were evidence to support the argument, the only question was how small was small?

Undoubtedly the Plymouth Society did not see itself as a small society and this was a busy period of expansion as new shops were opening all across the patch. In addition to new 'temporary' shops in Courtenay Street the Society opened new pharmacies in George Street, Devonport, and in Torpoint, and they announced that a new footwear shop was to be opened in Plympton.

On top of all this, work was now under way on a large extension to the Radnor Dairy following the acquisition of existing milk businesses at Bere Alston, Bere Ferrers, Millbrook and Kingsbridge in the second half of 1946 and at Ivybridge and Liskeard in March 1947.

Another venture towards the end of 1946 saw the redevelopment of the drapery in Embankment Road - on 10 October the premises was re-opened as a Cycle, Radio and Electrical branch. The move proved disappointing however and it closed eleven months later.

Interestingly enough, shortly afterwards William Gilbert, the man who had steered the Society through the troublesome years of conflict, was presented with one of the Co-op's 'Defiant' radiograms upon his stepping down from the Presidency after his thirteen years in the seat.

Mr Gilbert was succeeded by Arnold Stroud, another old stalwart, who had been vice-president. Stroud was elected unopposed, and CR Westlake became his vice-chairman.

Post-war sales were still increasing, as was the membership, but 'normalcy' was still some way off. Indeed a remarkable number of shops were still operating with boarded-up windows.

Supplies of plate glass were very limited and the process of restoring window frontages was painfully slow. At the end of 1947 the windows of Station Road grocers and butchers were dealt with, as were those of the groceries at Patna Place, Notte Street, and Tavistock Road and half a dozen or so other of the Society's stores. But there were still many more with corrugated iron where there should have been enticing displays.

A Revolution In Retailing

In the first three months of 1948 another twenty shop windows were re-glazed and to improve appearances yet further a programme of internal and external decoration and modernisation was begun. Within twelve months the programme of plate-glass renewals had almost been completed and a clear property-maintenance schedule had been drawn up. Henceforth all shops were to be externally updated every five years and internally updated every three years. There had however been another, more significant, more revolutionary, development on the modernisation front by that time, as the Society started to introduce the idea of Self Service.

There had been gradual changes in the shopping experience throughout the twenties and thirties, as suppliers steadily increased the number of foodstuffs that came pre-packaged, weighed and branded and backed up with national advertising. Bit by bit there was less for the shopkeeper to do, fewer items to weigh, wrap and recommend. As advertising campaigns became more and more effective so customers entered stores with ever clearer ideas of what they wanted; all that was left for the shop-keeper to do was pull the packet, bottle, tin or jar off the shelf and onto the counter.

In June 1942 the London Co-operative Society decided to try an experiment along the lines pioneered successfully in America by the Piggly Wiggly grocery chain started by Clarence Saunders back in 1916. Saunders introduced a turnstile entrance and a check desk at his store in Memphis

A typical post-war Co-op grocery - St Helen's, Lancashire, December 1948.

One of the first new Co-operative Self Service stores, in Portsea c.1949

and within seven years had built up an empire of 2,800 Piggly Wiggly stores across the United States.

In London, the Co-operative Society screened off a section of their grocery store in Romford, took away the counter and gave their customers a basket and then let them do all the selecting, making sure that they all went past a small counter close to the door where payment could be made.

Although adjudged a success it was not until January 1948 that the London Society opened their first, full-size supermarket - in Manor Park - but then the floodgates opened. In March the Portsea Island Society opened what they claimed was the first self-service shop in Great Britain - in Albert Bridge Road, Portsmouth – and towards the end of the year the Plymouth Society started to introduce the notion of self-service shopping to the city.

Beacon Park was the first grocery to be thus fitted out. The grocery at Courtenay Street was converted soon afterwards, and then, on 7 March 1949, the Jubilee Stores at Peverell re-opened as a self-service establishment with all new fixtures and fittings.

'In general, members approved of the change,' wrote Briscoe, who had become the Society's Education Secretary in June 1947, *'though some members regretted the passing of the counter service shop. There could be no doubt, however,'* he added, *'as to the much smoother service given by the new type of shop.'*

Smoother, and more cost effective, this was undoubtedly the shape of shopping for the future and before the year was out the Plymouth Society had introduced Cornwall to the new method of retailing as on 8 August 1949, the Launceston grocery was converted to self-service.

In this type of shopping, the Co-operative Movement, in Britain at least, were market leaders and by 1950 *'90% of all self-service shops were Co-operative'* (Birchall). It was a statistic that sent a chill down the spines of cornershop proprietors as invariably their premises were much smaller and less suited to conversion to self-service. Even in the bigger 'supermarket' stakes the Co-op was a major player. By 1950 again there were 50 such stores in Britain 40% of which were run by the Co-op. The future did indeed look bright.

Hall For One

One of the main practical problems encountered by the Society since the destruction of the Central Premises was where to hold meetings. During the blackouts afternoons had been favoured and Swarthmore Hall on Mutley Plain was a regular choice, with a fair attendance of guildswomen generally assured - even though the guilds themselves struggled.

Once the meeting reverted to evenings it became more difficult to attract good numbers and the situation wasn't helped by the relative inaccessibility of some of the venues - Ford Hall, Alexandra Road, Ford being one particularly unpopular location involving issues with bus journeys ... and fares.

Nor was the Society the only organisation looking for meeting places, the City Council too had been displaced as had other bodies and Central Methodist Hall served as a main 'temporary' base for many.

Another meeting-related issue however was the simple question of attendance as all too often monthly meetings struggled to attract a quorum. One thing they didn't fail to attract though were those who were unhappy with the falling 'divi': *'Members did not always recognise the difficulties in this early post-war period* (Briscoe).'

The new President, Stroud, did his best to explain how the Government's anti-inflationary policy, combined with less overtime, the evaporation of the period of demob-happy spending and the Co-operative Society's national price-reduction policy for bread and groceries, had conspired to put pressure on the revenue stream.

There was also the matter of Purchase Tax. *'During the war purchase tax had been introduced with a dual purpose: firstly, to reduce the demand for goods in short supply: secondly, as a means of raising taxation revenue. In addition, the tax on tobacco and cigarettes had been increased to such an extent that it now formed the biggest part of the cost. After the war, the increase in indirect taxation continued, largely for the first reason. It met with a certain amount of opposition from the co-operative movement and from the society, since indirect taxation has always been anathema to co-operators, who prefer that taxation should be based on an individual's capacity to pay'* (Briscoe).

The further gripe with Purchase Tax was that it necessarily meant that for those product lines concerned the surplus per pound of sales was less. Consequently, some Societies refused to pay a dividend on such purchases, most notably cigarettes. Plymouth, however continued to offer the 'divi' on these lines, and so there was bound to be an impact on the dividend rate.

However another move by Central Government was to have an uplifting on the Society's trade, and that was the introduction of the National Health Service. Within a month of the beginning of the NHS in September 1948 the number of prescriptions presented in Co-operative pharmacies across the city was roughly three times the amount it had been twelve months earlier. It's worth noting, however, that certain pharmaceutical lines did not qualify for the 'divi'.

Architect's drawing for what will become Co-operative House.

Laying the foundations for Royal Parade.

Straight away the Society did all it could to expand its dispensing service to meet the increased demands. Just a couple of months earlier, in anticipation, new pharmacies had been opened at Plympton and West Park. Plans were unveiled for a new pharmacy as part of the proposed new central premises along Royal Parade.

The long-awaited new HQ was still some way off though; more immediately of interest now was a new grocery warehouse at North Quay. Blighted by technical problems and various delays, work on the main piling operations drew large crowds when it did eventually get under way at the end of 1949.

Foundation stone laid for North Quay, 5 August 1950, by President Stroud.

Six months later the building licence for phase one of the new Central Premises was granted and the Society's Work's Department set to work on the site clearance and excavation work. Meanwhile the temporary stores opposite the Odeon had been cleared to make way for the street-widening on the other side (New George Street) of the block.

It was now five years since the end of the war and people's patience with the slow rate of progress of the new shopping centre was starting to wear thin. Nor was this just a local problem, nationally the electorate were starting to tire of all the planning and austerity. At the General Election early in 1950 the Labour Party was re-elected with a much reduced majority. Locally the Conservatives gained a majority for the first time in four years.

Any concerns that the Plymouth Society had about the change in local politics were soon manifest. As the President was to observe at the October annual meeting: *'I say so plainly and publicly, without fear of contradiction, now you know who your friends are.'*

The issue that brought the matter to the fore was the 'deliberate anti-co-operative bias' in the allocation of a new milk contract. The Society had been supplying milk to the Plymouth Hospitals for some years, and, as of 1 January 1950, that had been extended to District Hospitals, by which time the Dairy Department was also supplying milk to over 140 schools, processing - and pasteurising - more than three million gallons of milk per year. With work ongoing on the redevelopment and enlargement of plant and machinery of the dairy at Radnor Place, this was a very serious part of the Society's activities and any loss of business would have been keenly felt.

Tragically the Dairy Department manager, SJ Tarrant, died suddenly at the end of November 1950, very soon after reaching his 50th birthday and only 18 months after taking up his appointment. He was temporarily replaced by the retired manager, J Sheenan, pending a permanent appointment (John Akers from the New Swindon Society took up the reins the following March).

Meanwhile the Society continued its acquisitions policy. In February 1950 the milk and egg business of WJ Moore of Bere Ferrers was bought, in June, Giles' milk business in Down Thomas was added to the portfilio and in February 1952 a similar concern in Aveton Gifford was purchased.

Such is not to suggest that the Society was slowing down its expansion into other markets as new grocery stores, butcher's shops and mobile units were opened and introduced around the City and within it. King's Tamerton saw the construction of new grocery and butchery branches, while the Camel's Head and Treville Street groceries were both converted to self-service at the end of 1949.

These were busy and challenging times, but for a whole raft of reasons, despite increases in turnover, trade and membership, the dividend was gradually dropping. For the year ended September 1950, the 'divi' was down to a shilling, despite record annual sales of £4.54m and a membership roll of 93,000.

Dilemma In Devonport

If this was causing a degree of head-scratching in Plymouth, the situation was even worse in Devonport where an amendment to the Devonport Admiralty Extension Scheme meant that the group of shops in Albert Road and Ross Street, as well as the dairy depot in Ross Street were now outside the scheme and could be retained by the Society after all.

But then, in June 1952, the City Council served a compulsory purchase order on the Ross Street and Pentamar Terrace properties for housing. This meant the Society losing the Ross Street grocery (one of its oldest stores), the pharmacy warehouse, the dairy depot, garage and cold store.

However, on a brighter note, a licence was granted for the Society to rebuild the St Levan Road grocery, and some houses in Warleigh Avenue that had been destroyed in the war.

These were frustrating times for the traders and residents of Devonport: 'So far as reconstruction was concerned, the elaborate scheme of dockyard re-development decided on in the latter stages of the war and in the immediate post-war years, was considerably amended, and the greater part of the old Devonport area was 'in the melting pot' again' (Briscoe).

In the meantime none of the big players were making a move in this part of the city and as rebuilding in central Plymouth got under way all the people of Devonport could do was look on enviously.

Clearly the mobile stores were a lifeline for them too, although, here, as elsewhere there was competition for the Society. These were busy times for the travelling traders - even the CWS joined in, in May 1951, with their soft drinks division selling mineral waters, squashes, and cordials to the new housing estates to the north of the city, garaging their vehicles at the rear of the premises at King's Tamerton.

With roundsmen becoming an ever-increasing part of the Society's profile, the centralisation of garaging for the expanding fleet became a pressing concern and one which was most satisfactorily dealt with early in 1951, when the former Mumford Factory at Billacombe was bought up and brought into use.

Top left: A post-war Co-op coal lorry. Left: Radnor Dairy. Above: Peark's were one of the alternative travelling shop providers.

Roundsman Douglas Robertson leads the last horse-drawn grocery cart back to Peverell.

Horsey Horsey

William Mumford had built the unit for coach building in the 1920s and during the war the factory had been used for the manufacture of aeroplane parts. A vast site, offering plenty of room for expansion, the move there freed up the coach building/painting premises at Alma Road/St John's Bridge Road and garage at Vauxhall Street.

The move was symptomatic of another major change too, one that had been inevitable for years and which by mid-1952 was almost complete.

The Plymouth Society pulled up its last horse-drawn grocery vehicle in September 1951, meanwhile the greengrocery division brought more and more electric vehicles into service, so that by March 1952 they too had ceased to call upon their faithful quadrupeds. This left just the bakery department still using the odd horse-cart, however before long the stables section had been become extinct.

It was the end of an era, and one that had lasted a good deal longer than some might have expected, particularly in respect of the bakery department, which in other respects was one of the most up-to-date in the country. At the beginning of 1951 work had begun on demolishing seven large draw plate ovens on the ground floor of the Peverell Bakery and these were replaced by a massive, 60 Tray Uniflow Oven capable of producing almost two and half thousand pounds of baked bread an hour.

In February of the following year Peverell operation began slicing and wrapping their loaves, and soon they were supplying the packaged product to neighbouring societies in Torbay, Tavistock, Newquay, Bodmin, Lostwithiel, St Austell, Roche and, from 1953, Wadebridge – as well as their own immediate area.

By this stage the new four storey warehouse on North Quay was already in use and ready to serve the Society's 65 grocery branches. With half as much space again as the old warehouse, occupation enabled space to be freed up at the Preserve Works at Peverell, and this enabled the butchery small goods factory to be moved up from the cramped location at Water Lane, Stonehouse.

Left: Not only sliced, but it's wrapped too.
Below: A removal van out on the moors.

Two views of the impressive new Co-op warehouse on North Quay

All this increased activity was not enough to boost trading figures favourably enough to produce any more than a sixpenny dividend, the lowest to date.

It might have helped had everyone who worked for the Society also shopped with the Society. In his August 1952 newsletter, the CEO, Herbert Twigg, noted an encounter with an employee who had over twenty years service with the Society. In conversation it emerged that the said employee had never tasted the Society's bread ... or the Society's milk! Mr Twigg's response was not published.

One thing that promised to help the financial situation was the end of rationing. Clothes came off first, prompting the Committee to reverse a long-held view on extending credit facilities to members: 'Members of the Joint Guilds Executive Council had for some time been campaigning for the mutuality club, saying that the Society should provide credit facilities similar to those available from our private trade opponents and thus encourage poorer members to trade with their own society' (Briscoe).

Across the country the Co-operative Movement was becoming increasingly aware of its 'private trade opponents'. As the Co-op had been expanding its interests here there and everywhere, acquiring small private businesses, butchers, bakers, pharmacies etc. as well as opening new shops on the new estates, so other multiple traders were extending their sphere of influence, shedding the family firm image and becoming public limited companies. This process empowered such concerns giving them access to large capital sums, sufficient to allow them to start moving into substantial city centre sites around the country.

Just as the Plymouth Society was merging and amalgamating with smaller societies around and about, so too some of the multiples and other large businesses were working their way through a take-over and merger process. Dingles – the Co-op's biggest local competitor – whose impressive new post-war store had been the first to open on Royal Parade in 1951, had bought out Vickery & Co before the war, while the national retailer, Debenhams, had added Spooners (another large city centre business) to their portfolio way back in 1929. However, somewhat ominously, Woolworths, the American chain that had first extended its tentacles into Britain in 1909, and Plymouth soon afterwards, were the first to open a new store in Plymouth's reconstructed City Centre, in New George Street, in November 1950.

Top: 27 February 1954 saw the pensioning off of the last of the Society's horses and the old stable at the Peverell Bakery was converted into a repository for the storage of the members' furniture - furniture that had been rescued during the 'Blitz'. Popular with many customers, who liked to feed the horses on their rounds, the creatures were also popular with roundsmen around Christmas time, as they 'allowed' them the luxury of the odd tipple.

Right: One of the new mobile greengrocery vans.

Frustratingly, it wasn't to be for another two years, until November 1952, that the Co-op were in a position to open the doors to their new premises, or at least the first phase of their new building. However, they had had the advantage of still having a part of their pre-war emporium open throughout the post-blitz period.

A large crowd arrived to witness the event and to explore the ground, and lower ground floors. Generally people were heartily impressed with the size and scale of the new store, marvelling at the range of merchandise and the fixtures and fittings. The drapery department staff looked splendid in their wine-coloured dresses and attracted a great deal of attention.

Four weeks later, and just in time for Christmas, the first floor was opened up for the sales of millinery, fashions, carpets and lino, and four days after that – 8 December – the new tobacconist, on the corner of Royal Parade and Courtenay Street was open for business.

Top: President AN Stroud opens the first phase of the new Central Premises, with CR Westlake, Mrs Short, Mrs Moses and Mr Davey. Above: the new premises alongside the Emporium.

Top: PCS Coach. Bottom: Mobile Shop

Before long the second floor was ready for trading too, the furnishing moving up there and vacating the old emporium in the process (which in turn was swiftly occupied by the tailoring and pharmacy departments - although clearly this was to be an interim measure, until the later phases of the Central Premises were ready).

The third – top – floor of the new building was given over to storage, soft furnishings and drapery workrooms, in addition to a staff canteen, while the mezzanine, floor was occupied, from March 1953, by the ladies' hairdressing salon ... 'Perms from 15/- to 42/-, Shampoo & Set 3/6d'.

While a complete vision for the finished building had long been on the table, it wasn't until November that year that the building licence for phase two of the Central Premises project was issued.

Meanwhile, the Works Department had secured a contract to build 35 houses (at a cost of almost £50,000) for the City Council on the Ernesettle and Whitleigh Estates. The Council themselves were engaged, amongst other things, in the construction of a group of twelve shops to serve the Whitleigh Estate, the first of which they offered the Society for use as a much needed pharmacy - it opened on 18 January 1954.

The process was not an altogether smooth one, however, and it was only after a 'considerable squabble in the city council' that the Society was allocated a grocery branch on the Whitleigh Estate ... and then, with no dispute, a butchers.

'The Society had always taken the line that it had the right to serve its members on the new housing estates. It had never itself asked for a monopoly, nor could it acquiesce in the granting of monopolies or semi-monopolies, to others. The Society took the view that consumers were entitled to reasonable choice as to where they could shop' (Briscoe).

In the meantime the Society opened a pharmacy at Torridge Way, Efford and another at Ernesettle where the new shops on Ernesettle Green (the Society opened a butchery and grocery there as well) allowed for the closure of the grocery in the Cornish Unit house in Rochford Crescent. This had always been inadequate, in any case and had been supplemented by mobile shops.

Similarly, the Whitleigh members had been heavily reliant on mobiles and with the new shops being completed there, the travelling units that had served that estate were transferred to serve the needs of residents around Chaucer Way.

Back in Devonport, meanwhile, the tailoring outfit in Marlborough Street was closed – the lease was coming to an end and anyway there had been a significant decline in the non-food trade in this area, as a large number of those who hadn't been bombed out during the blitz were now being moved out through the clearance and redevelopment of the area by the Admiralty and the once prominent Devonport was becoming a backwater.

This truly was an era of great change around the city and clearly one of the consequences of rehousing the local population in the new far-flung estates that were being built around the northern boundaries of the old Three Towns was that fewer people were inclined to attend the monthly meetings – the journeys were longer and more expensive. An attempt to force the issue saw a resolution passed to the effect that if a quorum was not reached, business would be held over until the next meeting, and so on. Nevertheless it was another two years before the inevitable conclusion – to opt for quarterly meetings – was accepted.

The Co-operative Employees' Welfare Club.

CO-OP STORE (FIRST PART) **ROYAL PARADE—**

Shopping Centre of
Reconstructed Plymouth

*A store of beauty
and utility, comman-
ding the interest of
the discerning shop-
per and pride of over
93,000 Co-operative
members*

. . . .

*Expressive of ad-
venturous enterprise
in public service, and
coincident in opening
with a new era*

Completed in Coronation Year (1953) Elizabeth II

Not Easily Phased

One assembly that was still relatively well attended was the half-yearly meeting and the 1954 get-together was notable not only because it saw Arnold Stroud step down as President, but it also saw Mrs Ellen Roberts elected to succeed him. Mrs Roberts, a widow with no children, had first taken office in the Society over thirty years earlier and had been on the General Committee since 1929. Her appointment put a woman in the President's seat for the first time. It has been suggested that the ascension of Queen Elizabeth II to the throne a year or two earlier, and the appointment in 1950 of Mrs Jacquette Marshall (a long-standing member of the Co-op) as Plymouth's first Lady Lord Mayor, may have had some bearing on the voting. It is worth remembering, however, that Plymouth has had almost unbroken female representation in Parliament since Lady Astor became the first woman to take her seat in the Commons in 1919.

Another significant appointment that year saw the Society's CEO, Herbert Twigg, appointed President of 1954 Co-operative Union Congress at Scarborough - the highest bestowed honour available within the Movement.

Unfortunately, it wasn't the easiest year financially for the Chief Executive, with building costs moving ever upwards, the expenditure on the new Central Premises was straining resources and for the first time ever the balance sheet that September showed a bank overdraft of £93,000.

However there were plenty of reasons for cautious optimism and after the West Park grocery was converted to self-service – the 20th of the Society's stores to do so – Mr Twigg noted that converted branches were showing much larger trade increases than counter service shops and wage costs per pound of trade were lower over all – however, he added, there was nothing to choose between the two types of shop when it came to pilfering and leakage … shoplifting!

Self-service wasn't the only way that the Society was tackling its time and efficiency issues. Experience suggested that small butchery branches were handicapped when it came to staff finding the time, space and, sometimes, the competence to cut carcasses into small joints or selected pieces and so a 'Central Cutting Room' was established at the Peverell warehouse and henceforth outlets were increasingly supplied with ready cut meat.

The Peverell complex had undergone a number of changes recently, not least of which was the removal, in 1953 of the chimneys appended to the Bakery, Laundry and Preserve Works. For over 40 years they had been a familiar part of the landscape, however they had been redundant for some time and so were removed.

Not surprisingly the Preserve Works had enjoyed a boom period that year in the wake of the de-rationing of sweets - sales of boiled sweets, made at the factory increased spectacularly. However, in 1954 four of the Society's confectionery shops were converted to grocery branches and generally there was a move away from individual societies having their own establishments like this. So it was that in the summer of 1959, by which time Plymouth was the only Society left with its own Preserve Works, the factory was closed.

1954 also saw the first full year of the new 'divi' arrangements. The revised system, whereby members came in to collect their payment on a set day according to their share number, had been implemented the previous October, mainly to cut down the queues on the busiest days. From May 1954 payments were made from the first floor of the new Central Premises.

October 1954 the steelwork goes up on the next phase of the Central Premises.

Another Society-related event that attracted big crowds was the Co-operative Wholesale Society Exhibition on the Flora Street site alongside the Gaumont Cinema in Union Street in the summer of 1955.

The exhibition ran throughout the last two weeks of July and proved to be a great hit with tourists and locals alike, with over 50,000 visiting the show, 9,000 of whom turned out for the fashion parades.

The exhibition served to highlight the progress being made with phase two of the new Central Premises, the ground floor of which (all 16,000 square feet of it), had come into use in the middle of May. The pharmacy, optical and tailoring sections moved out of the old Emporium and into the new building. Meanwhile a dividing wall was constructed inside the old Emporium so that the western half (nearest to Raleigh Street) could be demolished, thereby allowing work to start on phase three.

Those departments that had been operating in the temporary shops on the eastern side of Courtenay Street - footwear, greengrocery and confectionery - were moved into the remaining half of the old Emproium which the Society then rented back from the Council.

By May 1956 an impressive forest of steel had been erected from phase one in Royal Parade, around Derry's Roundabout and along Raleigh Street, to link up with the New George Street corner block.

It was now possible to see how vast a project the New Central Premises was becoming. Comfortably the biggest store in the new City Centre; 'I am proud to be connected with it – and I hope you are too,' said the Chief Executive to his staff.

Curiously enough the angled design of the new building was echoed in the angled plate glass windows of the Society's new pharmacy at Crownhill which opened in May 1955 - the idea being to give customers a clear view into the shop without distracting reflections. This was just one of many subtle innovations the Society were introducing to the city. Another was the installation, in the greengroceries at Mutley and West Park, of display cabinets for frozen foods.

Clarence Birdseye's pioneering frozen food lines had taken off in America in the 1930s (although Birdseye had sold his interest back in 1924 for $22 million). And although Smedley had started the ball rolling over here before the war, it was Birds Eye products that the Society first introduced the Plymouth consumers to, as frozen fruit, fish and vegetables went on sale at Mutley and West Park in the summer of 1955.

Yet another initiative taken by the Society around this time, was the establishment of a 'Do It Yourself' shop at the rear of their hardware store in St Budeaux. The DIY phenomenon was very much in its infancy in the fifties, although clearly people had been painting, decorating and repairing things themselves for a very long time. This was probably the first designated DIY store in the area, although it's unlikely that many people then referred to it by the DIY acronym.

On a smaller scale another new move saw the installation of an externally mounted cigarette machine on the wall outside the Royal Parade tobacco outlet. Another, although somewhat different, external arrangement was the construction of a small kiosk (with telephone link to the travel office) at the City's temporary bus station in Station Road, off Union Street.

The situation had been occasioned by the work that was being carried out in Raleigh Street (which had previously been used as a pick up and drop off point for coach trips). It was to be a temporary measure as, in April 1958 with the completion of the new bus station at Bretonside, they moved their motor coach booking office there. By that time the Co-operative Travel Service (CTS), a subsidiary of the Co-operative Wholesale Society, had taken over the running of the Society's Travel Office.

Interestingly enough, in October 1955, the Traffic Department adapted one of the Society's motor coaches as a grocery mobile shop - it was to be the first of a series of such conversions.

Conversion and adaptation was a theme throughout the fifties; the success of the self-service butchery experiment at the Jubilee Stores at Peverell led to similar conversions at St Budeaux and Swilly Road in February 1956, while at the same time Edgcumbe Street butchery was closed and the space vacated was taken over by the existing greengrocery there.

Of course one important element in the handling of any type of foodstuff, meat, fish, fruit or veg, was that of hygiene, and on 1 January 1956 the Government issued a set of *New Food Hygiene Regulations*.

'A person engaged in the handling of food shall, whilst so engaged -
• *keep as clean as may be reasonably practical all parts of his person liable to come in contact with the food.*
• *keep any cut or abrasion on any part of the exposed body covered with a suitable waterproof dressing.*
• *refrain from spitting.*
• *refrain from the use of tobacco and snuff while near open food.'*

Happily the Society had been observing these new standards for years and their reputation for food was second to none in the City. Indeed just a few weeks before the Government had put the new regulations into force, the Society had opened their major new food hall on the ground floor part of the phase three development.

Accessed via Raleigh Street and New George Street, it wasn't properly completed until March 1959 when there was a formal opening - an event marked by great rejoicing on the part of City Centre food shoppers and Society members in general. With supermarkets still a thing of the future for the City, this was a major move forward for post-war Plymouth and the Co-operative House Food Hall set the standard for others to follow.

Inside the new Co-operative House Food Hall.

Selection of Fifties' vehicles.

171

Bigger And Better

The decision to name the new central premises Co-operative House, was taken at an interim meeting in 1958 when members also learnt of the Society's acquisition of the interests of the Dartmouth Society, a move which also gave the Society a branch in Kingswear on the other side of the Dart.

Two years earlier, in May 1956, the Society had also secured the transfer of the Cornwood Co-operative Society, interests which now meant the Plymouth Society exerted a considerable influence over south west Devon and south east Cornwall.

However there were still issues within the Plymouth City boundaries. Speaking at the January 1957 interim meeting, at which she stood down from the Presidency in order to gain election to the Committee, Ellen Roberts announced that the City Council had allocated the Society a shop at Congreve Gardens, Chaucer Way, and that further more this would become the Society's twentieth pharmacy. However she then added:

'While we are glad to avail ourselves of this opportunity, your Committee is frankly concerned about the general problem of the shopping services on Plymouth Corporation housing estates, and although we do not underestimate the difficulties of the City Council, we should like to see them so arrange their shopping centres as to provide for the main trades, a choice of service, whether co-operative, multiple, or small trader, to the residents on housing estates.

'At present, we think the shopping centres provided are too small, built at too late a stage in estate development and by no means particularly suitable in shop layout. Frankly, what we should prefer – and many councils are doing this – would be for the council to sell or lease us a suitable plot of land on which to build and equip shops to our own requirements subject, of course, to designs approved by the Council.

'This would relieve them of the burden of capital expenditure, and would, we think, give our members a better service.'

Mrs Roberts finished as tactfully as possible by saying; 'We are more than a little disturbed about the position here.'

A couple of months later, David Moore, who had succeeded Mrs Roberts as President, was able to announce that the City Council had allocated the Society extra accommodation at Honicknowle Green where everything had previously been a little cramped. Furthermore, he announced it was the intention to create a miniature food hall there.

The following year concern was expressed that the Society had not been allocated shops on the Austin Farm estate or at the western end of Whitleigh, however the President expressed pleasure at the Council's decision to reconsider the situation at Southway. It now emerged that when major development did come to be undertaken on that extensive new estate would-be developers would be leased sites rather than the have the Council build shops themselves and try and shoe horn businesses into them.

In the meantime the Society introduced another travelling grocery to serve that area: they now had eight mobile grocery vans in addition to their four travelling butcher's shops.

Walk in mobile Butcher's shop.

Robert Briscoe author of the Centenary History.

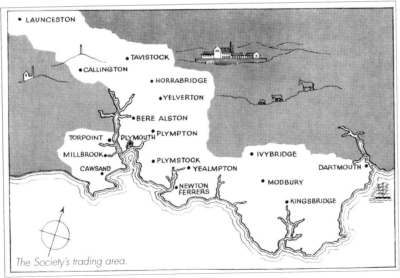

The Society's trading area.

172

End Of An Era

Sadly 1957 was marked by a number of notable deaths within the Society's ranks. In May, Ellen Roberts, who had only recently stepped down as President in order to take a more active role on the Committee, passed away peacefully in her sleep; the following month Albert Webb, nephew of John (a founder member and the Society's first historian), died at the age of 94; in August, Kate Sansom, daughter of the Society's first General Manager and an active Education Committee member from 1899-1938, passed on aged 95; another senior figure, a former President, known also as Uncle Jim (he wrote a history of the Society for younger members) was William James Gilbert who died aged 90. Most tragic and unexpected of all however was the sudden death, in October, of the Society's General Secretary and Chief Executive Officer, Herbert Twigg.

Twigg, who was just 57, had been appointed to his high office in 1941 and had been active within the Co-operative Movement since he was in his teens. As an economist he was head and shoulders above most of his contemporaries and his death was not only a great loss to Plymouth but to the Movement as a whole. It also meant that Twigg was not able to see the completion of Co-operative House, a project he had been so closely involved with since the dark days of the war.

In the event, Twigg was succeeded by Alan Wright, who had been the Society's accountant, and throughout the following year, 1958, there was a gradual move into the new building as different floors became available. By September the furnishing department was in complete occupation of the second floor and the admin and accounting offices had moved onto the third floor (the 'temporary' home at Thorn Park was sold in November).

There was increased satisfaction across the board as each new phase of Co-operative House was completed, although there was a degree of disappointment with regard to the large meeting hall. Intended to be a part of phase four, this was axed on the grounds that building costs had steadily been escalating. Doubtless the fact that attendance figures at meetings was, at the same time, decreasing, played some part in the decision, while on a happier note, the new boardroom and sub-committee meeting rooms all came into service in April 1959. After eighteen years of making do, at last the Society had a room worthy of entertaining distinguished guests.

Sitting around the new table at those early meetings in the new premises everything looked quite rosy, as the Committee inspected their 1959 Balance Sheet, which concluded 100 years of trading in the area. Sales were nudging £7.5 million, having increased around 5% on the previous year and membership was not far off the six-figure landmark at 97,577.

The dividend had been held firm at 9d, but the sums would have been better still had it not been for Finance Act of 1958. Nationally there was much disquiet at the Government's intention to increase Co-operative Societies' tax liabilities, under profits tax, from 3% to 10%, while at the same time relieving private traders of profits tax to the tune of £16 million. The gesture prompted the familiar rallying cry for the Co-operative Movement to sponsor their own representatives in Parliament.

Locally, meanwhile, there was the question of the centenary and how to celebrate it. The Society had appointed a specialist Publicity Manager, Geoff Bradford, at the end of 1958, his brief – to plan and co-ordinate events and publicity programmes – and now they were not only about to complete their grand new central premises, but they were about to enjoy one of the best excuses to celebrate that any business can hope for: one hundred years of unbroken and ever-expanding service to the community.

A Centenary Sub-Committee was appointed to oversee the programme and the Education Secretary, Robert Briscoe, was charged with writing a Centenary History. Meanwhile a major sale was scheduled to kick off the big year on Friday, 1 January. It proved to be the Society's most successful January Sale ever, with the queue stretching around from the front door on Royal Parade right into Raleigh Street. On the same day the *Western Evening Herald* published a four-page supplement of centenary congratulations from local civic heads and well-known personalities in the wider Co-operative Movement.

Herbert Twigg 1900-1957 General Secretary and Chief Executive Officer of the Plymouth Society 1941-1957 National Congress President 1954.

Co-operative House soon after opening, note the Co-op van, in the green and yellow livery, at the roundabout end of Raleigh Street.

CHAPTER 10: THE SWINGING SIXTIES: HIGHS AND LOWS

11 January 1960 saw the Lord Mayor, Percy Washbourn, opened the new Restaurant and Cafeteria in Co-operative House. Situated on the third floor overlooking Royal Parade, it was christened the Dolphin Restaurant and very quickly established itself as a premier centre for lunches and teas, as well as a first choice venue for evening functions. It also become the preferred location for members' meetings - the first being held on 26 April, 100 years after the Plymouth Pioneers had discussed their first ever quarterly balance sheet.

A service had been held in the newly restored St Andrew's Church on the actual day the Society celebrated its centenary. Despite disappointing weather, over a thousand members and employees had attended and the bells of Plymouth's mother church were rung in celebration.

A week or two later an Employees' Centenary Ball was held in the Guildhall, the restoration of which had even more recently been completed. Over 750 employees and friends attended and Patricia Luton was crowned Centenary Beauty Queen by the President, David Moore. Wendy Shiner and Mrs Pamela Hughes were designated as her attendants and the three were scheduled to appear at various events throughout the year.

An invitation to members with more than fifty years' continuous membership brought forth Miss E Shilson of Peverell, the great-grand-daughter of John Slade who had been allocated share No.4 one 100 years earlier. Mrs Blanche Scott also got in touch. She was the grand-daughter of Charles Goodanew (share No.1) and niece of Thomas Reynolds (No.3). All in all over 1,000 members attained the 50-year membership criterion and most attended one of four evening celebrations in June.

Society President David Moore crowns Patricia Luton Centenary Beauty Queen.

Alan Wright, the new CEO.

On the last night, the guests included pensioned employees and retired officers and, as each guest left the Guildhall, they were given a copy of Mr Briscoe's book 'The Story of the Plymouth Co-operative Society 1860-1960', as well as a chromium-plated tea caddy decorated with engravings depicting the old and new Central Premises.

Just a few weeks earlier, the biggest event of the year saw 1,200 delegates attend the four-day Women's Guild National Congress in the Guildhall. This was the first major congress to be held in the venue since its rebuilding and was adjudged a great success. Lord Mayor, Percy Washbourn, gave a civic reception there on the first day: on the following night the Society hosted a reception for international delegates: Wednesday saw a concert from the choral society and girls' choir: while on the Thursday the Western College Players gave a performance of *Come Back Peter*.

In July, International Co-operative Day was marked by a sports and social day at Unity Park at which Mr WP Watkins, Director of the International Co-operative Alliance and the son of a former President of the Plymouth Society, gave an inspiring address. He also warmly congratulated the Society on its centenary and the progress it had made.

Certainly the Society appeared now to be in a particularly strong position, Co-operative House dominated the western end of Royal Parade and every other picture postcard of the City seemed to feature that view looking from just west of the new Central Premises, up Royal Parade to the National Westminster Bank building at the eastern end of this bold new thoroughfare – a thoroughfare that was invariably lined with bright red shiny buses. Plymouth had the most modern shopping centre in the west and the Co-op was a very major part of it.

Far left, top and bottom: two of the original, in store, murals. Middle and right: the Account Office.

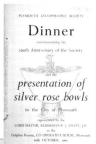

As the City looked forward to a more settled future with most of the major pre-war players now re-housed in the new bright City Centre, so the Society eased back into a central position, both geographically and economically.

They had come a long way from the opening of that first little shop in Catte Street a hundred years earlier. Growth, spectacular at first, had been an ever-consistent aspect of successive balance sheets as the Society had gone on to dominate the retail scene locally and nationally. However, latterly they had been facing increasing competition from the multiples, the chain store companies, and private operators who had been taking a keen interest in the Co-operative Movement: how it bought, sold and promoted itself. There were plenty of lessons to be learnt, but, despite a healthy and enthusiastic Education Department, it seems that other organisations were adapting to the post-war world more effectively than the dear old Co-op.

Top left: looking out from the third floor towards the Drake Cinema. Centre: President Moore and his wife with Lord Mayor Stott and the Lady Mayoress at the presentation of silver rose bowls at the dinner to commemorate the Society's centenary.

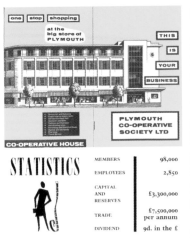

STATISTICS

MEMBERS		98,000
EMPLOYEES		2,850
CAPITAL AND RESERVES		£3,300,000
TRADE		£7,500,000 per annum
DIVIDEND		9d. in the £

Promotional booklet and Service Card indicator, and statistics produced for the Centenary Celebrations.

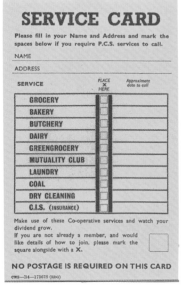

Competition Time

It wasn't just the large multiple retailers that were taking notes, as many of the small independent retailers started talking to each other, 'co-operating' even.

The larger retail chains were, by now, in a position to start flexing their corporate muscle and dictating terms to manufacturers. Previously the balance of power had been the other way round, manufacturers had produced goods at a certain price and had insisted that their 'manufacturers' recommended price' be observed by all. Now the retailers were saying they wanted a better price, and the bigger the retailer the better the deal they expected.

From the manufacturers' perspective this wasn't all bad, as now their ability to mass produce a consistent product was greater than ever before and the large multiples offered them a guaranteed market. The solution for the smaller independents was to form a loose co-operative where they would support a local wholesaler who would not only warehouse the leading product lines, but would also provide point of sale material and offer help and advice with respect to the layout and design, the fixtures and fittings of shops.

Like the Co-op, these wholesalers tended not to operate on a credit basis and locally the phenomenon would make a millionaire of the City's first 'cash and carry' man, Robert Daniel. It was also destined to create competition for the Co-op's smaller stores at the same time as the larger multiples were creating problems for the Movement's larger stores.

Nationally, the British Co-operative Movement had almost ground to a halt, in terms of overall growth, by the end of the 1950s. The bottom line statistics were undoubtedly impressive – over twelve million members, around a billion pound turnover and over 30,000 shops. Furthermore, with its 250 factories it was still the largest wholesaler in the country.

The Co-op could also be said to be leading the way towards the future of retailing. Over 60% of the nation's self-service stores were Co-op stores – and it was in the process of building some of the most state-of-the-art department stores yet to be seen – with Plymouth a shining example.

However, although the Co-op's share of the retail market was around 11% the multiples now controlled twice that – an increase of around 20% since the war, a figure that contrasted starkly with the corresponding 3% growth of the Co-op in the same period.

Even more worrying was the slight drop in the market share of clothing and footwear, and food and household goods, and this at a time when retail price maintenance was still in operation and members could get a dividend on all their purchases.

In Plymouth these concerns had to some extent been allayed by the post-war situation. As the new estates had sprung up all around the northern boundaries of the city, so the Society had managed to tap into the new markets with fixed and mobile outlets. Inevitably, however, this was bound to be partly at the expense of the volume of trade at those surviving pre-war outlets.

Another element in the equation was the ever-increasing use being made by housewives, particularly on the estates badly catered for by public transport, of the 'home shopping' service offered by the various mail order catalogue companies like Littlewoods, Freemans, Grattans and Kays. All of them had been around before the war, but now, with notably more women at work, they enjoyed even greater success.

There was every opportunity for the Co-op to compete in this market, but the individual retail societies did not give the CWS initiative enough support to make it viable. Nor were they prepared to let the CWS take on the 'bazaar' traders like Woolworths, for fear of it affecting their own retail set-ups. However, therein lay part of the problem facing the Co-operative Movement overall, there were perhaps too many independent Co-operative retail societies – over a thousand of them across the country. Given that many of these were also rather small, the situation begged further questions about the long-term viability of such operations.

Not surprisingly, given the level of concern about these various issues there were a number of in-depth investigations into the health and well-being of the Movement in the fifties and early sixties, the most significant of which was produced by a committee set up under the then deputy leader of the Labour Party, Hugh Gaitskell in 1955 (he would become Labour leader before the year was out). With another prominent Labour politician, Tony Crossland, as the Committee's secretary and a distinguished array of the best Co-operative retailing analysts of the time, the Committee put the Movement under the microscope.

Their findings were to have lasting repercussions nationally and locally and affected all aspects of the Society's business.

The south west was adjudged to not have enough grocery stores (while there were too many up north), there was also a perceived shortage of greengrocery stores and those selling wine and fish.

Non-food lines were a weakness all over the country, as was the quality of the shops themselves, although Plymouth, with so many new outlets, was something of an exception. However it was still felt that too much of the Co-op's considerable assets were tied up in investments – many of them outside the Movement – and therefore it might be time to unlock some funding and give some of the dowdier stores a facelift.

While the cosy, old Co-op image might suit the country store, there was a definite need to embrace the brighter, brasher, cleaner image that so many of the self-service stores were adopting. It was also felt that this move might appeal to the younger customer.

An undoubted feature of the fifties was the emergence of the teenager. A whole new market was opening up to relieve this generation of its newly found spending power. This was especially obvious in non-food areas like women's clothing and children's wear, where, traditionally the Co-operative was considered conservative, old-fashioned and not at all rock'n'roll.

Of course one of the main reasons for this was the management structure across the Movement. Some Societies had overly intrusive committees, others had committees that stood back too far. What was needed was a committee that concentrated on its main business, principal policy decisions, liaising with the membership and managerial appointments.

Although herein was another problem. Following the raising of the school

leaving age and the opening up of grammar schools after the war a lot of the more promising working class youngsters, who previously may have been picked up by the Movement's educational system, were now opting to stay on and perhaps even go to college. This left those who may not have been quite as dynamic, but nevertheless keen to get themselves a relatively prestigious job-for-life (which is how Co-op appointments were often perceived - even though the salaries were generally a little lower than those on offer in the private sector).

However, the most crucial issue of all raised by the Committee was a simple one ... why are there so many Societies?

A thousand organisations under one umbrella resulted in the duplication of resources on a grand scale, particularly with regard to warehousing, specialist staff and office space. This meant that the transport infrastructure was inevitably less efficient than it needed to be. It also meant that the Movement's considerable capital was spread right across the country, with some Societies sitting on sums they had no immediate use for, while others, who were in desperate need of re-investment, didn't have the wherewithal to do anything about it.

Looking at the food-based multiples around at the time they found that almost three-quarters of them had more than 50 branches each, while among the Co-operative Societies only about a third had that number. Applying the same criterion to the non-food stores, the contrast was even greater and the conclusion reached by the Commission was that the Movement would need to set up national specialist chains. One Committee member even produced a report suggesting a national Society (echoing an idea first put forward fifty years earlier but never taken seriously), however the agreed recommendation was that each Society should at least have 15 grocery stores, a proposal that would, in effect, reduce the number of societies from around a thousand to just two or three hundred.

They also proposed a national footwear and clothing chain (similar to the National Co-operative Chemist arrangement) and the setting up of a new national federation, a Co-operative Retail Development Society, that would pool the Movement's vast experience and have control over the Society's surpluses, allowing them to underwrite new development. It was estimated that the Movement as a whole had around 100 million pounds

Top: Scene from the Bakery and, Middle; Inside the Dairy, both from the Centenary booklet. Below: Brochure celebrating the opening of Co-operative House.

One-stop shopping saves time and energy . . . come Co-operative Shopping at the Big Store of Plymouth where everything you require is under one roof.

CO-OPERATIVE HOUSE

DERRY'S CROSS PLYMOUTH
TELEPHONE 62800
PLYMOUTH CO-OPERATIVE SOCIETY LIMITED

Christmas at Co-operative House

at its disposal across all its societies, with more tied up in the undervalued assets of the CWS.

Significantly, the CWS also came in for scrutiny: here the Commission recommended that the wholesale societies should focus on supplying the retail societies with goods, wherever they came from, rather than producing to supply. Then, if the CWS factories survived on their own merits, fine, if not - move on.

The Commission also said that the wholesale societies should be freed from some of the excesses of democracy - yes there should be a board, but it should be part-time, not full-time, bigger if necessary, but either way managers should be given more authority to actually manage.

Overall the conclusion was that the Co-operative Movement wasn't making the most of itself. It had vast capital resources it could call on to help it compete in the modern world, but didn't seem in a hurry to do so. Indeed they were only re-investing around 3% of their surpluses each year, compared to the 37% of their rivals. Over and above that of course, they were sitting on a fortune at the same time as they were gradually falling behind the competition:

'Between 1957 and 1961 retail trade increased by 15%, but the Movement only grew by 7%. Most of the increase was taken by the multiples, which grew by a staggering 29%, and the department stores, which grew by 16%, but even the independent shopkeepers recorded growth of 11%' (Birchall).

This was a boom time: *'Indeed, let us be frank about it - most of our people have never had it so good,'* said Prime Minister, Harold Macmillan at a Conservative rally in July 1957.

'Go around the country, go to the industrial towns, go to the farms and you will see a state of prosperity such as we have never had in my lifetime - nor indeed in the history of this country.'

The Co-op were not exactly lost, but they were losing out – something had to be done.

Happily it seemed as though there was a genuine appetite for change: the special congress convened to discuss the report voted to accept almost all of the recommendations, however, without the mechanism in place to effect change at local level, it seemed that evolution rather than revolution was in the air.

Plymouth Grasps The Nettle

Because of Plymouth's somewhat unusual post-war situation the Society here had already been investing more heavily in bright new stores than many of its counterparts across the country. Indeed the level of investment was something of a concern in itself.

With the final phase (phase four) of Co-operative House, under way, in the City Centre there were celebrations out of town, in Plymstock in October 1960 when four ground floor units were opened on the Broadway - the new shopping centre built to support the new houses being built in that area.

Just a few weeks earlier, however, the footwear shop in Morice Street and the Embankment Road greengrocery had been shut as a massive process of rationalisation was started.

In the wake of the closure of the Preserve Factory at Peverell in 1959, the Society's confectionery stores suddenly started to look particularly vulnerable. The Torpoint confectionery was the first to close, it went the following March, 1960. During 1961 a further six confectionery stores were axed: Cattedown Road, Peverell Park Road, Fleet Street, Albert Road, Camel's Head, and Union Street.

Meanwhile, underlining the Committee's finding on footwear outlets, the Plymouth Society closed four footwear stores and, at the same time, they became a shareholder member of Society Footwear Ltd, henceforth to be known as Shoe Fayre Ltd.

After 100 years of steady expansion, such closures seemed an odd way to be moving forward, however with the opening up of the whole of Co-operative House, and the escalating conversion to self-service across the Society's stores, such measures were entirely appropriate, particularly in the light of the Commission's observations on the Movement's national position.

All in all, the Society closed twenty outlets locally in 1961, among them the three properties in York Street which were compulsorily purchased by the Local Authority as part of the City Centre redevelopment, and properties in St Budeaux that were similarly acquired by the Council as part of their drive to improve the approach road to the new Tamar Road Bridge.

There were five further closures in 1962, and six in 1963, and thereafter throughout the rest of the decade there were never fewer than seven each year, with more than 50 stores across the Society's patch being shut down during that period.

The Society also sold their Motor Coach business in December 1961 (to the Embankment Motor Company) and March 1962, the bakery at Peverell, together with all of the door-to-door rounds, was transferred to the Bakery Division of the Co-operative Wholesale Society, where it stood more chance of competing with the large bakery factories that were now gaining ground in the private sector.

The rationalisation process did not just spell sell-offs and closures, however, and that same month, March 1962, the Society purchased three properties in Gilwell Street with a view to a major redevelopment of the Radnor Dairy.

Two years later the closures at St Budeaux were more than adequately compensated for by the opening of Tamar House, the Society's new department store for the area. With foodhall and off-licence on the ground floor and fashions, footwear, children's wear, furnishing and ladies hairdressing on the first floor, this was a major step forward for shopping in St Budeaux and a special two weeks' worth of 'double divi' heralded the opening.

Earlier, in 1962, the Society had opened the first-ever supermarket in Dartmouth, meanwhile, again in line with the suggestions from the Commission, the Society sought and were granted permission for off-licences in Yelverton, Callington, Newton Ferrers, and Plympton.

Top: Tamar House, St Budeaux. Above: One of the Society's new off licences.

Co-op Dolphin Restaurant.

Other initiatives indicating that the Commission report was being taken seriously included the modernisation of several stores, the scrapping of the practice of printing General Committee Minutes for approval at the Quarterly Members Meetings (from January 1963) and the abolition of the Sub-Committees system (as of 1 April 1963).

Meanwhile closer examination of the viability of certain aspects of the Society's trading led to the removal of the Traffic Department, in its entirety, from Billacombe to the recently vacated premises at Peverell. The Billacombe site was sold to Albany Meat Products in the summer of 1963 for £61,500.

Around the same time, the sale of Netton, Caulston and Lambside Farms added a further £120,000 to the year-end surplus. This wasn't a one way land slide, however, and in May 1964, £35,000 was spent on buying land, with planning for 70 houses, at Dudley Road, Plympton.

The anticipation was that each house would yield a net profit of £370 and

that dividend would be paid on the selling price minus the £500 per site for the land. The work was to be a major project for the Building Department. Interestingly enough, this announcement came hot on the heels of the dismissal of the Building Department's manager, which in turn followed a review of the senior management by a firm of outside consultants.

The Society's newly appointed accountant, Victor Barton, filled the post until a successor was appointed at the beginning of 1964. By the end of the year seventy of the houses had been built to roof level, and twenty of them had been sold. In December 1965 it was announced that all seventy-two properties had been sold. However, when the year-end figures were published it emerged that on this and on other smaller building projects (Chesterfield Road, Laira: Lancaster Gardens, Whitleigh: Kingsbridge and Bere Alston) the department had made a loss of £98,000.

'There is no doubt that the Society, in the space of about two years, had rushed into an activity which it was not capable of properly managing,' observed Barton.

Above: Dairy Service Commer van.
Below: Mobile Grocery Unit.

Building work well under way at Dudley Road.

The whole affair was vaguely reminiscent of the Society's first foray into the house building market, only on a much larger scale.

However, planning permission to build houses on land at Poole Farm was applied for at the beginning of 1964, although most of the land was subsequently sold for housing development, it was not carried out by the Building Department.

Nevertheless, early in 1965 a wholly owned company called Buttland Properties Ltd. was acquired and into it the value of the land north of Federation Road, Laira, was transferred. In May a parcel of land at Kingsbridge was also purchased and added to the Buttland Properties portfolio and the Society's house building programme.

Out Of Town Developments

Meanwhile at the end of May 1965 the Dartmouth Advisory Committee was disbanded, just as the Plympton Advisory Body had been a few years earlier. Initially it had been the intention for these Committees to replace the respective boards at Plympton and Dartmouth before they transferred their interests into the Plymouth Society. As time passed, however, they were seen as more of a hindrance and in a climate where the Co-op was looking to move on, they were superfluous.

Similar logic, but in a different context, was applied to the situation in Launceston in September 1962. The Plymouth Society had introduced Co-operation into that area during the war, however the CRS (Co-operative Retail Services) had blossomed throughout most of Cornwall and it was deemed that the framework would be better served if the Launceston grocery, butchery, furnishing and tailoring stores were transferred to the CRS Cornwall Group.

To the east of Plymouth on the other hand, the Torquay Society had been struggling for sometime when, in 1966, the members there 'sensibly chose Plymouth' (Barton), when faced with the dilemma of whether to throw their hand in with Plymouth or the CRS. Faced with competition from holiday camps, like Butlins and Pontins and cheap foreign package holidays, Torquay generally had been facing difficult times and it did indeed make sense for their Co-op to become part of a bigger organisation.

There was also talk of Newton Abbot and Paignton coming under the Plymouth umbrella, and despite a degree of hesitancy, they both did, before the decade was out.

In the event, it was the Finance Act of 1965 that actually precipitated the process. Under the terms of the Act, Corporation Tax was introduced for Companies and Co-operative Societies in place of Income Tax, furthermore, under Section 87 of the Act, cessation relief was allowed if a company ceased business before 1970.

Thus it was that, in early 1969, the Newton Abbot Society, along with those of Buckfastleigh, Paignton *and* Plymouth, all prepared to wind themselves up before the year was out. A scheme was hatched whereby the old Societies would cease to exist, but a new one would take over. However, this would only work provided that the new company was more than 75% different in its make up from the old one. The problem being that Plymouth's stake in the equation was 81%. This was ingeniously solved by Plymouth investing £500,000 in the CWS and the CWS in turn, investing £500,000 in the new company.

Thus it was that, technically, on 31 March 1969, the Plymouth Co-operative Society ceased to exist, after 110 years of trading. However on that same day a new organisation came into being - the Plymouth and South Devon Co-operative Society. Most members would not have been particularly aware of the change, however this little technicality was to secure the Society a refund not far short of £150,000 - well worth the exercise.

The bottom line in all this meant that, with the 53-year-old Tavistock Society also pooling their resources with Plymouth (in October 1967), the new Plymouth and South Devon Society had a membership of 143,316, property worth nearly £3 million, capital of over £4 million, reserve funds of over a million and another million and half pounds worth of investments.

It also meant that the Society had ticked another box on Regional Plan No.43, cutting down on the number of individual societies, furthermore it meant that the Society was well placed to participate in the a nationally driven period of re-investment and modernisation, one of the most conspicuous signs of which was the new national logo which made its debut in 1968 and was fully supported by the Plymouth Society.

Top: Early 1968 advert with logo. Bottom: The all-new logo at revamped Albert Road.

STAFF
TRAINING and EDUCATION 1967-1968

PERSONNEL DEPARTMENT, PLYMOUTH CO-OPERATIVE SOCIETY LIMITED

THIRD FLOOR, CO-OPERATIVE HOUSE, DERRY'S CROSS, PLYMOUTH Tel. 62390.

PLYMOUTH CO-OPERATIVE
SOCIETY LIMITED
STAFF TRAINING
COUNCIL
1967-1968

Message from
ALAN WRIGHT

*General Secretary and
Chief Executive Officer*

It is perhaps more true to day than ever before that success requires practical experience to be backed up by a sound theoretical training.

Throughout the Society and the whole of the Co-operative Movement, there is an increasing number of opportunities for the well qualified man and woman. The Society will provide every encouragement and opportunity for you to obtain these qualifications if you, for your part, are prepared to make the effort.

Complete and return the application form to the Personnel Department, which will be pleased to assist in any enquiries.

QUALIFICATIONS COUNT!

The Board of Directors has gone on record :-
"In making appointments and promotions, preference will be given, other things being equal, to candidates holding the appropriate educational certificates and diplomas of the Co-operative Union Ltd."

Top: April 1966 inside Plym House; Middle: An edition of the Staff newsletter from 1968. Above: A contemporary advertisement.

April 1966, Plym House, Plymstock Broadway opens for business.

A New Look

Prior to the arrival of the new national logo, the Society, locally, had, a year or two earlier, gone with a family-orientated visual device showing a mother and a father figure with a small child. It appeared on all of their revamped shop fronts and took centre stage of the new supermarket opened on Plymstock Broadway in April 1966.

A huge queue assembled for the opening of Plym House, as it was christened, and in addition to the grocer's, butcher's, off licence, pharmacy and greengrocery supermarket on the ground floor, there were also ladies hairdressing, clothing, household goods, a restaurant, bar and laundry facilities on the first floor. Once again the move represented a major boost for Plymstock, which was then in its last year as an independent community - the Plymouth boundaries would be extended in 1967 to encompass both Plymstock and Plympton.

Clearly the move also prompted the closure of the Co-operative shop units opened earlier on the other side of the Broadway, but there were no complaints from the customers, only from the management, who soon found that trade in the menswear and drapery sections of the clothing department was not sufficient to justify the floor space allocated to them. So it was that within two years they were removed and in their place what proved to be a highly successful frozen food department, appeared.

There could be no doubt about it, the Society was attempting to shake off its fuddy duddy image and swing with the times. Just as Plym House was opening its doors on the Broadway so the city centre store opened its doors to a new first floor boutique - a 'Young Ideas' section complete with dimmed lights and appropriate background music. The 'mod' culture, with its dedicated followers of fashion, had even managed to penetrate the corporate psyche of Co-operative House.

It was a good time to call time on old technology too, and that same year, 1966, saw the removal from the premises of the old Lamson Paragon Vacuum Suction System, that fondly remembered cash handling process that saw sales assistants put cash and a bill in a small container which would then be wooshed up to the central cash office on the third floor and then wooshed back down again with the appropriate change.

Left: Plymstock Broadway and the well-lit Plym House. Above: Ad, logo and wrapper from the late-sixties.

The times certainly were a-changing and better monitoring of their sales and service allowed the Society to make ever more prudent decisions. To wit, when it became apparent that the number of prescriptions dispensed in certain pharmacies was falling below the level at which it was deemed viable to trade, it was considered that over-the-counter sales might still make the operation worthwhile. So it was that late in 1965 the Society decided to form a wholly owned subsidiary company the 'Plymouth Co-operative Drug Stores Ltd' with a view to retailing non-drug pharmaceutical product lines.

The pharmacy at Torridge Way, Efford, became the first to be transferred to the new company, in December 1965, and was followed, within a few weeks, by the pharmacy in Beaumont Road. In March 1966, the Millbridge facility was similarly converted as the move gained momentum.

Meanwhile the pharmacy at Crownhill, along with the butcher's, was compulsorily purchased by the Local Authority, in advance of their plans to widen the road there, facilitating the creation of a new dual carriageway and flyover just behind the main shopping thoroughfare.

Another closure, again in line with what was happening nationally, spelt the end of the Society's footwear repair factories both in Seymour Road, Plymouth and in Union Street, Torquay. With the mass production of more affordable footwear generally, fewer and fewer people were taking shoes in for repair. Given that six of the original Plymouth pioneers were involved in the trade it very much heralded the end of an era.

The new cash register.

It was the end of an era as in its place the Society installed fifty Hugin cash registers at a cost of some £14,000 - not a decision to be taken lightly, but necessary if the Society was going to keep pace with the private sector.

It was to this end too, that, in March 1968, the Society's Accounts Department started down the path of computerisation. At that point in time it meant that data in Plymouth was punched onto magnetic tape and then taken up to CWS Computer Bureau at Nuneaton, where it was processed and sent back to Plymouth as hard copy. Shortly afterwards a Data Processing Officer was appointed in Plymouth and within a year the Society began to think in terms of establishing its own Computer Department.

Marking the end of a life with dignity, meanwhile was certainly providing the Society's funeral business with opportunities for growth and in the summer of 1968 five new Chapels of Repose were dedicated.

Above left: Mutley Pharmacy.
Right: The Chapel of Repose at St Budeaux.

However, perhaps the change in the public's perception of the Society during the sixties was the espousal of the modernisation process and the adoption of that new national logo.

Nowhere in Plymouth was that more simply or dramatically illustrated than at Jubilee Stores at the top of Peverell Park Road. Here there had been little change to the external appearance of the block since it had been erected 58 years earlier, indeed the sign above the shop fronts still read 'Plymouth Mutual Co-operative and Industrial Society Limited'.

Now, as of 10 May 1968, that had all gone, or at least been covered over, as clean white cladding disguised the surviving Edwardian features (although clearly some had been removed altogether) and the only wording that adorned this display was the striking blue and white 'Co-op' logo.

Clear and simple, it reflected the popular perception of the Society, for just about everyone called it the 'Co-op' anyway – or rather, in Plymouth, the 'cwop' – and only the most committed and conservative committee men – and women – would have called it the Plymouth and South Devon Co-operative Society.

It also conferred upon the Society an image and a title more in line with its supermarket rivals like Asda and Tesco (both of which, incidentally, like Morrisons had opened their first supermarkets in converted cinemas). Furthermore, although the Plymouth & SDCS was still very much an independent Society, the national branding gave the Co-op all sorts of opportunities for marketing itself on a much bigger scale.

Above: The revamped Co-op at Laira. All the other images show Jubilee Stores Peverell, before and after their makeover.

The new corporate Co-op logo flies high above Co-operative House

CHAPTER 11: THE SUPERSIZE SEVENTIES & EIGHTIES

The new logo was perhaps the most obvious indication that the Plymouth and South Devon Co-operative Society Limited was buying into the national movement's branding initiative, but it was by no means the only one.

In February 1970 the Society joined the National Dividend Stamp Scheme, a project that had been introduced by the Co-operative Wholesale Society nearly two years earlier (around the time that the new logo was unveiled), and which, so far, had met with great success among those retail societies that had already bought into it.

For the traditionalists it meant the end of the long-standing cash 'divi', which had been the main magnet for members since the Rochdale Pioneers had first come up with the idea back in 1844. However, the 'divi' had for some years been a disappointing 6d in the pound and looked set to fall further and the new system was altogether more instantly appealing to the customer, as both members and non-members could actually watch their dividend grow with the licking and sticking of their pale blue stamps. It also meant significantly less work for head office staff, allowing savings to be made there.

Stamps were issued to shoppers at the rate of two stamps for each shilling spent in store and completed books initially had a cash value of ten shillings … for members - and eight shillings for non-members. Some members with low share balances closed their accounts in protest, but the vast majority

were very happy with the new arrangement and the additional trade that the stamps encouraged more than made up for the deserters.

As a promotional tool it worked particularly well for the Society as it created the potential for 'double' and 'treble' stamp offers. However, although this was a CWS initiative nationally, the idea of stamps had been brought into the country by London printer Richard Tompkins who, when holidaying in Chicago, noticed how popular S&H Green Stamps were in stores over there.

In 1958 he started up his own Green Shield Stamp business in this country and five years later Tesco's founder Jack Cohen bought into the idea. Cohen had been spurred on by Fine Fare's decision to offer S&H Pink Stamps (Tompkins had shrewdly bought the name Green Shield from a luggage manufacturer and so was able to pinch the idea and colour of the stamps for launch in the UK before S&H tried breaking into the British market). S&H, named after their founders Sperry and Hutchinson, had already been going for over 60 years before Tompkins transported the concept across the Atlantic.

Observing the success that their retailing rivals were having with this marketing device, it was only a matter of time before the Co-op realised that the tool was tailor-made for their dividend scheme and made a move to grab a piece of the action for themselves.

Co-op stamp book and a 1970s promotion: 'Give your spare stamps to charity'

'Old Pence New Pence Co-op Shopping Makes Sense' - 15 Febrauary 1971 - Brtiain goes decimal.

Exactly twelve months on from the introduction of stamps to Plymouth Co-operatives an even bigger revolution took place, one that many consumers thought that retailers would exploit by putting prices up. However, the Co-op, across the board, were keen to ensure that that didn't happen.

'D' Day was 15 February 1971, as Britain turned its back on the old pounds, shillings and pence and went decimal. Under the terms of the 1969 Decimal Currency Act, the old currency, with 240 rather large pennies to the pound ceased to be legal tender, and in their place we had 100 rather smaller pennies to the pound.

Some of the old coinage had already been demonetised: the ha'penny had gone on 1 August 1969: the brown ten shilling note had gone two months later and in January 1970 the clunky old half-crown had followed suit (although none had been produced after 1967). From 'D' Day onwards, we also lost that big penny, the threepenny bit and the sixpenny piece.

Meanwhile, as of that auspicious day, we now had a new half-penny, one-pence piece and a two-pence coin. A new five-pence coin, superseded the shilling, although it was the same size and weight and the shilling was allowed to remain in circulation until 1990 – as indeed was the florin, or two-shilling coin which was of identical dimensions to the new ten-pence coin. This meant that there was no immediate need to change thousands of slot machines – especially parking meters. Incidentally, after 1990 both the 5p and 10p coins were significantly reduced in size.

There was one other decimal coin around at that time, the 50p piece, but this had already been in circulation for a year or two, having been first issued when the ten-bob note (ten shilling or 10/- note) was withdrawn. Again the original coin was heavier than its modern counterpart – it was trimmed and slimmed in 1997.

It was estimated that the cost of the change-over programme including: staff training, customer assistance, cost of conversion, change of office systems, payroll and other miscellaneous items - would be in the region of £20,000. Added to this was the capital cost involved in introducing new cash tills, automatic scales, and office machinery. The Society also purchased two Burroughs E4000 visible record computers and, three weeks prior to the event, sent an 'education vehicle' around Plymouth, Torquay and Tavistock. The vehicle attracted nearly a thousand shoppers and a great deal of publicity!

Top: another D-Day window at Co-operative House. Above and Below: the old money.

Top: Pre-decimal prices. Bottom: New p-p-pence P-P-Penguins.

A selection of branded Co-op vehicles.

The other major event at the dawn of the new decade was that the final piece of the Regional Plan 43 (that bit that concerned Plymouth and South Devon) was formally put in place, with the merger of the Society with Newton Abbot.

For some time this move had been fiercely opposed by the employees of that organisation. Fearful of losing their jobs they packed the meetings and swung the vote against the merger. There was even talk of joining the CRS rather than Plymouth and South Devon, however at a meeting of the Co-operative Union Standing Joint Committee in London, in August 1969, a clear steer was given in favour of the union and, eventually, faced with a shortage of capital and a desperate need to modernise, the members and employees of Newton Abbot gave the proposal the necessary backing.

Thus it was that as of 7 September 1970, with the lone exception of Brixham, the Plymouth and South Devon Co-operative had rationalised its region and was now in the process of rationalising and modernising its considerable number of outlets ... and on 9 January 1971 that meant the closure of ten grocery branches across the patch. It wasn't just the non-food stores that were experiencing difficulties.

Nevertheless, the trading year 1970-71 was to be a good one. Sales were up 12% to a new high of almost £16 million with a trading surplus of £863,000 compared with £465,000 the previous year. There was a £1 bonus for every member's redeemed book of stamps on top of the 50p value of each book - each book incidentally represented £30 worth of purchases on the part of the member. Clearly the dividend stamps were proving to be popular, more popular even than the old cash 'divi'.

The Society had every reason to be pleased with itself and in the Director's Report of December 1971 an appraisal by Britain's largest firm of Management Consultants had this to say:

'Plymouth and South Devon Co-op has an enviable record of profitable growth and is one of the most efficient retail Societies in the country.

'Plymouth has accepted the need for change and faced up to economic facts of life while not forgetting the needs of Co-op members and the human problems that arise from any reorganisation.'

Modernisation was very much the watchword of the early seventies. In 1971 the go ahead was given for the major overhaul of the departmental store in Newton Abbot; the grocery and butchery stores in Buckfastleigh were not only modernised but merged and provided with a food hall and ancillary stores; then, in February 1972, authority for improvements of the grocery stores at Mutley, Crownhill and Yelverton, was granted.

The big project, however, was the one in Newton Abbot and work progressed throughout the year on what was effectively a complete rebuild of the Queen Street premises - with some departments moving out temporarily to neighbouring buildings.

The overall cost of the scheme was eventually well in excess of £500,000, a sum that would have been well beyond the means of the Newton Abbot Society had they not joined in with Plymouth and South Devon. In the event the new store opened on 3 October 1972 and the town was able to celebrate that Christmas with its most modern store to date.

Above and bottom left: The refurbished store in Queen Street, Newton Abbot.

Meanwhile, back in Plymouth, other housekeeping measures were being put in place in the interests of fiscal prudence. A decision was taken to award the hard-pressed Education Department an annual budget based on their projected work, rather than a grant, which could go up or down, based on membership.

It's interesting to note that, as of March 1972, there were seven Junior Pathfinder Groups, seven Senior Groups, one Youth Club and three Woodcraft Folk Groups with a total membership between them of around 300 young people. On the female front, there were still 22 Women's Guild Branches, embracing some 700 members, but enthusiasm was waning. Plymouth No.1 Guild would celebrate its 90th anniversary in 1976, but a splinter group, activated by Lady Astor faltered in the sixties, and in their 1978 report the Education Committee expressed concern at the falling membership of many of the Women's Guild Branches and the high failure rate of new branches. It emerged that of the eight branches formed in recent years only four had survived, three of them Young Women's Guilds.

There were of course so many other activities vying for people's attention, not least of which was the goggle-box, that electronic portal on the world that had now invaded most homes and had recently acquired the added allure of colour (BBC 2 had led the way in Europe from 1967 onwards). With three channels on offer it was proving increasingly difficult to prise people away from their homes in the evening and the Society eventually had to acknowledge this.

In 1971 they formed a partnership with Pearce and Gray, a radio and television servicing business at Alexandra Road, Ford. The new company went under the name of Servatron Limited. At the end of the decade they went a step further, as, in October 1979 the Society opened its first TV Rental Shop in the City Centre, at No.6 Cornwall Street, in the premises formerly occupied by one of their Greengrocery units.

Curiously enough, the following month, November 1979, saw the Education Committee completely reorganised. A Special General Meeting of Members approved a decision that involved changes to six of the registered rules and the Education Committee henceforth became known as the Members Relations Committee, and the secretary, as the Members Relations Officer.

Top: One of the local Pathfinder Groups Bottom: Lord Mayor's Day float on the Hoe, the Co-op's entry promoting Activities for Young People, with the Girls Choir. Right: The Co-op was always a leading supplier of school uniforms.

Of greater concern however were the disappointing performances of certain stores. Shopping patterns were changing, people were looking more and more for convenience shopping ... and convenience foods ... TV dinners?

The all-in-one, self-service supermarket had firmly established itself and individual grocers, greengrocers and butchers were finding life increasingly difficult. All three were suffering, but the butchers in particular found that the going was getting tough.

In 1973 the grocery at Lipson was closed, as was the butcher's at Yealmpton, while the former butcher's at Crownhill was converted to a hairdressing salon. At the same time five mobile butcher's shops were taken out of service. The Armada Street butcher's was closed the following year, along with a couple of out of town grocer's - at Kingsbridge and Yealmpton. In 1976 two more butchers went, at Laira and in Paignton, as did the Mount Gould Grocery. Then, in 1978, four more of the Society's butchery stores closed: two in Plymouth – Fleet Street and Peverell – one in Buckland and one in Paignton. That year also saw the demise of the Plymouth & South Devon's last five mobile butchers.

Of course there was no single reason for all this: mobile shops had largely run their course, the estates they were introduced to service, now had their own shopping centres and butchers generally were faced with competition from the supermarkets and the freezer centres. The Society's experimental freezer centre on the Plymstock Broadway had been a great success and in 1975 had been extended. At the same time a freezer centre had been opened in Hele Road, Torquay, while later in the year the freezer centre in Ham Drive, Plymouth, was more than doubled in size. Four years later the Society opened another freezer centre in Plympton, on the Ridgeway, but by this stage there had been other significant developments within the P&SD retailing programme.

Clearly the Society had faced some major challenges, but shrewd management had meant there was never any cause for alarm - although the much-publicised failure of the Millom Co-operative Society in Cumbria had ruffled a few feathers – the BBC 'Nationwide' programme had run a feature on it in January 1970 – and the collapse, three years later, of the Belfast Co-operative had also caused a few furrowed brows.

Plymco takes shape at the bottom of the Ridgeway. Top: Fruit and Veg.

Interestingly enough, it was shortly after the Belfast incident that the Society decided to have its premises professionally valued, to see just how much their assets were worth. Messrs Body, Son & Fleury carried out the exercise and came up with a valuation of nearly £8 million, some £5.5 million more than had been estimated in the Balance Sheet.

With such a solid base, the Plymouth story was a happy enough one, which is not to say that it couldn't have been happier still.

Back in 1968 the Society had sought planning permission to build their first out-of-town superstore at Lee Mill, sensing this was the way forward, as had already been demonstrated by other retailing chains. Plymouth City Council, however, turned down the proposal. The Society appealed, and were again rebuffed, but after a second appeal they were granted approval. However, the City Council factored in several conditions and these became the subject of years of protracted negotiation.

The site in question, all six acres of it, was owned by Plympton St Mary Rural District Council and they were prepared to offer a lease to the Society, but only on the basis of five-yearly rent reviews, and given that back then out-of-town shopping centres were in their infancy the Society got cold feet.

Initially they had budgeted around half a million pounds for the project, including £100,000 for the purchase of the land. Now after the passage of time, estimates of expenditure had soared beyond the million mark and that was without ownership of the land. Furthermore there were concerns about staffing the superstore: public services to Lee Mill were poor, and the long opening hours were sure to be considered 'anti-social'. Besides this there was insufficient confidence in the number of customers who would be ready, or able, to jump into a car and venture out to Lee Mill to do their shopping.

Add to this list the facts that Plympton Council refused to allow for any change from retail to industrial use, should the venture not take off and that most food supermarkets were then relatively small by today's standards - and hence expertise on that scale, both in terms of management and buying, was thin on the ground, as was warehousing space. So the decision to pull out, although perhaps overly cautious, was at least understandable. However, the success with which Tesco subsequently picked up the proverbial baton

and ran with it, cast a large 'what if?' over the next few years.

With or without the Superstore at Lee Mill, in July 1974, a 24-page report was presented to the Directors recommending that a 'Food Trade Division' be created to amalgamate the struggling strands of butchery, grocery and greengrocery. The suggestion was that an overall 'Controller' should be appointed to head up the new body.

It was not the first time such an idea had been put to the Board. This was in fact the fourth attempt to promote such a notion, however, despite the support of independent Management Consultants, who endorsed the proposal as part of a long-term strategy for the Society to move into the superstore market, the idea was again rejected.

For the Chief Executive Officer, Alan Wright, this was the final straw. As far as he was concerned the writing on the wall could hardly be clearer – the sooner the Society started to think in terms of food generally and not meat, fruit and veg, and packaged produce as three separate businesses, the better. However, while *there is no doubt that the stubborn attitude of some directors played a part, internal politics also played a role, supported by the butchery and greengrocery departments who sensed a loss of their individual freedom* (Barton).

Wright, who had been with the Society since 1953, and CEO since 1957, tendered his resignation in November and took up a similar role at the more progressive Portsea Island Co-operative. Jack Parsons was appointed as Wright's successor, while Victor Barton was made Assistant General Secretary.

Announcing the changes at the Member's Annual General Meeting a few weeks later, Society President, David Moore, 'appeared his normal self, but inwardly the turmoil and anxiety caused by the change of top management must have been a mental strain. His passing, on 4 January 1975, after a short illness, was unexpected and a shock to the respectful many who knew him and admired him.

George Truscott was subsequently elevated from his Vice-President's role and George Bestier, a Director since 1955 and also a Director of CWS and of Shoe Fayre Ltd., was appointed the new Vice-President.

Dairy brochure, van and another contemporary advertisement.

COME CO·OPERATIVE SHOPPING

For all the family

co·op
Co-operative House
Derry's Cross Plymouth PL1 1HA Telephone : 62800
Plymouth & South Devon Co-operative Society Ltd.

Plymco One

In August 1975, with new personnel at the top the Society, the Committee again considered the recommendation that a Food Controller be appointed: this time, for whatever reasons, they gave it their blessing. Grocery manager Sydney Cole was appointed Food Trades Officer and the butchery manager, Ted Milnes, was appointed Deputy Food Trades Officer:

'And so at long last, the Society had a food managerial structure to take it forward into the large supermarket and superstore era. All it now needed was a food distribution/warehouse centre in place of the outmoded grocery and greengrocery centres at North Quay.'

Twelve months later it was announced that outline planning approval had been obtained for the building of a large supermarket at the bottom end of the Ridgeway, Plympton, together with land for car parking. Plans were also unveiled for a 48,000 sq ft, food distribution centre at Bell Close on the Newnham Industrial Estate.

Work started almost straight away and by the middle of January 1978 the food distribution centre at Newnham was ready for action and six weeks later Plymco One - the Society's first Superstore, began trading.

It was an instant success. Furthermore the car parking gave the whole of the Ridgeway a welcome boost as a shopping centre and the following year the Society bought No.s 29-31 The Ridgeway to open as a Pharmacy. Later that year the aforementioned freezer centre at the bottom of the Ridgeway was opened in the former International Stores shop, and above it, a ladies' hairdressing salon - Melanie - was established.

Meanwhile the opening of the new food distribution centre meant that the post-war, four-storey grocery warehouse on North Quay was now redundant. Although a striking building visually, its four floors made it difficult to service. In the new building everything could be warehoused on one level, albeit with help from mechanically aided pickers - forklifts. The antiquated wooden warehouse that served the greengrocery department in Lower Street, was also now freed up, although the butchery warehouse, for the time being, at least, remained where it was in Recreation Road, Peverell.

Plymco for all the family - but it helps if you've got the flares for shopping.

Plymco 1 opens for business on Plympton's Ridgeway on 7 March 1978

The new Food Distribution Centre at Plympton

Three In One

The long overdue coming together of the butchery, greengrocery and grocery departments soon found other applications across the Plymouth and South Devon region.

In September 1975, after a six month rebuild, the new grocery self-service, incorporating a butchery and off-licence, opened at Eggbuckland Road, Higher Compton. With four times the floor space of its predecessor, and with the bonus of some parking spaces at the rear, it too proved a hit with the local community, the increased sales swiftly justifying the cost of the refurbishments. The adjoining, yet still separate, greengrocery and florists were also given a makeover.

A little over six months later, the Kingsteignton store was greatly extended and converted into a combined grocery, butchery and greengrocery foodhall. While in Torquay the grocery and butchery branches at Barton Road were merged with great effect, although the arrangement was short-lived, as before the year was out, the Society had opened a much larger supermarket in the same place.

At Ipplepen, the erstwhile Mace store was added to the Society's portfolio and proved a popular replacement for their previously under-sized branch. Torpoint too was quick to benefit from the new approach and in August 1978 a considerably enlarged and modernised supermarket was opened with an element of excitement. As was the greatly revamped Tamar House at St Budeaux, which re-opened for business on 22 March 1977.

There were other improvements here and there too as the Society attempted to move with the times.

Tamar House St Budeaux re-opens 22 March 1977. Top: TSW's Ken McLeod arrives on a dray. Bottom: Lord Mayor Arthur Floyd with wife Pat and Society CEO Jack Parson.

Internally, on 1 January 1976, the Society's impressive new ICL 2903 Computer became operational for the first time. The CWS Computer Bureau had grown to such an extent that, following a feasibility study, it was deemed prudent for the Plymouth & South Devon Society to acquire its own computer, even though the cost was a staggering £61,000. It was a decision not to be taken lightly, but with a turnover now in excess of £34 million and a trade surplus of £1.64 million, there was every reason for confidence in the future.

Moving On

Having said that, however, the trade surplus was slightly down on that of the previous year. Concern primarily focused on the dividend stamp liability which was creeping up year on year, prompting, in 1979, a devaluing of the dividend stamps, with the rate halved from two for every 5p spent, to just one.

Other cost-cutting measures throughout the seventies had seen the running down and closure of the Furniture Removals and Storage facilities in 1973 and in 1975 the sale of ten acres of land north of the Society's holiday facility at Stoke Beach.

Poole Farm was also formally relinquished, having been under a compulsory purchase order threat for some years, the land being required for the proposed Estover Housing programme. The order came into effect in 1976 and the livestock there were transferred to Longbrook Farm at Milton Abbot.

On a more positive note, in 1977 the Transport Department at Recreation Road, opened a small retail shop selling vehicle parts and offering advice and a tool hire service. 'The Motoring Centre' as it was dubbed, became a popular centre for car enthusiasts.

Meanwhile, for those interested in the back pages of the Society, a room was taken above the pharmacy on Mutley Plain and converted as a Social History Museum, under the guidance of the Education Committee - which was then, in 1979, in its last year in that guise.

Also in its last year was the Television Servicing relationship with Pearce & Grey. In 1980 a new venture was launched with Sharp & Savage - it was the Plymouth Television Repair Service.

Meanwhile celebrating their 50th anniversary were the Co-op sponsored Western College Players, the amateur dramatic club based in Western College but then mainly staging their productions in the Athenaeum. Founded back in 1929 by a group of ladies from Women's Guild No.1 as the Plymouth Co-operative Players the troupe had also used the Central Premises (until its destruction) and the Swarthmore Hall on Mutley Plain.

Angela Rippon, an alumnus of the Western College Players, with fellow thespians. Inset: Western College.

Opened in November 1911, the Society's Laundry and Dry Cleaning operation at Peverell closed in the summer of 1981.
Top: A scene from the 1930s. Right: Looking much the same several decades later. Above: 1959 Co-op Laundry van.

Bigger and Bigger

On 6 June 1981, the longstanding Laundry and Dry Cleaning Department at Langstone Road was closed, after almost 70 years of service. The domestic washing machine and the local launderette had taken their toll, nibbling away at the market to such an extent that what was left was no longer commercially viable. In its heyday it had employed hundreds as had numerous other Laundry operators around the country.

What was happening here was happening everywhere. Generally, though, it was the smaller operations that were proving to be increasingly uneconomical; in September 1980 the butchery at Ernesettle was closed. However, a week later, and on a larger scale, the Society opened their new Carpet Warehouse and Retail Showroom in Vauxhall Street.

In Torquay, on 5 September 1981, a number of small units were closed, however this was but a prelude to the opening, the following month, of the long drawn-out rebuild of Tor House Departmental Store in Union Street.

Opened with a big flourish, the new store attracted much favourable publicity and was undoubtedly *'the best store in the town'*, moreover the whole project had been completely financed from internal resources.

It was a pattern that was being repeated across most of the Co-operative Movement. When the influential Independent Commission published its report at the end of the 1950s there had been some 30,000 Co-op shops across the length and breadth of the British Isles, but by the early 1980s over 20,000 of those had been closed.

Meanwhile, the average size of those shops that the Society did have trading had increased spectacularly. The Movement now embraced over 1,750 supermarkets (the criterion being over 4,000 sq.ft) and some 43 superstores (identified as being over 25,000 sq.ft). There were also a further 256 department stores and a significant number of small neighbourhood shops and small supermarkets, but the trend was unmistakable.

'The Movement's shops had by now fallen on average to a third of the size of those of the multiples, the top four of whom were doing nearly twice the Co-op trade from only 1,300 outlets. Strenuous efforts were made by

societies to respond to the new trend, by borrowing heavily, closing their small shops and building new superstores' (Birchall).

The Plymouth and South Devon Society were no exception: they undoubtedly had the resources to invest and, with the notable exception of the ASDA Superstore at Estover, they also had a headstart, and something of a monopoly, certainly within the Plymouth area - they just needed confidence and, of course, the necessary planning consent.

Plans and Appeals

In 1981 the Society submitted planning applications for a superstore at Transit Way, Honicknowle (on land acquired from Westbrick) and a large foodstore at Recreation Road, Peverell, where the Preserve Factory, Bakery and Laundry had all been based. Both applications were refused. The reasons given being that the proposals were: contrary to retail policy; constituted the loss of residential land and were likely to generate traffic problems. The Society decided to appeal.

'The Appeals commenced on 13 July 1982,' noted Victor Barton, who was about to be appointed the Society's Chief Executive Officer following the retirement of Jack Parsons. 'The Society was represented by Mr Moriarty QC supported by expert witnesses for planning, traffic and highways, environmental impact and architecture.

'Held in the Lower Guildhall over the course of two days, the Chief Planning Officer for the Council expressed concern at the impact on Crownhill Shopping Centre, a preference to see Crownhill Centre enlarged, and a preferred development at Roborough. Opposition to our Appeal also came from traders at Crownhill, and the Highway Authority. As part of our case, we undertook to carry out required roadworks and improvements to approach roads at Transit Way and Recreation Road, Peverell.

'We also agreed to keep open our shops at Crownhill, Ernesettle, Whitleigh, Honicknowle, Jubilee, North Prospect, Peverell, and West Park. At the end of the hearing and site inspections (including showing the Inspector the dreadful road system at Crownhill) his decision was reserved, leaving us with nothing but a six month agonising wait.'

Plymouth and South Devon Co-operative Society Dairy Queen, 1979-80 at Radnor Dairy.

Supporting the Lollipop Ladies.

Branded double-decker at
Milehouse Depot

Aerial view of the Pomphlett site, the old quarry to the right and the former mill pond to the left.

202

In the meantime the Society agreed to buy five acres of land at Pomphlett Mill, Plymstock, subject to retail planning approval, as well as 32 acres of development land at Abbotskerswell, near Newton Abbot (the latter purchase being made via the subsidiary Buttland Properties).

There were also further developments at Torquay with the openings of new supermarkets – in St Marychurch Road, in July 1982 and at Hele Cross in October. The following month, though, saw Torbay Planning Authority turn down permission for a superstore on land at Hookhills, Paignton, on the grounds that it undermined the structure of local shopping; interfered with pedestrian flow to the local school and swallowed up eight acres of land that could be used for housing. The Society decided to appeal.

In February, in response to the appeals on Transit Way and Recreation Road, Plymouth, the Secretary of State declared consent for outline planning approval for a 50,000 sq.ft superstore at Transit Way, but turned down the plan for the Food Hall at Peverell.

Thereupon a decision was taken to shelve the Peverell proposal but move ahead with the superstore at Transit Way. This was by no means a straightforward matter:

'Certain conditions were laid down to improve access to the site, the most important being the road junction with Crownhill Road. This involved buying the Jehovah Witnesses freehold land and place of worship (Kingdom Hall) at the junction corner and re-accommodating them further along Transit Way.'

'To do this, the Society acquired Roadway House, owned by the Road Haulage Association, converting part of it to meet the requirements of the religious order – including an indoor baptismal pool. They also had to provide car parking and improve the bend in the road in front of the Securicor building. Furthermore four acres at the western end of the site had to be dedicated to the City Council as a Public Open Space' (Barton).

It was all a far cry from buying a site and, subject to a few basic stipulations, building on it. Local Authorities were right to be concerned; there could be no denying the impact that superstores were having on the old corner shop, however it was equally clear that people were voting with their cars

rather than their feet and that the public increasingly were looking to do one major, weekly shop, rather than nipping out for supplies on an almost daily basis.

Clearly it was a costly business to sort out the infrastructure, but the Co-op was keen to stay ahead of the game in this part of the world, as, across the country, the competition was fierce. Thus it was that when the Nottingham-based developers Errill Properties announced that they were going to build three large non-food retailing units at Cot Hill, Plympton, the Society agreed to take on the middle one. A 20,000 sq.ft space, they earmarked it for a 'Homemaker' store, selling furniture, furnishings, carpets, electrical goods, televisions, glass, china etc. The two units either side were destined for DIY and carpets.

In the summer of 1984, the failure of the Society's Freezer Centre that had opened on the Ridgeway, Plympton, five years earlier, saw the frozen food element transferred into Plymco 1 while the Freezer Centre itself was taken over by the Pharmacy Department. These were times when fortune favoured the brave but it wasn't always easy to make the right decision.

Around the same time, Plymouth City Council invited tenders for a 40,000 sq.ft superstore – plus a number of smaller units and a car park – on a 12-acre site at Roborough. Tempted, the Society ran it past their expert consultants who *'were of the opinion that the site would not be viable so no tender was submitted. In view of the housing development at Woolwell and success of the Tesco Store ... how wrong can you be?'* pondered Chief Executive Barton some years later.

Meanwhile, when the Secretary of State dismissed the Society's appeal on the Hookhills development at Paignton, that same summer, the decision was taken to lodge a further appeal in the High Court. The Society also lodged a new application, this time with Teignmouth District Council, for a 40,000 sq.ft superstore with a 35,000 sq.ft non-food store and space for 560 cars, on railway owned land at the back of Newton Abbot Station.

Devon County Council recommended to Teignbridge that the application be turned down, and consequently the latter authority resolved to defer the application until the potential highway issues that Devon had complained about, had been addressed.

Staff Journals from the 1980s.

As it transpired the Society weren't unduly bothered: *'unknown to Devon County, we were also in talks with Teignbridge District regarding a good site at Penn Inn, Newton Abbot, which Teignbridge preferred to see developed rather than the station site'* (Barton).

By this stage work on Transit Way was under way and to further embellish the project now dubbed 'Plymco 2', the Society applied for permission to erect a petrol filling station there. Meanwhile, the Society also decided not to submit a tender when another retail development in Plymouth was mooted - this time on former railway land at Friary Station (the station closed to passenger traffic back in 1958 but had kept going as a goods yard for many years after that).

The site was subsequently filled with carpet, furniture and DIY warehouses, meanwhile a hole in the road at Transit Way provided a hiccough in the progress there. The void, which extended down to a depth of six metres, was dealt with by Devon County Council - it was their responsibility and they picked up the bill for £35,000.

Another natural phenomenon that had a disproportionate impact on events was the slight snow flurry that brought Plymouth to a virtual standstill on Friday, 18 January 1985. Apart from the impact on that day's retail activities – most people went home early, many of them getting stuck in traffic, the Society were worried about the inauspicious start it would give to their first Homemaker unit, which opened the following day at Cot Hill. While the opening day's sales may have been disappointing, the store quickly rewarded the faith shown in the original decision.

The following month the Teignbridge affair was back in the spotlight as an agreement forged with the District Council there saw the Society commit to a £1.5 million scheme at Penn Inn – subject to planning approval. It also saw the abandonment of the other proposal at Forde Road, behind the station at Newton Abbot.

It has to be said that the Society was not enjoying an easy ride in that area, at that time, Trago Mills had put in a higher bid for the site, but the Society already had an enforceable contract with Teignbridge, so they won the day. However, Trago weren't finished and offered the Society to lease or purchase part of their site at Heathfield, rather than pursue the Penn

Top: Check out - the haircut. Bottom: The new Homemaker, Electrical, Furniture and Furnishings, at Cot Hill.

Inn option. However, the Society's projected figures gave them a trading loss at Trago, where they would only be permitted to sell food. At Penn Inn, where, as Victor Barton put it, *'we could sell what we wished'*, the calculated annual profit was in the region of £500,000. Consequently *'the Trago offer was politely declined!'*

It was around this time that Victor Barton took the early retirement he had requested the previous year, and David Greener, who had been appointed Chief Executive Designate in January 1985, formally took office in September.

It had been a busy year, particularly for the drawing office. March 1985 had seen the Society submit a plan for a 40,000 sq.ft superstore - with parking – at Pomphlett Mill and reach agreement with Clarke Construction to build Plymco 2 at a projected cost of £6.28 million. No sooner had that been approved than another application was submitted for Transit Way, this time to add another Homemaker to the property portfolio. Planning approval was granted but with all the new developments, it was only a matter of time before warehousing was going to be a serious issue. The City Council and the Society, with assistance from the CWS, started to give the matter some thought.

'The former four-storey grocery warehouse on North Quay was being used for furniture and electrical storage, and the single storey warehouse in Vauxhall Street for carpet storage and sales - neither of them first class facilities. In addition the pharmacy warehouse and offices were in poor premises on North Quay close to Harbour Avenue.'

It was time to move on, and happily, in August 1986, the planning officers were given authority to approve the Society's application to market the three properties with residential and commercial potential. Within a year the old buildings had been sold and everything had been moved into a large single storey building in Marshall Road, Plympton.

These were heady times, things had moved on a long way from that tiny tentative first shop in an upstairs room in Catte Street. In the trading year to the new year-end of January 1986 (the change from a September year-end accounting period had been effective since 1983) some £6 million had been spent on capital development - most of it on Transit Way. A

million pounds worth of investments had been withdrawn, while trade and bank borrowing had taken care of the rest. Meanwhile an arrangement had been made with the Co-operative Bank for a loan facility of up to £5 million, if required.

The Society had to keep pace with their rivals and in the mid-1980s that meant a lot of crystal ball gazing, trying to predict consumer patterns and, inevitably, massive re-investment.

'The face of retailing in Plymouth was changing dramatically, the shopping trolley was taking the place of the basket, stiff competition was on its way, - self selection, pile it high, sell it cheap. Bulk shopping by car was the in-thing' (Barton).

Up until now the Society's only serious competition in Plymouth had been that superstore at Estover. Now, with the opening of Transit Way still many months away, there were two new superstores in the city. On 10 February 1986 Tesco opened on the Roborough site that the Society had turned down, and just seven days later Sainsbury's opened the first inner city superstore at the top of Armada Way, in the city's much heralded new shopping centre, the first truly indoor mall in Plymouth.

Above, retiring CEO, Victor Barton, below: his successor David Greener

In truth, the Drake Circus shopping centre, which had opened in September 1971, had been an earlier attempt to create a kind of shopping mall, but it wasn't enclosed. It did, however, contain the largest Tesco store in the country at that time, but it fell just short of the mark to make it a superstore and was, rather, an extremely large food hall. Predating that development by a few years, Ford and Lock also had a large supermarket at the western end of Mayflower Street, opposite the site that the Armada Centre came to be built on.

Tastes Change

City centre food shops and even food halls generally started to struggle as the new superstores appeared. When first completed and occupied, the post-war Cornwall Street had been full of food shops, from one end to the other: butchers, bakers, grocers etc. and most of the major department stores had substantial food halls. Woolworths, Dingles, British Home Stores, Littlewoods, Marks and Spencer, Spooners. One by one they closed, Spooners (Debenhams) and Dingles were among the early casualties, with only Marks and Spencer still offering food today.

Clearly this wasn't just a Plymouth thing either. In April 1986 a decision was taken to close the still relatively new food hall in Tor House, Torquay, *'which had been in a loss situation in each of the previous three years'* (Barton). The space was closed, stripped and refurbished, and re-opened the following month, with fashions, furnishings and footwear.

This was not an inexpensive process and with various planning proposals on the table and more in the pipeline, the question of financing the ongoing and future projects was inevitably an issue: *'Property not used in trade came under scrutiny. Should any be sold to provide funds or continue to be let and accumulate future equity gain? A survey of such properties was undertaken. To sell or not to sell!! (Barton)'*

Farms and other land holdings, including Unity Park and Peverell, were all professionally surveyed and in March 1986 the decision was taken to dispose of agricultural land that didn't have any obvious potential for development. In July there was a major auction staged at the Novotel at Marsh Mills, and fifteen lots were offered for sale. Only one item, a house and adjoining 31-acres of land at Longbrook, failed to reach its reserve

Top: Transit Way nears completion. Bottom: Drake Circus c.1971

price (it was subsequently sold privately). Whympston, Hareston, Tuxton and Gradna all went under the auctioneers hammer and brought the best part of £1.6 million into the Society's balance sheets.

Meanwhile, although not exactly cost cutting, another couple of measures were put in place in the interests of long-term financial prudence. In January 1986 the Society's dwindling Solid Fuel trade was passed over to the CWS and around the same time, the process of franchising the Society's 180 milk rounds was started. Devonport and Tavistock were the first areas in which roundsmen took over ownership of their rounds, while continuing to take supplies from the Society. Attempts to advance this process met with considerable opposition from the Trade Unions nationally, however, after the local membership were balloted, it was agreed to continue and in October 1986 a further twenty rounds were included in the scheme. Within another two years almost half the rounds had been franchised out.

Above; February 1986, the newly opened Armada Centre, inside and out.

Whympston Farm

A Matter Of Convenience

Tuesday, 21 October 1986, was another auspicious day in the history of the Plymouth Society, as the multi-million Transit Way superstore, Plymco 2, was officially opened. There was no grand procession of Co-operative vehicles through the town, no vast crowds assembled to witness the event: *'The President, Mr GFV Bestier, unveiled a commemorative plaque listing the date and names of the Board of Directors. No other special ceremony was thought necessary'* (Barton).

Architecturally uninteresting, the new building won the top award for Energy Management at a ceremony in London in April 1987. The building was also judged the winner of the Electricity Generating Board Award for the most efficient use of energy, both locally and nationally. The superstore originally comprised a grocery, butchery, delicatessen, greengrocery, bakery, fish counter, florist, pharmacy, dry goods, optical centre, restaurant and petrol station. A shopping mall was added later.

When the accounts were presented for the year end January 1987 they revealed that over £8 million had been spent on major developments, substantially more than had been spent in any previous year since the Society had started. The accounts also revealed a total trading figure in excess of £100 million, a truly notable landmark.

The stakes had undoubtedly been raised and the Society was now in a proper position to compete with Asda, Tesco, and Sainsbury's.

As ever the Society hadn't been operating in isolation, and by the mid-1980s the Co-operative Movement nationally had become the third largest operator of superstores in the country. However, those societies *'who were stuck with large numbers of small shops were in trouble. The small size of shop has been blamed for the relative weakness of the Movement in Scotland, and was a major factor in the takeover of the largest society - London - by the Co-operative Retail Society; after the takeover, 80% of the Society's grocery shops were closed'* (Birchall).

It was a situation the Plymouth & South Devon Society were only too well aware of. In August 1987, despite a plea from a special meeting of members in Buckfastleigh, the Board re-affirmed their decision to close the

Top and bottom: Transit Way is open for business ...and play.

Transit Way by night.

**BOARD OF DIRECTORS
ANNUAL REPORT**
FOR THE 52 WEEKS ENDED 26th JANUARY 1985

CO OP P&SD

drygoods store there. They also closed the groceries in Bridwell Road, Plymouth and Tweenaway, Paignton, the butcher's shops in Station Road, Plymouth and Shiphay, Torquay as well as the tobacconist on Royal Parade and the optical store on Mutley Plain, although the latter re-opened as a hairdressing salon before the year was out. The following year, however, the pharmacy at Mutley Plain was another victim of the cuts as was the Albert Road butcher's and the grocery at Camel's Head.

It was as though the writing on the wall for the small shop could hardly have been bigger and it wasn't just the Co-op that was affected. Small food shops, handy corner shops, small grocers, greengrocers, butchers and bakers were all feeling the pinch.

For owner-occupiers it was often the end of the road, for the Co-op it was time to pull out and re-invest elsewhere. The corner shop was convenient, but it tended to be more expensive because small scale independent traders struggled to get good prices from wholesalers, even via the cash and carry route.

A typical scenario would see one of the big superstores selling a product line, say a tin of beans on special offer at a price that was below what the small independent retailer was paying his or her wholesaler for the same product. How could the small store compete, unless, like the Co-op, they could benefit from being part of a big buying-in organisation? And, unless they were offering a service that the superstores weren't providing.

Therein lay the heart of the problem ... and ultimately, for the Co-op at least the answer to it. Imagine having a shop on your doorstep that stayed open after the superstore had closed, a shop that wasn't so big it couldn't be manned by one or two people. After all, television had all but destroyed the traditional tea time; people's eating patterns had changed greatly since the war, families no longer always ate together. Microwave ovens, instant meals and takeaways played their part in the process. Fish and chips on a Friday was no longer the nation's favourite alternative to mum's meat and two veg, there were now curries and pizzas just a phone call away. Everything was geared to the customer's convenience so why not a convenience store, one that was open all hours?

The Co-op was by no means the first to realise this, there were already thousands of 7 Eleven stores all around the world, having originated in America back in the 1920s, while in the 1930s the Dutch Spar company - So Near So Spar - was established. Then in the 1950s Londis (from London District Stores) entered the market-place.

Typically these convenience stores - there were many others in America - sold basic lines, 'emergency' items and alcohol (causing them to be dubbed 'party stores' in many parts of the States). Thus you would pop in for milk, bread, cereal, soft drinks, cigarettes, confectionery, hygiene products, magazines, newspapers, toilet paper, cat food, dog food and the like.

With the benefit of hindsight such shops were bound to complement the superstore, and yet the Co-op had, over the last twenty to thirty years, just gone through the painful process of closing over 20,000 shops. Nevertheless they still had thousands of small stores on their books, the length and breadth of the country, most of which had survived because their situation meant that they were still commercially viable - most of them were therefore ripe for conversion.

The CWS lead the way setting up two 'C-Stores' on a trial basis. Following the success of that experiment they then established a franchise operation with a dozen such stores. The Regional Societies were swift to follow suit:

'Instead of seeing their small stores as a liability, they found that in some locations (but not all) they could be refurbished and made highly profitable. For instance, by 1987 the Norwest Society was taking half its turnover from ten 'Shopping Giant' superstores, but another 10% from 15 'C-Stores'. And the conversion of the stores was very rapid; the North Eastern Society converted 127 shops in one year. In fact, so successful have the Co-ops been in utilising their small-shop base, that they are now the leading 'C-store' operators, leaving behind both the independents, who are less well organised, and the multiples, who cannot easily find good sites' (Birchall 1994).

Happily the Plymouth & South Devon Society still had plenty of good sites for C-stores or their 'Plymco Late-Late Shops', as they preferred to call them.

SPAR originally operated under the name DE SPAR (the name is an acronym of the Dutch phrase Door Eendrachtig Samenwerken Profiteren Allen Regelmatig - that is: 'through united co-operation everyone regularly profits'). The phrase was deliberately contrived as in Dutch - and in Afrikaans, German, Danish, Swedish and Norwegian - 'spaar' or 'spar' means to save (money), while De spar mean 'the fir tree' - hence the corporate logo.

Top: A typical Late Shop interior. Bottom: Jubilee Stores conversion. Right Babbacombe.

Above and left: the extended Food Distribution Centre at Plympton. Below: Plans for the new Penn Inn superstore.

The 'Big' Push Continues

None of this was to affect the pace at which the Society was pressing ahead with it superstore plans however.

Following an offer to acquire some 6.5 acres of land owned by Mexbro Concrete at Paignton, with a view to building a 50,000 sq.ft superstore there with over 600 car spaces, the Society had submitted plans to Torbay Planning Committee in the summer of 1986. On the grounds that it would, amongst other things, impact adversely on existing local shopping facilities, the proposal was turned down. Three years later, however, and following an appeal, the Society was granted permission for a 57,000 sq.ft building.

Meanwhile, by the end of 1986, outline planning consent had been obtained for the Penn Inn development. Detailed plans were submitted and approved by Teignbridge Planning Committee in October the following year. Whereupon tenders were invited for the work.

In the event, just weeks before the Society's second and largest superstore was ready to open, some two years later, disaster struck - although it could have been so much worse. On the night of the ninth of August, a large water tank (holding 60,000 gallons of water) ruptured. The force of the water burst doorways, caused the roof to lift – dislodging tiles – buckled steelwork and demolished an internal wall. Fortunately the water didn't reach the sales area and luckily no-one was on site, otherwise the consequences may have been very serious indeed. But no-one was injured, the manufacturers accepted responsibility, the insurers covered all costs and the liability and the building opened on schedule, on Tuesday, 24 October 1989.

Four hundred staff were employed there, including some from the Food Save-It Discount Shop in Kingsteignton, which closed on the same day and was later demolished. The adjacent sites were subsequently purchased and, in time, the Society would construct a new Homemaker store on the site.

Back in Plymouth, plans for a Homemaker, together with seven shop units, at Transit Way were approved in the summer of 1988, while the existing Homemaker at Plympton was extended to meet the demand for selling space. There was also an extension, creating an extra 30,000 sq.ft of warehousing, at the Plympton food distribution centre.

Plympton was very much a growth area in other respects too. Chaddlewood had been designated an area for housing development in the Devon Structure Plan back in 1972, and since the mid-1970s hundreds of acres had been developed for residential properties. However, in the same way that the other post-war estates around Plymouth had been slow to be granted local facilities, it wasn't until 1987 that approval was granted for a district centre, incorporating some 15,000 sq.ft of shopping, plus a pharmacy, post office and car parking. Two years later the Society bought eight acres of development land for £3.5 million.

The Society had also bought land and property the previous year, at Bell Close, Plympton - on the Newnham Industrial Estate - in order to move the Transport Department out of their outdated premises at Peverell. Together with the vacated small goods factory and the former butchery warehouse, this provided the Society with a sizeable redundant space at Peverell, space that was substantially added to when the Freezer Centre at Recreation Road was closed at the beginning of January. However, an application to develop the site for housing was refused and so a decision was taken to split the buildings into separate industrial units for letting - short term letting, so that they could keep their options open.

Meanwhile, in the City Centre, in the wake of the pedestrianisation of much of Armada Way and New George Street, the City Council issued a brief, outlining proposals for the development of the Colin Campbell Court area with the possible inclusion of Co-operative House - the first of a series of schemes for the regeneration of the east end.

The pedestrianisation of the City Centre had been a major move on behalf of the Local Authority and on 22 July 1988, the Queen had paid a visit to the City, partly to honour the 400th Anniversary of the defeat of the Spanish Armada and the opening of the Hoe Dome, but also to view the new City Centre layout.

The creation of car-free areas was an attempt to rejuvenate the central shopping area in the wake of all the out-of-town superstores and warehouse-style units that were attracting custom away from the traditional high street.

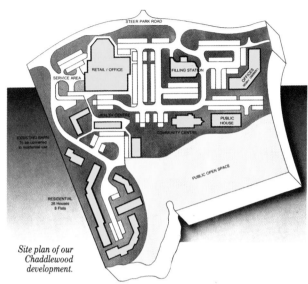

Site plan of our Chaddlewood development.

Top left: Pedestrianisation of New George Street takes shape. Top right: Plans for Chaddlewood.
Above: Co-operative House closed between 11.45am and 1pm on Friday 22 July 1988, partly to allow staff to take part in the celebrations and partly to reduce any potential security risk posed by crowds flocking onto Royal Parade.

Staff Journal 1988.

Top: The Society's holiday accommodation at Stoke Beach.
Middle: The shoe department inside Co-operative House.
Bottom: Part of the limousine fleet.

Other Eighties Odds And Ends

It certainly wasn't a time for standing still and in addition to the major schemes the Society was also constantly reviewing its existing facilities.

For a variety of reasons, not least the escalating cost and diminshing profit on certain lines, a decision was taken to stop issuing dividend stamps on petrol, cigarettes and tobacco as well as transport, catering, TV rentals and hiring holiday accommodation at Stoke Beach.

In 1987, concern over the future trading growth of the Footwear Department in Co-operative House, prompted open negotiation with Peter Lord Ltd., the retailing arm of Clarke Footwear, with a view to franchising the business. Shoefayre (the CWS subsidiary) felt they were unable to maintain the strong brand profile which Clarke already had in Co-operative House, but would be able to take over branches as separate units.

Meanwhile, later that same year, disposal of the warehousing facilities at North Quay meant that, in addition to providing the new Food Distribution Centre, a home had to be found for the fleet of funeral cars and limousines. To that end a purpose-built garage was erected on Society-owned land at Coxside, alongside the Works Department.

The following year, incidentally, that arm of the Society was expanded significantly with the purchase of the Westlake Funeral Business. Formerly known as Westlake and Searle, the company had been run, latterly, by Bill Westlake, however, following Bill's death at the end of 1986, the firm passed to the company accountant who was keen to sell the business as a going concern. Consequently the Society agreed to purchase, and to keep trading under the Westlake name.

Around the same time it was agreed to surrender the Society's 4,000 TV hire agreements to the newly established CWS national TV rental scheme which was operating under the name of Super Hire. However, two years later, following the retirement of the Managing Director of Plymouth Television Repair, the Society, who already had a 51% stake in the company, decided to purchase the retiring Mr Sharp's remaining 49%, giving the Society total control. Whereupon they clawed back the rental accounts from the CWS.

Electrical goods generally, however, were not a strong feature of the Society's trading and in the summer of 1989 the short-lived Mutley Powerpoint store was closed - again the big new warehouse style Comet and Curry stores were proving stiff competition, while other casualties that year were four grocery stores - at Honicknowle and Whitleigh (two of the stores the Society had agreed to keep open when pushing for permission to build the Superstore at Transit Way) and at Efford and Ivybridge.

Interestingly enough, opposite the grocery in Ivybridge, the Society owned two derelict shops with accommodation above, as well as two adjoining cottages and in 1988 they had these demolished and built two larger units in their place, one of which they opened as a Powerpoint shop, the other a Funeral Parlour.

Another change, at the end of the eighties, saw the Travel Agency that had been run by the CWS in Courtenay Street, moved into Co-operative House and taken over by the Society; although it was agreed that links with CWS Travelcare would be maintained to ensure that they could hold onto the membership of ABTA (the Association of British Travel Agents) and the recognition of tour and flight Operators.

Above: Plym House rebranded and refurbished.

SOCIETY UP DATE
EIGHTY NINE

A Review of Plymouth and South Devon's Largest Retailer

co op PSD Plymouth & South Devon Co-operative Society Ltd.

REVIEW OF 1988

According to the feedback I had as a result of last years edition of the 'Update', this manner of telling you what is happening in our Society appears to be well received and as we have a successful story to tell I had no hesitation in helping prepare this years 'Update'.

You will be able to see from the following pages that our profitability last year increased substantially over the previous year. Indeed, the profit achieved set another record level, but when I talk about 'records' I am always reminded of the well known saying in the retail trade - 'you are only as good as last years profits'. This being so, we must not become complacent at the achievement, however commendable, but use the newly created high as a bench mark for future potential.

Looking therefore to the future, you will also be told in this 'Update' of the many developments we are currently undertaking and as the majority of additional profit we made last year came from relatively new ventures you will see the importance of ensuring that every potential profitable retail development has to be pursued, the

alternatives being inaction, stagnation and ultimately, business failure.

The next few years will see the launch of at least one major shopping unit per annum and I classify 'major' as being within the superstore category. This year we will be opening a Plymco Superstore at Penn Inn, Newton Abbot and commencing a large new non-food project at Transit Way, Plymouth, where we expect to be trading in the Spring of 1990. This will be followed by a superstore development at Brixham Road, Paignton for a launch hopefully mid 1991 with Pomphlett Mill, Plymstock tagging on the end.

Whilst all of this is going on we will be endeavouring to ensure that ample opportunity exists for those years beyond the current known schemes and I have no doubt that we are set to go from strength to strength.

Finally as well as thanking you for your individual help in the overall effort in achieving such good results I once again ask for your further support and co-operation to ensure that we continue along this path.

David Greener
Chief Executive and Secretary.

The site for the Pomphlett Mill Superstore.

A Superstore at Brixham Road, Paignton will open on this site in 1991.

Penn Inn is now well underway for its Autumn opening this year.

PLYMCO SUPERSTORES South Devon

Our ongoing development of superstores ensures that we go from strength to strength.

Top: Mutley Powerpoint.
Bottom: Travelcare moves into Co-operative House.
Left: Update, in house magazine.

PLYMCO SUPERSTORE

TRANSIT WAY

VAT Registration No. 143 5434 82

PLYMCO SUPERSTORES

Making Shopping Surprisingly Simple

TRANSIT WAY
HONICKNOWLE · PLYMOUTH
Tel: 795929

RIDGEWAY
PLYMPTON · PLYMOUTH
Tel: 347272

SHOPPER
BUS
*Timetables Available
In Store*

140

140

SHOPPER BUS

PLYMCO

PRIVATE HIRE

CONTRACT

Branded buses weren't always a common sight.

CHAPTER 12: THE BUBBLE BURSTS

'The favourable trends shown in previous years have been maintained during the past year despite the evident down turn in the economy as a direct result of penal interest rates. The Society's development programme focused upon the Non Food Division and, as indicated further on in this report, an additional 50,000 square feet of space had been created.'

So ran the opening paragraph of the Board of Directors' annual report for the year ended January 1991. The British economy was in recession and the Society was doing well to keep its head above water, or so it seemed. However, as we read on we learned that: *'fortunes were mixed, with the main effect of the depressed economy coming in Non Food durable trade. With virtual stagnation in the housing market, demand for furniture, carpets and electrical goods has been weak ... but we are confident that with the gradual reduction in interest rates, we will see some improvements, possibly in the Autumn of the coming year.'*

It wasn't to be, however, and the following year turned out to be *'one of the most difficult years the retailing industry has seen in more recent times'.* Despite new developments Non Food was finding it hard to maintain turnover, while the core trading area - Food - was *'more than compensating'.* What was undoubtedly helping the Society cope with the difficult financial circumstances, though, was the Pharmacy, Optical and Funeral Services which were *'reasonably buoyant and provided diversification within the total group which helps sustain turnover when other specialist retailers suffer.'*

These were difficult times though and another income stream, that from property lets, was way down, there being plenty of empty units in the market-place at the time.

Of course it didn't help that the big capital expenditure programmes of 1989 and 1990 had occasioned so much borrowing, which, of necessity led to massive interest charges. Capital expenditure for 1991 was therefore restricted considerably to less than half of either of the previous two years' totals. Nevertheless work at last got under way on the Superstore at Brixham Road, Paignton, but, for various reasons, the Pomphlett Mill and Chaddlewood developments remained in the planning stages, as did the proposal to extend the food superstore at Transit Way.

Meanwhile, there were a further five conversions to Plymco Supermarkets or Late Shops: Devonport Road, Salisbury Road, locally, and Hele Cross and Babbacombe in Torquay and Kingskerswell, Newton Abbot. These were in addition to the eight stores - Tamar House, Torridge Way, Peverell, Fleet Street, Efford, Station Road, Albert Road and Buckfastleigh - that had received make-overs the previous year and which were now open six days a week and twelve hours a day

At the same time the Non Food store at Cot Hill was upgraded and re-branded as a Plymco Homemaker Store, the triangular motif, doubtless inspired by the Transit Way design, now a feature of the generic Plymco brand.

Cot Hill becomes a Plymco Homemaker Store, 1991. The Plymco branding was a way of acknowledging that the Society was part of the Co-operative Movement, but separate and distinct from it at the same time.

Transit Way from the inside

Data Processing.

Of course consumer patterns weren't the only area of change in society around this time, as increasingly the computer was coming to play an ever greater part in the home and in the work place. Number-crunching, data-processing machinery had been gradually getting smaller and more affordable and in 1991 the Society began bringing in specialised computer equipment with a view to introducing their first tailor-made operating system the following year.

Consequently, 1992 saw major steps forward, including the introduction of scanning equipment to identify the increasing number of bar-coded products at the checkout till. There had been ongoing attempts to try and find a way of conveniently coding grocery items for the best part of forty years, however it wasn't until June 1974 that someone pulled out an item from their shopping basket – it was a multi-pack of Wrigley's Juicy Fruit chewing gum – in a supermarket in Ohio, and had it successfully scanned.

The potential was clearly enormous and it was not long before stores with scanners were finding an increase in turnover and a reduction in operating costs, and throughout the eighties their use became more and more widespread.

IBM were at the forefront of this technology and, interestingly enough, in 1992 the Society's Data Processing Department were awarded an IBM Planning Certificate in recognition of the work they had done developing a disaster recovery facility at Transit Way, to be used in the event of the central computer being out of action for any length of time. It was the first time that such a certificate had been awarded by IBM to any organisation.

Of all the numbers the Society needed to crunch, however, the biggest - and most worrying was the loan. For the second year running this figure was in excess of £29 million, an enormous sum for a Society that had been built on a cash only foundation.

Surpluses had to be made and they had to be substantial, and they had to come soon ... a major lift was needed from somewhere.

Going Down

'The continuation of the economic depression throughout 1992 had an adverse effect upon consumer demand to the point that convenience food expenditure fell back to the previous year's levels' (Annual Report 1993).

There was an increase in overall turnover and it was ahead of the rate of inflation, and for the first time in a number of years there had been no large-scale development completed to boost the figures. So ostensibly things weren't too bad in a difficult market place. However, the Society was now trading seven days a week which clearly had a significant effect on staffing, heating, lighting and other on-costs.

'For the year to 23 January 1993 turnover amounted to £192.6 million, with a trading surplus of £3.8 million, but this did not cover the issue of dividend by way of dividend stamps and interest payable, and only the sale of the Pharmacy Branches created a transfer to reserves,' observed Douglas Fletcher, who was then the Administrative Controller and who would go on to become Chief Executive. He adds: *'This probably illustrates the first year where the unsustainable expansion into superstores began to 'hit' the financial performance, particularly with the unfortunate strategic decision of selling Pharmacies to the National Co-operative Chemists Limited.'*

'Unfortunate', because, while the sale kept the pharmacies within the Movement, *'the community pharmacies could have formed an important part of the Society's operations.'*

Indeed the previous year had seen the Pharmacies turn in a respectable surplus and two existing Pharmacy shops - at Plainmoor, Torquay and on The Quay at Kingsbridge, had been added to the portfolio.

The newly acquired and quickly sold Plainmoor Pharmacy.

Sunday Trading

The Society's decision to start Sunday trading, along with many of their competitors, came in advance of the Government's Sunday Trading Act of 1994, which in turn followed the defeat of an earlier bill in 1986 to enable widespread Sunday shopping. In the meantime many stores had flouted the regulations and the practice was already in place in Scotland (where Sunday trading had already been deregulated).

Nevertheless, the bill may have failed to go through Parliament had the shop-worker's Union (USDAW) not agreed to support the bill in return for a promise that not only would larger stores - i.e. those over 3,000 sq.ft be restricted to six hours of opening between 10am and 6pm, but that such work would be strictly voluntary and that premium pay scales would be offered for Sunday hours.

Most supermarkets opted for the six hours between 10am and 4pm.

The difficulties occasioned by massive borrowings did not stop what Fletcher refers to as the *'unsustainable expansion into superstores'* as work continued on Brixham Road, Paignton, and the Society completed the land assembly programme for the proposed development at Pomphlett.

Meanwhile, there had been disagreement with Plymouth City Council and the Planning Inspectorate over proposals that were on the table for two superstores at Marsh Mills and an appeal was lodged with the Court of Appeal. It was the beginning of a protracted saga that would rumble on for some years.

Away from the drawing board and back with the main Board, it was clear that the Society had entered an era that was well outside their comfort zone.

Historically the Society, like so many of their counterparts the length and breath of Britain, had built up their business on the basis of providing good quality products at fair prices, with any profits being ploughed partly straight back into expansion, and partly into the pockets of their members through the all-important dividend payments.

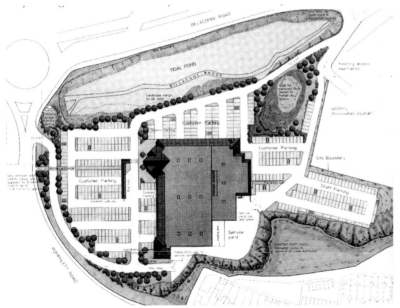

Pomphlett plans progress.

In the early days, in the absence of the privately run multiples, each Society had encountered little in the way of direct competition and, particularly in the bigger towns and cities (with perhaps the notable exception of London), they had come to dominate the market-place.

However, once private companies started to tap in to the economies of scale that the Co-operative Movement so effectively demonstrated and the multiples started to multiply, so the Society started to experience really serious competition. Clearly it was the ensuing difficulties that the Movement as a whole was finding in different areas around the country before and after the war that had prompted the Independent Commission back in the late 1950s.

Central to the CIC's recommendations had been a suggestion that the Movement rationalise and merge and, not to put too fine a point on it, look to make every effort to benefit from economies of scale on a national basis, just like their competitors, so that the Co-operative Movement as a whole could keep pace with the other big players, both in Food and Non Food.

To some extent that did indeed happen, the number of Societies in Britain was reduced from over 1,000 in 1958, to less than 60 by 1994 with less than half of those Societies accounting for around 90% of the trade … and with an annual turnover of more than £7 billion per year that meant the Movement was the second largest retailer in the country.

However, the Movement's market share had, in that same time, dropped from 11% to around 4% and although they were leaders in the food department, the CIC's advice in non food had, with the notable exception of Shoefayre, Travel and the expanding Pharmacy operation, largely been ignored by Societies anxious not to lose their autonomy.

'Where buying was co-ordinated nationally (as in electrical and television trade) it flourished, but where local societies insisted on doing their own buying (as in fashion clothing) the Co-op market share continued to decline' (Birchall).

In almost every instance it was a case of the independent Societies missing out on marketing opportunities, national campaigns and the like; although the CWS-driven 'Come Co-operative Shopping' had been a great success across the country back in the late-sixties, as had the subsequent 'It's all at the Co-op - Now!' initiative.

The CWS, having been directed to change from being a 'seller to' to a 'buyer for' the retail Societies, had done extremely well. Loss-making factories had been closed, production had been concentrated on a few sites, private companies had, in some instances, become involved and Co-op own brand products had held their own in the market-place. There were even instances where, if the product could be sourced cheaper than the CWS could manufacture it, Co-op labelled products were made outside the Movement.

But if the Co-operative Wholesale Society was big, so too was the Co-operative Retail Society - indeed it had become the largest retail Society of all back in 1977, by which time it had absorbed some 162 erstwhile independent Societies. However, while the idea of merging the CWS and the CRS has long been mooted, *'lurking at the back of the talks has always been the fear that the wholesale interest might take power from the retailers; again, in another form, the defence of local society autonomy reappears'* (Birchall).

It is almost certainly this resistance to rationalising all of the Co-operative Movement's resources that has hindered the Movement's chances of putting this noble organisation of the people at the forefront of British retailing. It was certainly what thwarted a principal recommendation of the CIC back in 1958, namely to set up a Co-operative Retail Development Society.

However, in 1993, four of the larger Societies set up the Co-operative Retail Trading Group to ensure that all food products and promotions were centrally purchased and arranged. But:

'The Plymouth Society turned its face against such a group believing that it could purchase and promote better. It was missing its historical point of economy of scale; it was missing the point of the national brand; and it was missing the fact that it was developing stores that were too large and which the competition would kill. It compounded the error by purchasing Normans Limited in 1995 which were a group of stores that were poorly located and which had received little or no investment for a number of years - although had a very willing and committed staff' (Fletcher).

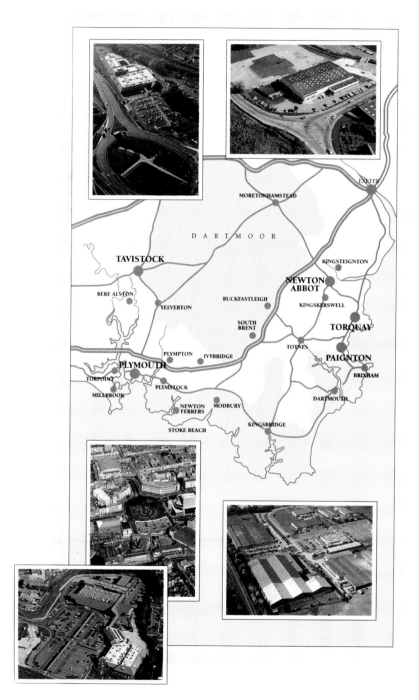

The Society's trading area with aerials photographs of, clockwise:

Plymco Superstore, Penn Inn, Newton Abbot

Plymco Homemaker Kingsteignton

Food Distribution Centre, Bell Close, Plympton

Co-operative House

Transit Way, Honicknowle

Down, Down Deeper and Down

The 1994 Annual Report began, not with the anticipated note of optimism but with a sentence that echoed its counterpart from two years earlier:

'The financial year just ended was possibly the most difficult trading period we have experienced over more recent years.'

It was a far from rosy picture. Turnover, thanks to the sale of the pharmacies and despite the opening of the Society's second largest superstore to date, at Brixham Road - was down by £9 million, borrowings had risen to over £31 million, interest payments were up to £2.9 million and the total trading surplus was down for the second year running to a figure that was barely a quarter of one per cent of the turnover.

With the market not showing any growth, and the lowest rate of inflation for years, the major multiples were all desperate for business and there was a damaging price war - a war which saw some lines being sold for less than cost price. *'As a result of the trading situation there were extensive economies forced on the business, including a number of senior management redundancies and forced retirements'* (Fletcher).

To further compound the financial gloom, there was an actuarial deficit in the Pension Fund, necessitating an increase in the funding level by the Society. Nevertheless plans to press on with the superstore at Pomphlett were progressing, with the Society at last receiving planning consent from the City Council. Permission was also granted to transfer the Post Office facility the Society had at Honicknowle, to the Transit Way site.

As 1994 itself progressed, the economic situation showed no great improvement, indeed the Annual Report sought to inform members, if they weren't already aware, that *'consumer spending in the South West was further hindered by cuts in defence expenditure ... forcing all retailers to chase a static market more vigorously than hitherto.'*

Once again the turnover was down, this time by the best part of £5 million, as was the trading surplus, which was just £368,000 out of a total trading figure of £178.8 million.

Brixham Superstore.

More of the family silver had to be sold, this time it was the Dairy business, which was taken on, not by the CWS or CRS, or even Unigate with whom negotiations had taken place the previous year, but by Cricket St Thomas Dairies Limited. Like the Society's Pharmacies and Optical operations these branches were considered, by the Board, to have no significant future: *'Suffice to say, the decision was taken in the best interests of our overall business long term'* (Annual Report 1994).

The Board and the CEO, Greener, clearly still saw a significant future in the big store and during the year the Society were successful in their bid to tender for a 12,000 sq.ft supermarket in Wolseley Road, and a 10,000 sq.ft unit in Dartmouth. Plans for Chaddlewood were also approved and the Society opened negotiations to sell the land with planning consent and to take a lease on the proposed supermarket, to help save cash.

The housing market, meanwhile, was also going nowhere, all of which meant hard times for the Non Food operations. People weren't moving house and they were being careful with what money they did have, all of which meant that sales of new furniture, floor coverings and electrical goods were suffering.

A Dead Cert

One of the few areas that was clearly recession-proof, however, and which gave the Society an interesting potential for growth, was the Funeral Business. Although modern technology and better standards of food - and living - were enabling men and women to live longer, we were still merely delaying the inevitable.

Perhaps because it's a subject people are not in a hurry to shout about, or even give a great deal of thought to, the funeral service is one of the few major businesses that has been slow to go global, multi-national or even national. Most people prefer a local provider, as a large faceless organisation is the last thing you'd want for the last rites of a loved one. Which is exactly where the 'caring sharing Co-op' scores so convincingly.

A stable contributor to the Co-operative coffers across the country, the Plymouth Society made a number of significant moves in the 1990s to increase its presence in the local market place - starting with the launch of a prestigious development named the Crowndale Funeral Home at Crownhill.

Recent Development The Crowndale Funeral Home at Crownhill Plymouth

The Crowndale Funeral Home at Morshead Road, Crownhill Plymouth.

Above: The Reception at Crowndale.

Above: The Chapels of Rest.

Funeral Services page from the Annual Report.

223

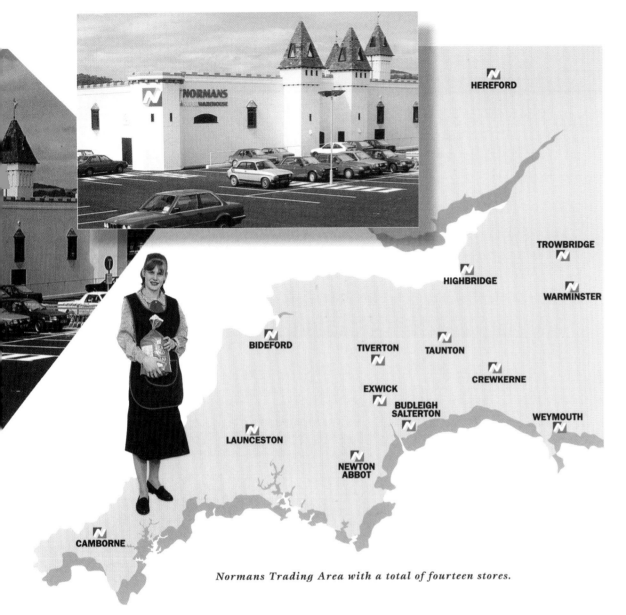

Normans Trading Area with a total of fourteen stores.

Inset; the Norman's store at Newton Abbot. Although the chain became part of the Society's portfolio none of the stores, at this time, were re-branded.

HEREFORD

TROWBRIDGE

HIGHBRIDGE

WARMINSTER

BIDEFORD

TIVERTON

TAUNTON

CREWKERNE

EXWICK

BUDLEIGH SALTERTON

WEYMOUTH

LAUNCESTON

NEWTON ABBOT

CAMBORNE

Somewhere Somehow Something's Gotta Give

With the figures for the year ended January 1996 showing a turnover that had fallen by over £20 million and the Board reporting that the *'outward signs of the much talked about economic recovery are as illusive as ever'* it was obvious that something had to be done.

Admittedly the main reason for that fall in trade was the sale of the Dairy business, and the figures were further complicated by the purchase, mid-way through 1995, of the Normans Discount Food operation. However, by eliminating these elements the Annual Report suggested that there had been a modest increase in turnover of 1.23%. What it didn't show, though, was the Comparative Price Index for the year which for 1995 was running around 2.6%, giving a truer picture of a decrease of 1.37%.

The statistics were not kind, the surplus for the year was a miserable £167,000, less than half what it been the previous year and the net interest payable on loans, before benefits to members, was £2.6 million.

Nevertheless construction work on the new supermarkets at Dartmouth and Wolseley Road got under way and work started on the plans to redevelop Co-operative House. Progress, however, was slow on the Chaddlewood and Pomphlett schemes.

Meanwhile, the ill-advised Normans arrangement started in July 1995 with the acquisition of one store on the Trago Mills site at Newton Abbot and a second at Exwick, Exeter. In November the rest of the group was added, extending the geographical spread as far west as Camborne, north to Hereford, and east to Weymouth and Warminster. However, it also brought another management structure with it and in the wake of the takeover, Martin Moyser was appointed Retail Controller for the whole of the Food and Non Food operations. There followed a sensitive re-appraisal of the management structure of the whole Society.

Indeed with the Co-operative Bank exerting pressure to ensure that the Society's borrowings were reduced, there needed to be a thorough review of almost every aspect of the Society's operations and, following the abrupt departure of the Chief Executive, David Greener, in December 1996, that's exactly what they got.

Things Can Only Get Better

Douglas Fletcher had been with the Society for over 20 years when he succeeded the man he had been shadowing for some time. Under his stewardship the Society entered a period of significant change, following the previous strategic direction of focusing, almost exclusively, on large food store expansion. In other words ... the big push was over.

'The rest of the Co-operative Movement had recognised this position a few years earlier and was moving towards operating smaller stores in the community and there appeared to be a realisation that being a 'community retailer', particularly in food, would be important in the future' (Fletcher).

The first major step in this direction had been the sale of the Society's Superstores in Newton Abbot and Paignton, in September 1996. Blink and you would have missed the reference to these sales in the annual report, and the undisclosed sale price to Sainsbury's Plc, but clearly it significantly relieved the pressure on the bank borrowing. The Brixham Road operation had been severely compromised by the opening of a Safeway superstore by Paignton Zoo, just a stone's throw away - trade had fallen overnight by 30%. It was an unhappy time for Greener who had been committed to the large stores.

Another move, instigated by David Greener, which was to have an even greater long-term impact on the Society's trading position, however, was the *'monumental'*, and frankly questionable, decision to sell off the Society's virtual freehold of Co-operative House. With the best part of fifty years still to run, on a peppercorn lease, the decision was taken to renegotiate a twenty-five year lease for a reduced-sized store. At the same time negotiations were set up to sell the Society's new arrangement to a private body, thereby securing a cash 'windfall'.

The whole process enabled Co-operative House to be completely refurbished and, at the same time, put a seemingly substantial amount of money into the account. The true legacy of the arrangement, however, was that the Society now had to start paying market value rents on the property, reviewable every few years, at a cost that would soon outweigh those short term benefits, moreover, they no longer had 'ownership' of their own premises.

And then there was a question raised over the total refurbishment cost predicted by the professional architects. In the event this was significantly higher than forecast and legal advice was sought from the Society's solicitors, Bond Pearce.

Small wonder, that at the Member's meetings in January 1997 Fletcher, as the new Chief Executive had to face significant questioning regarding the sale of the superstores in Torbay and whether the Society had any strategic direction.

One way or another though, the Society had turned a corner. The bank loan had been reduced by over £10 million and, as the new broom, Fletcher had set in motion a more consultative approach to management and forward planning.

'We commenced the process of radically transforming the Society's whole approach to business planning and the management of people within the organisation. Considerable effort has been devoted towards developing the Society's strategy for all round business improvement. A critical requirement of this strategy is to move away from the traditional hierarchical structure of management in the Society and develop a participative and team-base management style' (Directors Report 1998).

Below: The Wolseley Road store - open until 10pm. Above: Linda Gilroy, MP with members of her campaign team.

Meanwhile, the new stores at Western Approach, Wolseley Road, Whitleigh and Chaddlewood were performing well and the ongoing work on refurbishing Co-operative House was progressing. There was further expansion of the Funeral business with the acquisition of Ivor Burch's Plymstock operation and for the first time in several years the trading surplus topped the million mark. What is more, in the General Election of 1997, Linda Gilroy, the Co-operative candidate, was successfully elected to Parliament for the Plymouth Sutton Ward, while the local Co-operative Councillor, Tudor Evans, became leader of the Plymouth City Council.

First Choice

"Our **aim** is to be the customers **first choice** in their **local community**"

1998 saw the conclusions of the self-examination process rolled out to staff as a coherent set of strategies, aims and values, all of which went under the collective banner of 'Project First Choice':

'Our aim is to be the customers' first choice in their local community' was the battle cry of the Annual Report. And how different that report now was, with the house style having been set the previous year with section by section accounts of each of the main areas of individual activity: Food, Non Food, Finance, Property, Personnel and Management.

It was all there as part of the new move - to empower, include and take heed of individual's suggestions right down through the structural hierarchy - took effect. No longer faceless administrators, now members could see the movers and shakers within their Society. Members could also see, more readily, and more clearly, just how well the Society was doing.

The economy was still some way from making a full recovery, but various measures were starting to have an effect. Rather than look to do their own food and drink buying, and thereby ignore that fundamental economy of scale principal, the Society joined the ever-growing food-buying and procurement group, the Co-operative Retail Trading Group.

There was also a steady rationalisation of the portfolio with the some of the former Normans stores (at Crewkerne, Warminster and Exwick) being sold to GP Stores and others (at Weymouth, Trowbridge and Hereford) being closed (and later sold for housing). Meanwhile, a couple of existing convenience stores, at Hele Village and Barnstaple, were acquired, and work began on the refurbishment and rebranding (as Plymco stores) of Plym House (Plymstock), Embankment Road and Bideford.

Douglas Fletcher, Chief Executive & Secretary, centre, with senior staff, from left: Tony Giddy, Funeral Division, Brian Pedder, Retail Division, Bill Bourne, Buying & Marketing and Martin Moyser, Retail.

226

Inside Derrys Department Store

The major refurbishment of Co-operative House was also completed – after almost two years – and the store was relaunched as Derrys Department store, in September 1998. Nowhere in the building had escaped disruption, as the Restaurant had been first through the hoop, opening the previous summer; soft furnishings and linens were ready make a clean start in August and in December the new-look electrical department was opened in the basement.

Two months later, a four-position Post Office was opened, along with a Travelcare unit. Meanwhile, still within the confines of the Co-operative House building, an independent Argos catalogue shopping facility was opened on the ground floor, facing Royal Parade, while on the other side of the building, at first floor level, a section of the building was taken over by JJB Sports. To accommodate all these alterations two new entrances were created for the building

New signage went up outside the building with the now familiar Co-op clover-leaf logo appearing like the dot of a non-existent 'i' above the 'rr' of Derrys. To further accentuate the fact that the building had been given a makeover the front elevation was bathed in subtle night lights.

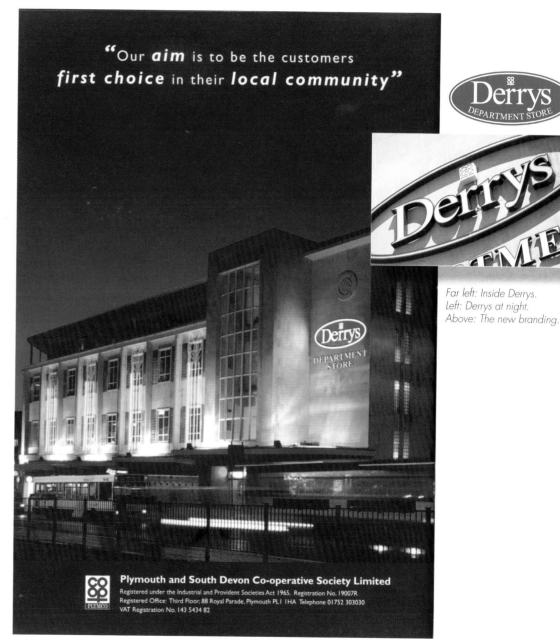

Far left: Inside Derrys.
Left: Derrys at night.
Above: The new branding.

227

Rest In Peace

The former Crown Post Office in Brixham is converted to a Chapel of Rest. June 1999.

One way or another the Society were ringing the changes and clearly the tills were ringing too, for although, through various closures and disposals, turnover was down, trade, comparatively, was up, as indeed, for the second year in a row, was the surplus. In fact it was up more than 50% on the previous year, so a degree of optimism was back in the air.

Indeed nowhere was that more apparent, ironically, than in the Funeral Division, where, hot on the heels of the Burch purchase, family businesses in Okehampton and Launceston, Cullompton, Callington and Bideford were acquired. The Division also opened new premises in Pomphlett Road, Plymstock, and Callington Road, Saltash, while in Brixham the former Crown Post Office building was added to the portfolio and planning permission was sought - and granted - to turn it into a Chapel of Rest.

Because of the difficult and intimate nature of the business most funeral businesses had tended to be family affairs, and through their success expanding into this area the Co-op were clearly showing that, with their reputation as the Movement of the people, they were readily accepted as an appropriate organisation to handle this 'trade'. Also there was no hurry to rebrand the newly acquired businesses.

'The cycle of people requiring funeral services tends to be around seven years, and if people have had good service from a provider, they aren't usually in a hurry to change. We would take on an existing firm and the name would stay up for a number of years; after a period of time we may have the name and add "part of the Plymouth and South Devon Co-operative Funeral Services". Then after a few more years that might switch to 'The Plymouth and South Devon Co-operative Funeral Service, incorporating ...", before, many years down the line, becoming, solely Society branded.

'This was an area we had been looking to expand for a number of years, however, with all our resources going into the big store programme, there was little or no room to invest in other areas. Once we had refocused our corporate strategy, we told the Funeral manager Tony Giddy, who knew all the businesses in the area anyway, to go out and knock on doors and ask the private operators how much they wanted to sell to us' (Fletcher).

The following year Perrings Funeral Service, operating out of Totnes, Dartmouth and Ivybridge was bought, and then the Tiverton firm of Cross and Beale, followed in February 2000, by S & J Westacott of South Molton.

It was around this time that the Society started selling 'pre-need Bonds' for people who wanted to purchase their funeral provision in advance so that they - or indeed anyone else, family member or otherwise - had peace of mind when it came to contemplating the cost, and the worry, of funeral arrangements. The service was becoming an ever important part of the Society's funeral service and the number of bonds sold was soon being measured by the thousand.

Other areas continued to experience difficulties however, and the turnover for 1999 was down again, over £16.5 million, but once again the surplus was up significantly, by 45% to £2.386 million. Partly this was down to sales and closures again but it was also due to good shop-keeping.

'It isn't always about turnover,' says Chief Executive Fletcher, *'as Bill Bourne, the Food Division manager would say to me, "I can put prices down and increase the turnover, but we'll all be busy fools", in other words working harder for less return.'* And running a business where all the surpluses either go back into the business or get shared amongst the members via the dividend or distributed as grants, donations and sponsorships back into the community, via Member Relations, then a healthy surplus is always the sensible goal.

The situation was particularly well-illustrated in the 2000 Annual Report, the year the Society celebrated its 140th anniversary and a name change - to the Plymouth and South West Co-operative Society - to better reflect *'the trading area in which the Society operates.'*

After a lengthy introduction commemorating the anniversary and a summary of the key points from the previous year's trading, the report highlighted, across two pages, the support given to local initiatives and organisations. Normally this information was to be found in the Member Relations section at the back of the report, but here it was a little more prominently displayed.

The Original Community Retailer

'Your directors ensure that the original concept of supporting local communities for 140 years continues, being the original community retailer. In the year we have assisted communities in the following manner.'

There followed a list of undertakings, headed up by the Co-operative Way, *'a 13.2 mile figure of eight walk through the rural and urban areas of Plymouth, to provide a permanent commemoration of the Society's 140 year existence.'* This was an ongoing project that was being executed in conjunction with Plymouth City Council.

Next on the list was a reference to the continuing sponsorship of the Plymouth Raiders basketball team: *'As part of our sponsorship agreement the Raiders held a competition to identify six local schools who would like to benefit from free coaching by the Raiders and the six chosen schools received the coaching sessions during the spring.'*

Then there was news of the Young Consumer of the Year Award for which the Society had been the sole sponsor in 1999; a paragraph on how, by not purchasing Christmas cards, the Directors and Senior Management had made savings that allowed the Society to donate £4,000 to local charities; details of a newly launched Community Grants scheme for environmental projects; and a note about the renovation of Derry's Clock, to which the Society contributed and provided the services of their monumental mason, David Lee who restored the carved inscriptions around the base of the clock (which was almost the same age as the Society).

All of this was in addition to the usual support provided for pre-schools and playgroups, Co-op clubs, the Western College Players, the Plymouth Philharmonic Choir, the Paignton and South Devon Choral Society, the Co-op Choir and the Guilds. The Society's President, Dennis Pidsley, and other Directors, being present at the 60th anniversary celebrations of the Stonehouse Guild.

Other events overseen by the Member Relations Department included various fund-raising activities, the inaugural Bob Briscoe Memorial Seminar and the first Fair Trade Fortnight at Transit Way, where free cups of Clipper Tea and Cafe Direct Coffee were on offer.

Clockwise: Douglas Fletcher, with DHS Girls; Raiders in School; Fair Trade fair; Mutley cyber-cafe; CEO and Council officials; Derry's Clock tower refurbished.

Investors In People

Having abandoned the superstore route and undertaken a thorough review of current activities and working practices, the way was cleared for a fresh approach to the existing portfolio.

David Greener, in his quest to make the Society into a West Country version of Tesco or Sainsbury or Asda had persuaded the board to channel almost all of the surpluses and borrowings into enterprise, and as long as the smaller stores had been ticking along nicely they had, to a certain extent, been sidelined. Now there was a need to refresh these facilities, to invest in them and in the people who ran them.

'We wanted to position ourselves as a good employer and that was difficult if stores were in need of refurbishment; if stock control wasn't as effective as it might be and if the right systems of management weren't in place. Until we could be sure that all three of these components were in place it was unreasonable for us to expect our staff to operate efficiently and effectively. Once everything had been set up properly, then it was difficult for anyone to complain and then you could start to move forward' (Fletcher).

So it was that Personal Computers were introduced in all stores so that store managers could make more accurate sales forecasts, and monitor waste in fresh food areas, so that stock levels were appropriate to each store and customers would be less likely to be frustrated by finding certain lines had sold out.

Training programmes were introduced for staff as a policy was implemented of providing home-grown managers. With stores now open from very early in the morning to very late in the evening it was not possible for a single store manager to be on site all of the time, and so rather than looking to recruit at manager level, the head of Human Resources, John Riley, looked to train up an ever-increasing number of duty managers and thereafter groom them into assistant managerial, then managerial positions.

Top: Trago Mills, Newton Abbot. Middle: Mutley Plain. Bottom: Plympton.

'There were always those who would argue that spending good resources on training staff and getting a reputation for it would backfire as staff would look for other jobs as soon as they had been trained to a certain level. But they didn't. Some did, of course, but that's inevitable. We offered a good package, rewarded our staff as appropriate and it led to first class stability levels' (Fletcher).

So it was that the major refurbishment and enlivenment programme initiated in January 1999 was continued into 2000. Four of the Normans stores (Bideford, Budleigh Salterton, Launceston and Trago Mills, Newton Abbot) were rebranded to Plymco Supermarkets; Ridgeway and Mutley Plain had major refurbishments at a combined cost of one million pounds and at Ridgeway a trial home delivery 'Store to Door' was commenced. The results exceeded expectation.

The Crownhill, Devonport Road, Plymouth and Torpoint supermarkets were also refurbished and the small store group went through a gradual rebranding exercise to resurface as Plymco Local stores with major enhancements, including the provision of newspapers and magazines, greeting cards, snack'n'go cabinets, and an increase in the amount of fresh foods, including the introduction of Cuisine de France fresh bakery.

Opening hours were increased too and a curious spin-off of the whole process was that through the inclusion of the news and magazines sections, the Society became the largest newsagent in the Plymouth and Torbay areas: it had come a long way since those dark days when the newspaper wholesalers refused to have any dealings with the Co-operative Movement.

Other significant developments that year saw Derry's - now open for all-year-round Sunday trading - enjoying continued growth, although the trade at the refurbished Snips hairdressing salon was disappointing. The Society's TV rental business was sold to Granada, and the Homemaker unit at Kingsteignton was doubled in size.

Left: Plymco Store To Door van.
Above: The new 'It's A Local Thing' lorry.

As the twentieth century came to a close, the Plymouth and South West Co-operative was, thanks to a series initiatives implemented off the back of the strategic review of 1999, was gradually getting itself back into shape, and more significantly back into the black, posting a reasonable surplus year on year. They had continued with the exit strategy, out of the food superstore marketplace and further focused their attention on the smaller food units - in addition to the two Torbay superstores, the superstore site at Pomphlett had now been sold on. Now, the largest stores left in the portfolio were Transit Way and the old Normans store in Camborne.

'It was the Board's decision that there was no likelihood of returning to better financial returns in the future, indeed the intensive marketplace in which these stores operated was gradually suffocating the financial return from these stores. Camborne was sold to Lidl and Tesco purchased Transit Way.'

The Directors' report suggested that it was their view that the market-place would polarise between the cut-price out of town stores and the convenient local community retailer.

'The Co-operative Movement has been well established as the nation's major community neighbourhood food operator. The Society believes that there is an opportunity to meet the needs of those consumers who want to use conveniently located neighbourhood stores based on high streets or local centres.

'There was a significant inflow of cash from the sale of the fixed assets mentioned above and the proceeds have been used to partly reduce borrowing and place money in an interest bearing deposit account and the remainder would be recycled into capital developments and acquisitions.'

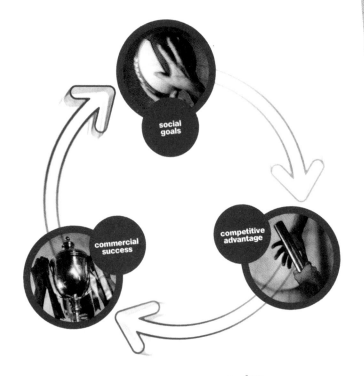

the co-operative advantage

Creating a successful family of Co-operative businesses

social goals

commercial success

competitive advantage

The Report of the Co-operative Commission
January 2001

businesses that trade profitably and for a social purpose

Chapter 6 – The Social Economy and Co-operation

Cover and an inside page of The Report of the Co-operative Commission, *2001.*

CHAPTER 13: BACK TO BASICS

The difficult conditions and the difficult decisions faced by the Plymouth and South West Society were by no means unique within the Co-operative Movement as a whole and on 14 January 2000 the Chairman of the UK Co-operative Council, Lord Graham of Edmonton, together with the Chief Executive of the CWS, Graham Melmoth, the Chairman of the CWS, Len Fyfe, and Pauline Green, the Chief Executive of the Co-operative Union, sent a letter to the Prime Minister, Tony Blair, requesting a thorough review of the situation.

'For 150 years the Co-operative Movement has sought to provide high quality ethical services to consumers and to involve itself in community developments. As it faces the new millennium, we believe it needs to review its strategy and structures in order better to meet its historical goals, and to do so in a modern setting.'

The Prime Minister's reply was prompt and positive: *'I am pleased to respond to your request to help set up and sponsor a Commission to investigate and propose ways to modernise the Consumer Co-operative Movement.*

'I agree with your desire to modernise the Co-operative Movement. I also agree that this means that the Co-op should be successful both as a business and in making a significant contribution to political education and community development … I am delighted to help in the establishment of the Commission, and to support your desire for a fundamental review.'

The Prime Minister appointed 54-year old John Monks, the Secretary of the Trades Union Congress, to Chair the Commission: other members included the aforementioned Len Fyfe, the Chairman of the CWS: the then recently retired former leader of the European Parliamentary Labour Party, Alan Donnelly: the Salford MP, Hazel Blears, and Lord Simon of Highbury, who would go on to become advisor to the Cabinet Office on the modernisation of Government.

The launch of the Commission was publicly announced in February and met for the first time on 29 February 2000.

Members came from a variety of backgrounds. Many were not overly familiar with the workings of the Co-operative and armed with a reasonably broad list of *'areas for discussion'* they structured their investigations around one fundamental question:

'What is the vision of the Co-operative Movement as we enter the new century - in terms of commercial objectives and socials goals?' This in turn generated two supplementary questions. *'How close to delivering this vision are we?'* and *'What structures do we need to close the gap between the vision and the reality?'*

Over the following weeks and months evidence and information was gathered from many experts and interested parties and there were submissions from all the major Societies and many individuals.

the new vision of co-operation for the twenty-first century

Chapter 7 – Mission Statement and Next Steps

The fact that the Commission was taking place was enough to stimulate action in many of the individual Societies. Plymouth, of course, had already gone some significant way down this path, others, however, were struggling, some were floundering.

Curiously enough the long-mooted merger between the CWS and the CRS did finally take place, just a matter of weeks after the Commission was set up, in April 2000, but work on this arrangement had been ongoing for some time. Already the two largest organisations within the Movement, the merger created a national Society and one which accounted for over half of the Movement's total business, the rest being spread around ten large regional Societies and thirty or so local and community Co-operatives.

On the face of it this was a massive organisation: *'The sheer size of the Co-operative Movement still surprises those not familiar with it. The Co-op is a significant retailer, with a turnover of over £8 billion, a customer base of 10 million, upwards of 90,000 employees, and assets with a market value of perhaps £5 billion'* (Commission Report 2001).

The Co-op was also Britain's leading Funeral service provider, the largest farmer and in the Co-operative Bank, ran one of the most successful organisations in that field. The Society was also reasonably successful in its provision of optical services, travel, dairy and pharmaceutical services. Overall, however, and particularly in regard to food, the returns received on capital expended and invested was well below that of the major plcs, like Tesco, Sainsbury, Asda, Safeway and Morrisons all of whom had seen returns on capital that were at least double that of the Co-operative and in some instances much, much higher.

Furthermore the Commission found that in some instances, and Plymouth and the South West was one of them, dividends were being paid to members when the annual trading figures simply didn't support such a gesture. The same applied to the sponsorship of community events and projects. Rather than halt such worthy activities *'some Societies have continued to meet their social goals by the sale of assets'*, this, said the Commission, *'is a matter for serious concern, not congratulation.*

'The Co-operative Movement cannot be sustained simply on the basis of its social commitment … It is essential for all Societies to generate annually expanding trading surpluses.'

'The best defence is to run a successful business,' was another obvious observation from the Commission, but there could be no denying that it was time to state the obvious.

'In some areas of business, notably in attempting to compete with the large multiple stores and supermarket chains, the Movement has failed to perform adequately. Indeed, there has been a long-term, significant under-performance in the majority of the Retail sector within the Movement, caused by a lack of vision: a failure of co-operation, and poor direction and management of businesses across the sector. The commercial failure has forced remedial changes in management structures, mergers and closures. However, these forced developments have been inadequate to prevent substantial loss of market shares and the majority of the Retail Movement is facing an uncertain future.'

To a certain extent the Society had been living off, and in, the past. It could not carry on selling the family silver if it was going to continue to be a major force for the future. The findings of the Commission revealed that the profits being made across the retail sector were below the rate of inflation, clearly the position was not sustainable.

The reasons for this under-performance were manifold, and although some Societies were better than others, when the Commission assessed the evidence presented to them, all would have had to plead guilty to at least one or more of the following failings:

• Inadequate strategic direction of businesses by the Societies' Boards.
• Lack of quality management and inadequate employee training.
• An inability to motivate and involve Co-operative employees fully in Co-operative business.
• Concentration on meeting social goals at the expense of, without reference to, commercial performance.
• Unwillingness to take commercially necessary decisions, e.g. closure of perennially loss-making activities.
• Failure to innovate in terms of products, services or organisation.
• Failure to adopt modern, successful marketing methods and practices.
• Failure to keep pace with business sector competitors.
• An inability to take advantage of the cross-selling potential of the Movement as a whole.

• An, as yet, unfulfilled potential of the Movement to communicate its capability to respond to developing consumer demands for trust and social concern in the delivery of goods and services.
• Failure to measure and set clear goals for both commercial and social performance.
• Lack of the active involvement of properly informed members in the affairs of the Co-operative businesses.
• Lack of pressure on management and Boards for change.
• Lack of focus on commercial performance.
• Reluctance to change poor management or recruit new management externally.
• Fragmentation of the Movement.
• Lack of co-operation between Societies.

While the Plymouth and South West Society had undoubtedly identified a lot of these issues already, and indeed started to take steps to address them, there was still a long way to go.

'The recommendations of the Commission informed all the decisions we were to make over the following years,' says Fletcher, who was all too mindful of the fact that the findings of the previous Commission over forty years earlier, had not been adequately acted upon, indeed, had they been the Movement would almost certainly not have been in the predicament it now found itself in.

The world had certainly moved on since 1958. Then there had been 1,000 Societies dotted around the UK, now there were only 46. The 1958 Commission had recommended that the ideal number of Societies was between 200 and 300, however it had taken 14 years to get the number below 300 and more than 20 years before the total was nearer 200 and then it was mainly by a 'large number of failures and forced mergers'.

Even back in 1967 the folly of ignoring that 1958 report had been picked up by the Co-operative Union, in their Regional Plan: 'If the serious warnings of the Independent Commission had been heeded, the Movement would be in far better shape to withstand the impact of new problems which have developed.'

left to right: Graham Melmoth, John Monks and Tony Blair at the launch of the Co-operative Commission, February 2000

Co-operative Commission

the commission's work is now complete; it is up to the co-operative movement to decide whether it is prepared to grasp the opportunity and to put these proposals into practice

Graham Melmoth, John Monks and Prime Minister Tony Blair.

The view of the team compiling the 2001 report was just as firm: *'That earlier report had been prescient in its analysis, and right in nearly everything it had recommended: and yet the Movement had failed to implement it. That must not happen this time.'*

Concluding his team's findings, Chairman, Joe Monks, wrote: *'The Commission's work is now complete. It is up to the Co-operative Movement to decide whether it is prepared to grasp the opportunity and to put these proposals into practice.*

'If it fails to do so; if it picks and chooses between the recommendations rejecting the radical and the difficult, or if it adopts our recommendations but fails to implement them, then I fear for the future of the Movement.

'But if it adopts them with enthusiasm and commitment and implements them in full, then I believe the prospects can be as bright as at any time in the Movement's history.'

So what were the recommendations? Essentially they revolved around the need to generate profits: to become leaner without being meaner, to train, educate and inspire their managers and employees; to set performance targets; to strengthen the make-up of Boards, and the training of Directors (who should henceforth be retired when they reach 68); to strengthen democracy within the Movement by introducing postal balloting; to work with politicians locally and nationally; to improve their general marketing and point of sale delivery; to embrace new technology (as the Co-operative Bank had done so successfully with their **smile** internet banking initiative); to shed their old fashioned and parochial image *and* embrace a national branding and a new logo and to join the Co-operative Trade Retail Group.

Above all the Commission spoke of the Co-operative Advantage, indeed it was the title they gave the report and it underpinned their mission statement, which was: *'to challenge conventional UK enterprise by building a commercially successful family of businesses that offers a clear Co-operative advantage.'*

By which they meant the provision of: *'Excellent products or services with distinct competitive benefits derived from our values and principles, our rewards for members or our commitment to the communities we serve.*

'The Commission recommends that the Co-operative Movement should prepare for its renewal in the twenty-first century by re-interpreting and re-invigorating the principals that it has always stood for, to make them relevant to the present day.'

Reaction

The Prime Minister welcomed the document: *'This Government believes that enterprise and fairness must go hand in hand if we are to achieve our goals of building a successful economy and a strong society. The Co-operative Movement is a living example of these twin values in action to the benefit of its employees, its customers and the entire community.*

'I congratulate the report's authors for this serious attempt to build successfully on what can be called the co-operative advantage. I promise the Government will study their recommendations and urge everyone who had the best interests of the Co-operative Movement at heart to do the same.'

In Plymouth the report was readily adopted as a blueprint for action. Pleased to see that many of the recommendations concerned issues they were already addressing - with visible results - there was no real difficulty in getting everyone behind the report.

When the Commissioners wrote that, *'in certain sectors and certain types of operations, e.g. large department stores and superstores, it is unlikely that the decline can be arrested. The customer offering in these activities is seen as inferior to conventional business competitors,'* then the writing was already on the wall for Derrys.

'Hard decisions are likely to have to be taken here, and the Movement may have to countenance moving out of large department stores and superstores, altogether, as have some Societies already,' wrote the Commissioners.

'I always knew, when I first took the job, that Derrys would have to be disposed of,' said Chief Executive, Douglas Fletcher eight years later, after announcing the sale to Vergo - but in 2000 that was still some years ahead.

Following on from the publication of the Commission's report there were a number of streamlining managerial appointments: Bill Bourne was appointed Retail Controller, overseeing both Food and Non Food, while John Riley was made Personnel Services and Corporate Relations Controller. The latter being tasked with, amongst other things, producing a membership strategy taking heed of the Commission's recommendation that: *'All Societies should up-date and refine their membership records urgently to delete the names of*

10 DOWNING STREET
LONDON SW1A 2AA

THE PRIME MINISTER

I welcome the report of the Co-operative Commission. It is a serious study which, I hope and believe, can help chart the route towards a successful future for this Movement.

I believe, too, that it is important that the Co-operative Movement does continue to prosper in the new century. The values on which it is built – values such as community and social responsibility – are also the values of the Labour Party and are as relevant today as they have ever been.

This Government also believes, of course, that enterprise and fairness must go hand in hand if we are to achieve our goals of building a successful economy and a strong society. The Co-operative Movement is a living example of these twin values in action to the benefit of its employees, its customers and the entire community.

I congratulate the report's authors for this serious attempt to build successfully on what can be called the co-operative advantage. I promise the Government will study their recommendations and urge everyone who has the best interests of the Co-operative Movement at heart to do the same.

Tony Blair

Out go the Dividend stamps, in comes the Dividendplus card and the new logo and out goes the Plymco brand

obviously dormant members and establish a membership file that accurately reflects the current membership.'

A national membership card was also suggested in the report and almost immediately the Society experimented - in five stores in Newton Abbot - with a points-based membership card, in place of the dividend stamp scheme. The following April it was extended right across the Society's outlets.

Again demonstrating the steps that the Society had already been making towards the recommendations that would come out of the Commission, in April 2000 Plymouth and South West Co-operative were awarded the Investors In People accreditation following an external assessment of the Society's training and development policy, including the way in which the training policy and practices support the overall strategy of the business.

In the meantime the drive to acquire smaller, convenient, food stores and to modernise existing premises continued. In Devonport the grade II listed building at the top of Duke Street, was opened as a food store. Built as a chapel, it had been a pub for 200 years prior to the conversion. A couple of months later the store in Moretonhampstead was significantly extended and refurbished - the first time in forty years that any serious money had been spent on the property.

Your Local Co-op

Stores in Shiphay, Modbury, Millbrook, Buckfastleigh and Buckland were all refurbished, as were, the following year, 2001, those in Newton Ferrers, Bere Alston, Torpoint and Stoke village. At the same time new stores were acquired in Efford and Ipplepen, while in Torpoint a Somerfield Supermarket was acquired, and in Kingsteignton, an Alldays store was bought – both of them as investments. However, three former Normans stores, in Budleigh Salterton, Taunton and Tiverton, were sold off - all three had significant non food elements. The Plymstock food store was also relinquished - Iceland took the lease.

Meanwhile the Society continued to expand its policy of responsible retailing and to that end they introduced a range of medicines with Braille labelling, a pledge on honest labelling generally, and the sourcing of a greater number of Fairtrade and RSPCA Freedom foods.

Cot Hill Homemaker

Inside Cot Hill Homemaker

As a result of the suggestion that Societies should reappraise their branding, a trial scheme saw two stores - in Devonport Road and Torpoint - with new signage which read: 'Your Local Co-op'.

The experiment was deemed a success and the decision was taken to re-brand all the Society's food stores that way over the next few years. In the same way, Cot Hill Homemaker store logo was redesigned without the 'Plymco' element and the Plymco brand, like the 'divi' stamps, was quietly phased out.

Later in the year the Homemaker at Errill Retail Park, Plympton, was given the same treatment, while another Plympton unit to experience a makeover around the same time was the Snips Salon in the Ridgeway: the Crownhill Hairdressers was also done, however it was decided to close the coiffeur's at Newton Abbot on account of low levels of financial returns.

One of the points made by the Commission was that there was no real place for failing businesses and sentiment. If the business wasn't generating sufficient returns then it had no place in the Movement. It was only possible to uphold the Co-operative advantage when surpluses allowed the Society to pursue its social goals.

On a brighter note, despite a falling mortality rate generally, one of the Society's most successful appendages continued to be the Funeral Service and, in 2000, with the purchase of the family business of J & K Davey, in Kingsteignton, the Society became the largest funeral operator in Devon and Cornwall. Their position was further enhanced with the acquisition of two more family-run concerns the following year - T Clark in Teignmouth, Gill and Eales in Buckfastleigh, plus another private business in Kingsbridge.

Extra-curricular, community-orientated activities saw the formation of a History Department under the umbrella of Member Relations, and the formal launch of what had now become a 15-mile figure-of-eight walkway through largely rural parts of urban Plymouth (taking in several of the Palmerston Forts) known as the Co-operative Way.

Meanwhile the ongoing sponsorship of the Young Consumer of the Year Award saw the team from Devonport High School for Boys go through to the local final, and on to Cardiff where they won the national title.

THE CO-OPERATIVE WAY

A programme of guided walks organised by the Plymouth & South West Co-operative Society Limited

Serving the Community the Co-operative Way

The Co-operative Way. Top: Douglas Fletcher, Alan Qualtrough, Dennis Pidsley and Keith Loze.

239

Moving On

The first full year of post-Commission trading saw the Society significantly improve its surplus in the face of a slight drop in turnover:

'Members will note an improved financial performance towards which all parts of the Society have contributed. We have invested in our physical assets, our people and our infrastructure.

'Although pleased with our progress, we still have some way to go before we can be fully satisfied with our financial returns. Nevertheless there is a growing belief in our prospects of success.'

As previously mentioned, the Society had already embarked on a re-appraisal programme that was in line with many of the Commission's recommendations, nevertheless, it was a source of satisfaction to see just how many boxes were being ticked.

The refurbishment process was continuing apace, with fourteen stores being upgraded at a capital cost of £2.7 million, meanwhile a further batch of stores were re-branded with the 'Your Local' fascia, which now meant that around half the Society's portfolio conformed to the new look.

'Your Local' Whiteleigh goes blue, with the button badge.

As part of the drive for customer convenience, more stores were equipped with cash machines, and now, thanks to an arrangement with the Co-operative Bank, a third of all the Society's stores had cash-points.

Again as part of the cross Movement consolidation even greater use was being made of the Co-operative Retailing Trading Group, with the addition of frozen foods, chilled products and green grocery now meaning that all food was sourced through the CRTG.

Three more of the former Normans stores were moved on or closed - in Launceston, Tiverton and Highbridge - while new food stores were acquired in Babbacombe, Wellswood (Torquay), Milber (Newton Abbot), Marlborough (nr Salcombe) and Southside Street on the Barbican. While the property department added a number of investments to its portfolio in Dorchester, Exeter, Torquay and Plymouth and thereby became local landlords for a number of national high street operators.

Other property matters concerned Society land at Chittleburn, between Elburton and Brixton, which had been earmarked by the South Hams Local Authority for a substantial new housing settlement to be known as Sherford. The Society had held the land since 1944 and were keen to make their own representations on how the development might shape up.

On the staffing front the Food Store Duty Management Programme had borne fruit, with ninety fully trained Duty Managers coming through the scheme, while the introduction of a new Food Store Development Programme produced six new Store Managers and also provided an excellent follow-on programme for the new Duty Managers.

Meanwhile, as part of the policy to pursue sound corporate governance a decision was made by the Board to separate the roles of Chief Executive and Secretary. Consequently, Fletcher, himself a former deputy Chief Executive but who had been working without a deputy, now had the former Controller of Personnel Services and Corporate Relations, John Riley, working alongside him as Secretary.

In tandem with these changes came a response to the Commission's recommendation that, having revised the membership data base *'Societies should thereafter maintain regular contact with their membership'* - it took the form of issuing Quarterly Reports and user-friendly Summaries of the Annual Reports and Financial Statements.

What's more, during the year, following the successful introduction of the DividendPlus card, the Society opted to introduce a new members' magazine – *DividendPlus News*. This was to be issued three times a year to the 'revised' membership which now stood at over 100,000, and included over 66,000 who had not previously been members of the Society, all of whom had joined the scheme since 2000.

Amongst the news items reported in the new publication was the launch of another Co-operative card - the Community card. This facility allowed community groups to accumulate points on 'their' card in the same way as individual members would. Devon Air Ambulance were the first charity to be singled out in this way and many thousands of pounds were raised for the cause in the first twelve months of the scheme.

Top: Torridge Way before and after the makeover. Middle: Handing over cheques to charities - the Air Ambulance Trust and Give A Child A Chance - monies raised via the Community Cards, left.

Top: Dennis Pidsley. Bottom: Modbury.

Interestingly enough the main report for the new financial year, 2004, contained reports from both the President, Dennis Pidsley, and the Chief Executive, Douglas Fletcher – it was the first time the annual reviews had been personalised in this way and again was part of the move towards greater accountability and transparency.

Coincidentally, it was also to be Pidsley's last report as he stepped down that April, after 40 years' service as a Director, which included 10 years as President. All the more pleasing therefore for him to be able to announce a trading surplus for the year that exceeded £3.6 million - *'the best financial result achieved by the Society for over 20 years'.*

Acknowledging that further improvements still needed to be made, he was able to tell members: *'we are now seeing the results of the decision made several years ago, to focus our strategy on the key areas of convenience food stores, non-food stores, funeral services and property investment.'*

Mention was also made of the extensive refurbishment programme which meant that the *'Society has a modern group of stores with a strong co-operative identity and distinctive co-operative branding.*

'The name Plymco,' he added, *'has served the Society well in the past, but it has now all but disappeared and will cease entirely in 2004.'*

Overall business was up, on a like for like basis, by 5.32% which compared very favourably with the average increase in prices that year of around 1.7%. The convenience stores were doing good trade, and the Homemaker stores were generally performing well. The newly opened Homemaker at Launceston had *'established itself throughout the course of the year'* while a new mini-Homemaker had been opened on the first floor of the Bideford store. However, *'Derrys Department store, like many other High Street stores, found trading more difficult.'*

On an even gloomier note, a number of the Society's stores during the course of the year were the subject of armed robberies: *'We find it very saddening and also very frustrating that our employees, who are providing a valuable service to the public, are put at risk in this way,'* said the Directors. Fortunately there were no serious injuries incurred and the Society threw their weight behind the USDAW 'Free from Fear' campaign.

Location, Location, Location

'Having improved the working conditions of the staff, and trained up a number of duty managers and properly equipped them with PCs and stock monitoring technology we could start to move forward.

'They were the important ingredients to get in place, once they had been sorted the rest was relatively straightforward. Convenience stores are not about price, they are about the quality of the service, the availability of the product and the convenience of the location,' observed Chief Executive Fletcher, who added, *'I sometimes used to drive around looking for locations. On one occasion I saw a petrol station that I thought would make a fine outlet. I spoke to the owner. He didn't want to sell, so I used to ring him every year, just to see how he was placed, then, one day, after about seven years he rang me, out of the blue: "I'm ready to sell", he said.'*

By this stage there could be little doubt that the change of focus was working, turnover was up 7.7%, but even more significantly the trading surplus was up for the third year in a row, this time by almost 10%.

Certain costs had risen, and there were some exceptionally high legal costs as the Society was pursuing its interests in Sherford and it was fighting a protracted court case against the architects who had, the Society alleged, severely underestimated the costs of the Derrys refurbishment between 1996 and 1998.

The Society was also spending on property: advancing its portfolio by making a number of strategic purchases. As 2004 progressed 14 former Conveco stores were bought, bringing the food store total to 66 outlets. In addition to these acquisitions further stores were bought in Wilton Street, Plymouth and Waterside, Paignton, along with two petrol stations, at Staddiscombe and at Kingsbridge.

The refurbishment programme also rattled along, in Yelverton, Elburton, Embankment Road, St Andrew's Cross, St Budeaux, Wolseley Road, Wilton Street, Dartmouth, Marlborough and Kingskerswell. While in Modbury the Society moved out of their existing premises and into a new, larger foodstore in another part of the village.

The Property Department had a good year too, at long last securing planning permission for housing on the former transport department site at Recreation Road (it would be sold to Barratt Homes, in 2005). Matalan were secured as tenants of the former Normans store at Taunton, and a defensive planning battle was fought over Aldi's proposals to set up a store near Mutley Plain. Meanwhile discussion and debate over Sherford rumbled on.

It was a good year for the hairdressing division as the turnover for the five combined Snips salons across the patch topped one million pounds for the first time.

The news from the Non Food Department was less encouraging, however, and there could be little doubt that the disruption caused by the development of Drake Circus was having an impact across the City Centre.

Other notable items from the year in the life of the Society included the staging of the first postal ballot for the election of Directors - 603 members took part in what was, essentially, a limited affair.

Membership, via the number of DividendPlus card holders, was up to 122,000, while the total number of employees on the Society's books, rose to over 2,300 thanks to the influx of an additional 150 personnel via the Conveco purchase. And while on the subject of staff, the Society was successful in retaining its recognition as an 'Investor in People' for the fourth year in row.

Judgement Day

2005 saw the apparent conclusion to the long drawn-out court case between the Society and the property lead consultants in the Derrys refurbishment. With legal costs running at over a million pounds it was a great relief when judgement was awarded in favour of the Society and the defendants were ordered to pay £2 million. Although not granted leave to do so, the defendants nevertheless determined to lodge an appeal with the Court of Appeal.

On 10 January 2006 in what had became a particularly significant legal case in terms of the 'quantification of loss in cases of professional

negligence', his honour, Judge Thornton QC, ruled that the fact that the Plymouth and South West Co-operative could not supply sufficient documentation to substantiate their claim for the degree to which they were out of pocket, should not be a bar on their attempt to recover damages.

Essentially the consultants, Architecture, Structure & Management Limited (ASM) who had been charged with overseeing the Derrys redevelopment back in 1993, were deemed guilty of providing insufficient design work and detail in the early stages of the work. Because of the provisional nature of so much of the work over 7,500 variations were issued and major overrun costs were incurred.

ASM were unable to provide any detailed explanation for the £2.2 million increase to the original budget figure and despite the 'almost complete absence of relevant documentation', Judge Thornton decreed that 'Plymco cannot be reasonably blamed for any failure to produce a more detailed case as to its loss since the documents it would need to do so were not available due to ASM's default in undertaking its professional services.'

Society President, Barbara Dure (who had succeeded Dennis Pidsley), commented that 'the commitment of the Board and the Chief Executive to pursue the legal case against ASM, was eventually justified following a victory for the Society, which resulted in an inflow of funds and brought this matter to a successful conclusion.'

The final figure saw an award by the Court of £1,995,000, in the Society's favour, while a subsequent settlement on costs saw a further payment to the Society of £1 million transferred into the accounts.

For Chief Executive, Douglas Fletcher, it was a very welcome conclusion to one of the biggest court cases in the Society's history:

'Once again it was Bond Pearce who acted for us, just as they had done 100 years earlier. Christine Hanley was the Senior Partner leading the team and her tenacity, and her determination to pursue the case was admirable. Due credit to her, for there were times when we were a bit battle weary and two sets of advisors said we wouldn't win, but Bond Pearce were solid, and I couldn't bear the thought of the arrogant London lawyers winning the day, so we fought on.'

Top: President, Barbara Dure.

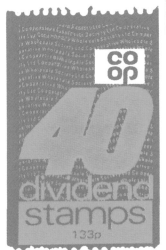

Top right: Tamar View Community Store, Barne Barton. Bottom right: The Official Opening with Pat Patel (Tamar View Community Centre's Company Secretary; Val Newman, Store Manager; Barbara Dure, President; Alison Seabeck MP; Douglas Fletcher, Chief Executive.

Brixham Come On Board

While 2005 generally may have been a difficult year for the Society and for retailers generally there was much, over and above the court case, to celebrate. After paddling their own canoe for so many years, the management of Brixham Co-operative Society eventually agreed terms with the Directors and decided to transfer their engagements to the Plymouth and South West Society - the arrangement was completed in March 2006.

At the same time, in order to better benefit from economies of scale, the the Society sold the Food Distribution Centre and Transport Depot at Bell Close, Plympton. This was a consequence of the Society becoming an early participant in a national project for the Co-operative Movement as a whole to improve its supply chain. The Co-operative Group Retail Logistics took over the running of the warehouse and distribution fleet and invested in upgrading the facilities to establish a new local distribution operation intended to link into a new national network.

Overall the changes here and those occasioned by the difficult times in retailing, saw the Society shed around 100 of its staff. Four former Conveco Stores were put up for sale - Seymour Road and Marlborough Street, Plymouth and Totnes and Tweenaway, Paignton. Eleven more stores were refurbished during the course of the year and, in the social enterprise sector, a major new development saw the opening of new store at Barne Barton.

A First For The Society?

Previously described as a *'food retailing desert'*, the project was the joint initiative of the Society and the Tamar View Community Association, a registered community business at Barne Barton.

'Having worked together on the design, construction and opening of the store, the partnership will continue as the Society is committed to sharing a percentage of the profits made by the store with the community association. We regard this as a first in the country for such a venture and believe that it demonstrates how local social enterprises can work together to mutual benefit and the benefit of the local community. The new store opened on 26 November 2005 and is exceeding sales targets' (Annual Report).

Success Through Change

By reassessing their business and social goals, the Society had undoubtedly turned a proverbial corner, not just crudely, in terms of turnover and profitability, but more importantly, in terms of what ultimately underpinned both of those elements. By looking at the working conditions and training of their employees, the Society had created a happier and more contented workforce - one which was ready to translate those personal positives into corporate and thus commercial positives.

'Thanks to the efforts of a lot of people, notably John Riley, we had positioned ourselves as a good employer, and, when we presented that story to local business people, we were more than delighted to win the "Success Through Change" category of the Devon and Cornwall Business Challenge awards' (Fletcher).

There were improved trading figures across the Food, Funerals and Property groups, however, Non Food again was struggling, and the situation was getting worse. In Plymouth the opening of Drake Circus had had a devastating impact at a time when consumer demand was already weak. There was also increased demand from superstore operators in the non food zone, as well as ever-increasing competition from internet sales.

The Food group continued their refit programme and bought a convenience store in Exeter Street, Plymouth, as well as creating a new and totally refurbished store at Ernesettle, where two of the Society's units were merged into one. There were changes at Plympton Ridgeway too, including the opening of a new facility - Cafe Pronto. While the Funeral services group relocated to a new unit in Totnes, which followed hot on the heels of the purchase the previous year of the family business of BG Wills & Son, of Dawlish.

Overall, membership numbers were up significantly to over 150,000 (which included 4,750 from Brixham). The number of employees was also up and there was an encouraging number of postal votes (almost 14,000) in the election for new Directors and members of the Members Relations Committee. Contributions to local charities were also up with £30,000 going to the Give A Child A Chance appeal and another £8,000 going to the Devon Air Ambulance Trust.

Top: Exeter Street. Above: Natalie Burridge, Nicola Warn, Tara Christmas and Colette Bowden at the Plymouth Respect Festival. Right: Cafe Pronto.

INVESTOR IN PEOPLE

Reading The Signs

In the summer of 2007 the Society purchased a former motorcycle dealership in Albert Road, Devonport, and by November it had been converted to a 2,000 sq.ft convenience store, replacing a smaller unit a few doors away. The branding was the now-familiar two-tone blue colour scheme - the clover-leaf button-badge a prominent feature of the facade. The Marlborough Street and Duke Street stores were also refurbished, along with the Trago Mills supermarket.

However, as the Dartmouth supermarket was being sold to Marks and Spencer and the former Conveco garage and food store at Tweenaway was being closed, members were also informed of the decision to trial the new Co-operative branding.

A direct result of the Commission's recommendation for a universal logo across the Movement, one that represented a re-appraisal of what the Movement was all about, a new motif had emerged and it did, indeed, restate the most fundamental principle of them all. The new logo was simply two words - The Co-operative. Co-operation was exactly what the Movement was about, and through it came exactly what the Commission had sought to quantify and promote - 'the co-operative advantage'. Not desperately trendy or self-consciously clever, just clean and simple and in a classic, yet modern typeface - Helvetica.

At the time of the talk of the trial of the new branding, few would have thought that within a year or two year there would be talk of a merger with the Co-operative Group. However, with the rebranding of food stores in Brixham Great Rea, Ipplepen and most noticeably in Chaddlewood during 2008, the message was clear. However, it wasn't until the review of the 2008 year's trading was published in the Annual Report for the financial year ending January 2009, that it was spelt out in black and white.

In what was her final Presidential Report, Barbara Dure wrote: *'Perhaps the biggest thing that I have learnt from my involvement with the Co-operative Movement is the need for constant change and adaptation. We are living in a new era of optimism for the Co-operative form of enterprise and against this background your Board of Directors takes the view that the time could not be better for the Society to seek a merger with the Co-operative Group.'*

Left: Success Through Change. Top: Albert Road. Bottom: New branding at Chaddlewood.

She went on: 'Founded in 1860, our Society has deep historical roots in Plymouth and South Devon. Your Board believes that combining from a position of strength with the Co-operative Group is the best way of ensuring that our business continues to thrive and develop for the next 150 years. A merger will not only secure business development, it will also maximise the rewards to our members, employees and the local community.'

The Plymouth and South West Society had, undoubtedly been doing well with its food stores and its funeral services, very well, in fact, but Derrys and other non food outlets had been struggling. Derrys like so many other City Centre stores had been badly hit by the opening of Drake Circus and it was no real surprise to see it sold, along with the rest of the Non Food Group, to Vergo Retail Limited in March 2009 (although two of the Snips Hairdressing units were bought out by their respective staff).

Notwithstanding the performance of Derrys though, all the figures had been excellent. Overall turnover was up significantly, to over £150 million, the first time it had reached those dizzy heights since the sale of the superstores, more importantly however the trading surplus was well in excess of £6 million, far higher than in any point in the Society's history - and although this makes no allowance for inflation, it was significantly up on recent years' performances and a remarkable 173% up on the 2007 figure which in turn was well above most of the surpluses generated in those supersize years.

And so the Society was indeed looking to act from a position of strength, not just financially but in other respects too. Towards the end of 2006 'conscious of its wider community role,' they had taken a significant step towards reducing its carbon footprint, by replacing a previous electricity supply contract with one which was based on power from 100% certified green sources, primarily from hydro generation, but also from wind turbines and other alternative sources.

In 2007 the principal project for the Food Group had been the implementation of a new point of sale and back office computer system, known as In Control and in 2008, as part of refurbishment of Chaddelwood, self-scanning tills were introduced. Clearly just as the self-service experience transformed shopping sixty years earlier, this was an indication of the shopping experience to come (in October 2009 a Tesco Express in Nottingham became Britain's first entirely self-service store).

Above: Vivien Pengelly, Leader of Plymouth City Council: Chris Robinson: Douglas Fletcher with a trail board from a series of five Co-op-sponsored City walks.

Above: The last full year's accounts of the Plymouth and South West Co-operative Society.
Below: Torridge way gets yet another revamp.

Right: Two views of the new Co-operative store in Hoegate Street which stands just a few hundred yards from Stillman Street (the erstwhile Catte Street where the Plymouth story began in 1860) - see plaque and picture below.

Another environmental issue was highlighted in 2007 when the Society supported an initiative led by Rebecca Hosking in Modbury. Rebecca wanted to make the town plastic carrier bag free and the Society's food store in the town played a key role in a campaign that received world-wide publicity and which spurred many other towns and cities to consider similar initiatives. Locally the Plymouth and South West Society carried the campaign a stage further by removing plastic carrier bags from six other food stores - Millbrook, South Brent, Ipplepen, Wellswood, Newton Ferrers and Mortenhampstead.

Meanwhile they continued to recycle packaging waste through the Co-operative Group's Retail Distribution Centre at Plympton. The non food warehouse sorted this out for the non food stores resulting in, in 2007 alone, some 10 tons of plastic being recycled, along with 17 tons of polystyrene and 123 tons of cardboard.

The Society were also pleased to report support for the local Respect festival, celebrating ethnic diversity, the Freedom from Fear campaign, aimed at addressing retail crime. Ten thousand pounds was donated to Crimestoppers to support various activities, including the 'Rat on a Rat' campaign to encourage communities to inform about illegal drug related activities. Further sums were donated to Give A Child A Chance and Devon Air Ambulance, bringing the combined total allocated to them since the Community Cards were launched, to £87,000. In 2008 a further £44,000 was donated to charities.

Meanwhile the Members Relations Committee (the Education Committee of old) was disbanded, as the Board were looking to increase the accountability for Membership and, following the amendment of a rule in July 2008, the requirements for the Committee were removed and the responsibility was transferred to the Chief Executive and hence onto the Marketing Department, with the creation of a new position - Manager of Membership and Social Goals.

The most important goal of all for the Board and the Chief Executive however was the proposed merger. Having come to the decision that this was the best way forward for the Plymouth and South West Co-operative Society, they now had to convince the membership base.

The Final Chapter

The situation was quite clear. The Plymouth and South West Co-operative Society was doing well but as suggested 50 years earlier, and reiterated in no uncertain terms just ten years earlier, like many other regional Societies it would be doing much better if it were to merge and become part of an even bigger, National Society.

As the debate was progressing, the Co-operative Group flexed its muscle with the acquisition of the Somerfield food group and the merging of its financial services interests with the Britannia Building Society. An improvement of dividend for members followed. If anyone needed convincing on the merits of the merger of the Co-operative Wholesale Society and the Co-operative Retail Services here was the proof.

As the Chief Executive noted in his 2009 report: *'It is evident that, for the future, our financial capacity to grow the businesses that we operate, to provide our stakeholders with dividends and rewards that at least match those of the Co-operative Group, as well as correcting the under-funded pension schemes, is likely to be beyond the Society without disposing of assets or reducing our overhead base considerably. These actions would be to the detriment of Members and staff alike. The Co-operative Group will meet these challenges ...'*

The inheritance of a substantial pension deficit had influenced the decision-making process, but notwithstanding that, the advantages of becoming part of a larger organisation, acknowledging those basic economies of scale that had formed a solid foundation for so many societies in the first place, before the plc invasion, were too obvious to ignore. Merge and thrive or in the longer term be submerged and sink were the realistic options.

A two thirds majority was needed to carry the resolution. In the event members voted overwhelmingly in favour - by 91% at Special Meetings held in conjunction with the Annual General Meeting in May 2009. The following month, at specially convened Members' Meetings the voting was 93% in favour and the die was cast.

'And so in leading up to its 150th Anniversary the proud independent Plymouth Society had carried out actions that it had encouraged others to do during those 150 years - that is to consolidate thereby creating economies of scale in order to ensure that a Co-operative retailing presence, and model, continues for many years to come' (Douglas Fletcher, Chief Executive).

For Fletcher and a number of administrative staff, it was the end of the road, however, for the vast majority of staff and for almost all of the membership it was business as usual. They are now part of the largest Co-operative consumer Society in the world and they can relax in the knowledge that Co-operative retailing is as strong it has ever been.

It had been a truly remarkable journey and it's hard to know what those Rochdale Pioneers from 1844 would make of it all today. At the dawn of the twenty first century there were over 750 million members of co-operatives across a hundred countries of the world. Over 440 million of them in Asia, while one in three American citizens is a member of a cooperative.

Outside of Britain the largest consumer co-operatives are in Japan, where a replica of that first building opened by the Rochdale Pioneers, has been created at the Japanese training centre in Kobe - it is twice the size of the Toad Lane original. In Moscow there is a Rochdale Street, while the official name the former British Guyana in South America is the Co-operative Republic of Guyana.

More remarkably perhaps than all of that, is the fact that in the first 150 years of the Co-operative Movement in this country at least £40 billion of profits (at current prices) was distributed to members in dividend payments and other benefits.

The Plymouth story largely mirrors that national picture and doubtless Charles Goodanew and his friends would be amazed by what they would see today if the ghost of Christmas past was able to bring them into the City now. Meanwhile who can begin to say what the situation might look like in another 150 years?

Toad Lane, the Mecca of the Co-operative Movement. Co-operators from all over the world make pilgrimages to this modest red-brick Rochdale building.

150 YEARS of
The **co-operative** in Plymouth

Charles Goodanew *Founder*

John Webb *First Secretary*

Thomas Densumbe

Joseph Young

William Millman

1859 Christmas Day
First meeting in Charles Goodanew's
house in Tin Street

1860 Society formed
1860 Charles Shovel (President)
1860 First Shop in Catte Street
1860 Kinterbury Street Shop

1862 Premises leased in Cornwall Street
1865 Coal business started
1865 Samuel Lockwood (President)
1868 First bakery in Neswick Street
1869 Footwear Department

1870 Drapery store in Cornwall Street
1871 Shop in Bilbury Street (Treville Street)
1872 Joseph Young (President)

1876 Joseph Young (Managing Secretary)
1877 Ross Street, Morice Town opens
1877 William Lethbridge (President)

1880 Thomas Densumbe (President)
1881 William Millman (President)
1881 Society buys their own Schooner
1882 Dairy opens in Treville Street

1888 Farming Department

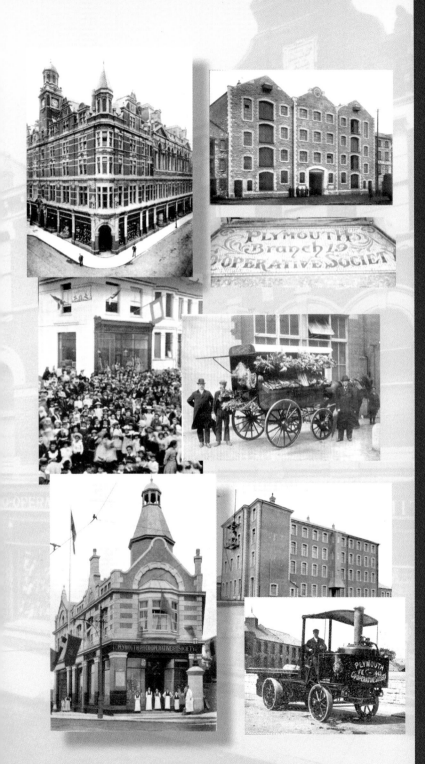

1886 Women's Guild Founded

1888 Poole Farm purchase

1889 Mutley Plain shop opened

1894 Central Premises opened

1898 Henry Heddon (General Secretary)

1899 Albert Wonnacott (General Secretary)

1900 Abattoir opens at Stonehouse
1901 23rd Grocery Station Road Keyham

1902 Funeral Service
1902 Society builds houses at Peverell

1903 First mobile grocery shop
1903 Weston Park Rd & Peverell Park Rd

1905 New warehouse built on North Quay

1906 New Bakery at Peverell
1906 Co-op starts a football team

1908 Jewellery goes on sale in drapery
1908 Society buys a local flour mill
1908 Co-op steam lorry takes to the road

1910 Jubilee Celebrations
1910 Jubilee stores Peverell opened

Albert Wonnacott

150 YEARS of
The co-operative in Plymouth

William Watkins

James Hayne Pillar

William Gilbert

William Lapthorn

Henry Drake

1911 Laundry built at Peverell

1914 William Watkins (President)

1915 Preserve Works
1916 Whympstone Farm and Stoke Beach

1918 Motor Coaches
1919 James Hayne-Pillar (President)

1920 Radnor Dairy is opened
1920 Preserve Works at Peverell

1921 Charles White (President)
1921 Golden age charabanc begins
1921 Pharmacy

1922 James Hayne-Pillar (President)

1929 23 charabancs gooff to Tavistock

1932 Unity Park opened for sport

1932 Courtenay Street furniture emporium

1934 Henry Drake (President)
1934 William Lapthorn (President)
1935 William Gilbert (President)

1935 William Gilbert (President)

1937 Ewart Francis Cocks (General Secretary)

1940 New store Fore Street Devonport
1940 First bombs fall on Plymouth
1941 Herbert Twigg (Gen Sec/CEO)
1941 Plymouth and Devonport 'Blitzed'
1940-44 40+ premises destroyed/damaged
1943 City Council buy Co-op land for housing

1945 Lee Mill merges with Plymouth
1946 100 new vehicles
     Mobile shops service new estates

1947 Royal Parade laid out
1947 Plympton joins with the Society
1948 Arnold Stroud (President)
1948 Co-op introduces Self Service shopping
1949 Jubilee Stores all new Self-Service

1950 New warehouse on North Quay
1951 Last horse drawn grocery vehicle
1953 First phase of New Central Premises
1954 Last horse is pensioned off.
1954 Ellen Roberts (President)
1955 Frozen food at Mutley and West Park

1956 Merger with Cornwood Co-operative
1957 Alan Wright (General Secretary/CEO)
1957 David Moore (President)
1958 Dartmouth joins with Plymouth
1959 Preserve factory at Peverell closes
1959 New Food Hall in Co-operative House

1960 Co-operative House completed.

Herbert Twigg

Alan Wright

Arnold Stroud

David Moore

150 YEARS of
The **co-operative** in Plymouth

Jack Parsons

Victor Barton

George Bestier

David Greener

254

1964 Tamar House, St Budeaux opened
1964 Houses built at Dudley Rd, Plympton

1966 Torquay Society joins with Plymouth
1966 Plym House, Plymstock Broadway

1970 The Dividend stamp arrives
1970 Newton Abbot & Buckfastleigh join

1971 Decimalisation

1974 Jack Parsons (Chief Executive Officer)

1975 George Truscott (President)

1976 The ICL 2903 computer starts work

1978 Plymco 1 on the Ridgeway opens

1981 Laundry is closed at Langstone Road

1981 Plans for Transit Way are submitted
1982 Victor Barton (Chief Executive)

1983 George Bestier (President)

1985 David Greeneer (Chief Executive)
1985 Homemaker at Cot Hill opens
1985 Plans for superstore at Pomphlett Mill

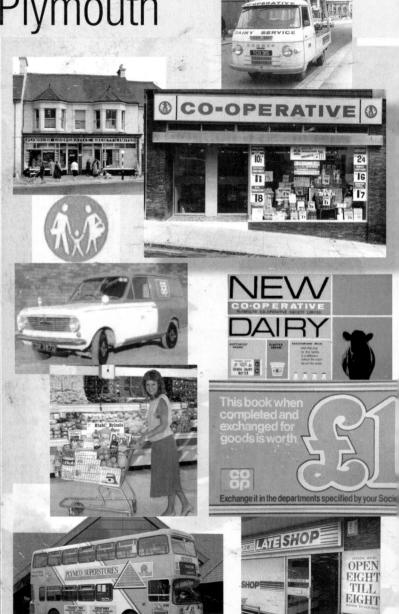